Critical Muslim 49

Scotland

T0386781

Critical Muslim is published quarterly by C. Hurst & Co. (Publishers) Ltd. on behalf of and in conjunction with Critical Muslim Ltd. and the Muslim Institute, London.

All editorial correspondence to Muslim Institute, Canopi, 7-14 Great Dover Street, London, SE1 4YR
E-mail: editorial@criticalmuslim.com

C. Hurst & Co (Publishers) Ltd., New Wing, Somerset House, Strand, London, WC2R 1LA

ISBN:9781787389588 ISSN: 2048-8475

To subscribe or place an order by credit/debit card or cheque (pounds sterling only) please contact Kathleen May at the Hurst address above or e-mail kathleen@hurstpub.co.uk

A one-year subscription, inclusive of postage (four issues), costs £60 (UK), £90 (Europe) and £100 (rest of the world), this includes full access to the *Critical Muslim* series and archive online. Digital only subscription is £3.30 per month.

Critical Muslim

<u>Subscribe to Critical Muslim</u>

Now in its thirteenth year in print, *Critical Muslim* is also available online. Users can access the site for just £3.30 per month – or for those with a print subscription it is included as part of the package. In return, you'll get access to everything in the series (including our entire archive), and a clean, accessible reading experience for desktop computers and handheld devices — entirely free of advertising.

<u>Full subscription</u>

The print edition of *Critical Muslim* is published quarterly in January, April, July and October. As a subscriber to the print edition, you'll receive new issues directly to your door, as well as full access to our digital archive.

United Kingdom £60/year
Europe £90/year
Rest of the World £100/year

<u>Digital Only</u>

Immediate online access to *Critical Muslim*

Browse the full *Critical Muslim* archive

Cancel any time

£3.30 per month

www.criticalmuslim.io

CM49

WINTER 2024

CONTENTS

SCOTLAND

SCOTLAND

INTRODUCTION:
HIGHLANDS AND LOWLANDS

Robin Yassin-Kassab

I'm heading for the mosque in Stornoway, on the Isle of Lewis, in the Outer Hebrides. The most northerly mosque in Scotland.

I'm not going all that way because I'm particularly religious, or because there are no nearer mosques either. There's one a mere thirty miles from home, in Dumfries, and there are plenty in the central belt between Glasgow and Edinburgh. No, I'm making Stornoway my target only because it's far away and not easy to get to, because most Scots as well as most Muslims would consider it to be a very distant and far-flung location. I aim to go so far into Scotland that I fall off the edge.

This issue of *Critical Muslim* is dedicated to Scotland. And why would *Critical Muslim* dedicate an issue to Scotland? For several reasons. First, there is a significant Muslim community here, which makes Scotland, like almost everywhere else, a part of the Muslim world. Second, Scotland's First Minister, Humza Yousaf, is a Muslim. This means that Scotland is the first western country (except for those with Muslim majorities, like Bosnia, Albania, and Kosovo) to appoint a Muslim as its leader. The leader of the largest opposition party, Labour's Anas Sarwar, is also a Muslim. Third, many of the issues facing Scotland have interesting echoes, reflections, and parallels in many Muslim-majority societies. These issues include competing versions of nationalism, the politics of minority language groups, arguments over land use and ownership, environmental degradation, and sectarianism – all of which (and more) are discussed in these pages.

So off I set. I live in Galloway, which is my journey's starting point. Galloway is in the far southwest. Therefore, I head north, with the Southern Uplands rising to the west of the road and endless sheep fields rolling to the east. It's a depopulated landscape which still bears traces of a more densely peopled past. In almost every field there's the ruin of a house once inhabited by subsistence farmers. There are ruins in the misty hills too, but those fallen stones are well hidden by the closely packed plantations of brooding Sitka Spruce. The summits bear mainly Gaelic (or Brythonic) names, though nobody around here has spoken any version of that language for at least a few hundred years.

Visitors from cities tend to assume that this is a natural landscape, but it's almost completely man made.

Some centuries ago, the lairds exported the subsistence farmers and imported the sheep, which gobbled up tree saplings to create a grass desert. The land became a workshop producing mutton, lamb, and wool. More recently, venture capitalists and the Forestry Commission took over the wilder pastureland and planted Sitka Spruce instead. Sitka comes from Alaska, and grows very fast in Scotland's comparative warmth. A forest can be cropped after a mere 40 years. The wood is low quality, and goes mainly for palettes and pulp to make cardboard, but the landowners benefit too from government grants for 'carbon capture'. Planting trees is rewarded, whatever the trees, however they are planted. Sitka don't root deeply, so in a gale they topple like dominos. You can't walk through them, they're planted so wrongly. Nothing much can live beneath them. And they acidify the soil and water.

Northwards as the hills rise, huge wind turbines turn. Then the road winds down through crumbling slopes all the way into Ayrshire. Into what used to be coalmining country. The landscape is flatter, with fewer trees. Depressed, grey, partially boarded-up towns string between decades-old slag heaps. One town is called Patna. So called after the capital of India's Bihar state, where William Fullarton, the founder of this Scottish Patna, was born. First, farmers were expelled from their land. Next, the dispossessed and landless congregated in mining and industrial towns, where they could at least find brutal work. And the mines, factories, and ship building yards in which they labored were funded by profits made from the British colonies.

The marks of all this are seared on the landscape and into the people in a way that they aren't quite in England, at least not in the south. There are lasting signs of traumatisation, of the violent renewal, and then the long decline.

The nexus of empire and industry shaped modern Scotland and made it more British. The end of empire and the death of old industry sets the context for Scotland's contemporary reality, which is increasingly less identified with Britain, or at least with the United Kingdom.

South of Ayr, I can see the Irish Sea in the distance. North of Ayr, my route joins the coast. Water shudders on the left, green and silver in scudding sunshine. Overlooking the beaches are holiday and retirement homes, and little palm trees growing in their gardens. It's not as cold on the west coast as you'd expect from the latitude. It snows more often in Damascus than in Ayr. And that's because the Gulf Stream bathes western Scotland in moist warm wind brought all the way from Mexico.

I see the Isle of Arran out there, not far away, rugged and towering. Looking like the Highlands already. Arran is obvious because of the height of Goat Fell, but it's difficult to tell the islands in the sea from the various bits of winding, curling mainland.

At Wemyss Bay I drive on to the ferry for the Isle of Bute. The boats leave at twenty-minute intervals. I lock the car and climb up to the deck. Very soon the engines are chugging us through the Firth of Clyde, the chief inlet and outlet through which Scots engaged with the world. Ships sailed through this channel carrying migrants to the New World and troops, administrators, engineers and teachers to the colonies. On the banks of the Clyde, Scotland's great industries were built, funded with profits made in the East and West Indies – including from slavery. Scots were thoroughly involved in the slave economy, as investors, owners, and overseers. Apparently Robert Burns – who now has 'national poet' status – was considering a job as a plantation book-keeper, and might have taken it had he not taken off as a poet. At the beginning of the nineteenth century, Scots owned a third of slaves and almost a third of estates in Jamaica. Profits from the colonial tobacco, sugar and cotton industries – all reliant on slave labour – built many of Scotland's grand buildings. Educational institutions, and the Wee Free Church (of which more later) were founded with funds from the slave economy.

Some Scots, of course, were active abolitionists, and on occasion Scottish communities took direct action against slavery. When in the 1760s, for instance, the slave Ned Johnson's owner brought him from Virginia to Glasgow, and then hung him up and flogged him, the neighbours cut Ned down, took him to a magistrate, and demanded he be freed.

The Clyde valley connected the Scots to the world, for good and for ill. 'A disproportionate number of Scots played a part in Britain's colonial administration,' writes Scottish-Sudanese novelist Leila Aboulela in this issue. Her essay focuses on three Scots who engaged with the Muslim world in very different ways – a colonial officer, an artist, and a convert to Islam. Their involvement with Sudan, Egypt, Mecca, complicates and in some way solidifies Leila's involvement with Scotland. Discovering a statue in Aberdeen of one of them – a British imperial martyr – she thinks: 'Gordon had been there, and I was now here.'

Scots and Muslims have been wrapped up together for centuries – Scots traveling to Muslim countries, and Muslims settling here. The Clyde valley, and Glasgow specifically, is where Scotland's largest Muslim community developed. Saqib Razzaq's, essay in these pages, describes the growth of that community in the twentieth century. She focuses on its largest component – Scottish Pakistanis – and on key figures such as Bashir Maan, Scotland's first Muslim councilor, and Atta Ashrif, founder of Glasgow's first Muslim Association, and eventually its first mosque.

But nothing so consequential as slavery, empire, industry, or community-building is happening on this stretch of water today. It's just the ferry chugging me and my vehicle across as I sip on a cardboard cup of coffee, just half an hour of chugging, and then I'm driving off the ferry into Rothesay, the only town on the Isle of Bute.

Rothesay is a bit battered these days, but in its late Victorian heyday it was a busy resort serving working and lower-middle class Glaswegian tourists. Some are still here, drinking in the daytime, or promenading with friendly grins (Glasgow surely being the friendliest city in the British Isles). As well as a few boarded-up shops, Rothesay boasts a mock-Mughal pavilion, and modestly elegant hotels, and mini-golf, and bright flowers in neat beds, and jellyfish, seagulls and seaweed.

So how should we judge Bute? Is it a terrible or wonderful place? Is it an island to retire to, or to commute from (the ferries are fast enough that some who work in Glasgow live here) – or to escape?

It contains enough of the characteristics of the rest of the country to seem like a microcosm. There is the same cracked grey council housing that covers much of the central belt, as well as high-ceilinged town houses of the sort seen in Edinburgh. There's a laird's palatial home and gardens, and agriculture, sea, some forest. The Highland fault runs through the island, so it is both lowlands and highlands, geologically speaking.

Terrible or wonderful? Extended to cover the nation as a whole, this question has governed Scottish culture since my childhood. Some decades ago, the general assumption was that the place was pretty terrible. Many or most Scots were not proud of Scotland. Mark Renton's monologue in the Highlands scene from *Trainspotting* summed up the attitude: 'It's shite being Scottish! We're the lowest of the low! The scum of the fucking earth! … Some people hate the English. I don't. They're just wankers. We, on the other hand, were colonised by wankers.'

Some people's language was cleaner, but this was a very common perception. Scotland was post-imperial and post-industrial, with a shrinking, ageing population, with (at one point) the highest murder rate in Europe, with high unemployment and a shockingly high rate of drugs deaths.

More recently, however, the self-perception of Scots has shifted in a positive direction. The general assumption now is that Scotland – despite the continuation of the problems listed above – tends towards the wonderful, or at least the potentially wonderful. There's been a Scottish cultural revival, expressing itself in literature, music, and art. The Gaelic language too is taken much more seriously than it was, and studied more widely. Scots of all political persuasions are happily aware of their national and cultural distinction from their English neighbours. And in the last twenty years, the Scottish National Party (SNP) has dominated the political scene, both in Scotland's devolved parliament, which enjoys limited powers, and at Westminster, where the SNP provides most Scottish MPs.

The party first achieved power in Scotland in 2007. In 2014, it organised a referendum on Scottish independence from the United Kingdom. The result seemed a foregone conclusion – at the start of the campaign, only about a third of Scots said they supported independence. Yet the campaign took off, and it mobilised sections of society that the SNP had never reached. These included young people, most ethnic minorities, and progressives represented by Common Weal and similar groups.

On voting day, 45 percent supported independence, despite all the big parties except the SNP, and all the media except one newspaper, urging people against it. In the days before the vote, British Prime Minister David Cameron and ex-Labour leader Gordon Brown (himself a Scot) promised 'devolution max' – that is, greatly increased powers for the Scottish Parliament – if Scotland remained in the union. This promise was forgotten as soon as the votes were counted. Forgotten by the English parties, but not by Scots. Shortly after the referendum, support for independence – according to opinion polls – passed 50 percent. Then in the 2015 Westminster election, the SNP won all but three of the Scottish seats.

The party's popular success continued, and only now is beginning to tail off. In the 2021 Scottish Parliament election, the SNP won the largest share of the popular vote and the largest number of constituency seats in any Scottish Parliament election – that is, it won 64 out of 129 seats. If the Scottish Parliament used the first-past-the-post system, like Westminster, the party would have won a landslide majority, but because Scotland uses a more democratic proportional representation system, the SNP governs in alliance with the Scottish Green Party – which also wants self-government.

Apart from the growing desire for independence, one reason for the SNP's success has been its skill at attracting disillusioned Labour voters. Once known as 'the tartan Tories', the SNP moved left as the Labour Party under Tony Blair's leadership moved right. Tony Blair's insistence on taking Britain into the 2003 Iraq War solidified the sense among many Scots that England under both major parties continued to be an imperialist power, while Scotland, at least in the new century, wanted to distance itself from its imperialist past.

The SNP, according to most perceptions, governed both well and in a manner which distinguished itself, and therefore Scotland, from England's very different political culture. As a result, unlike the English, Scots enjoy free medical prescriptions, free sanitary products, and free university tuition. The party is certainly to the left of both Blair and the current Labour leader Keir Starmer. And unlike the Labour Party under Jeremy Corbyn, it has been able to pursue leftist and socially liberal policies without collapsing into populism or support for authoritarian regimes abroad.

Yet for most of the years of SNP strength, England has been dominated by the Conservative Party rather than Labour, and the Conservative Party has moved ever more to the right. English politics has increasingly appealed to petty nationalist and xenophobic impulses which don't really operate in Scotland, at least not in the same way. Nigel Farage and his United Kingdom Independence Party (UKIP) set the agenda for English politics, but never took off north of the border. Two thirds of Scots voted against Brexit (but had to swallow it anyway). And most Scots are not frightened by immigration. It's true that only two percent of the Scottish population consists of minority ethnic people – as opposed to 15 percent of England – and therefore that Scots may become more xenophobic in the future if the proportion rises, but for now the country is much more welcoming than England. Or it would like to be – if it could control its own immigration policy.

Unlike all the major English parties, the SNP happily talks up the economic and cultural benefits of free movement and immigration. So in 2019, Nicola Sturgeon, then party leader, said: 'In Scotland, we know … that the Westminster approach to migration – as well as being deeply inhumane – poses an existential threat to our future prosperity.'

This goes some way to explaining why Scottish Muslims are more likely than not to vote SNP, and for independence. This often surprises members of minority groups south of the border, to whom the SNP sounds like the BNP – the British National Party, an anti-immigrant and blatantly racist outfit. People in England sometimes assume that any party with 'National' in its name must be based on an exclusivist ethno-chauvinism. But it should be remembered that two competing forms of nationalism are at work in Scotland. The independence-seeking Scottish version, at least under its current leadership, is an inclusive civic nationalism, whereas the unionist British version is much more likely to be exclusionary. A week before the 2014 referendum, the Orange Order – the Protestant identity group known for its provocative anti-Catholic and anti-Irish marches in Northern Ireland – organised an enormous unionist demonstration in Glasgow. On the day after the referendum, as the result came through, the same people celebrated in Glasgow's George Square. They painted 'Obey Your Queen' on the road, waved Union Jacks, and abused passing Pakistani-Scots.

But back to Bute – which hosts a new community of Syrian-Scots, 24 families to be precise. I knew about this before I visited, though I had no contacts in the community. I knew it because the story has been featured in the media. The apparent contradiction of 'refugees' and 'remote Scottish island' marks the topic for repetition (though Bute is not really remote – as already mentioned, it's commuting distance from Scotland's largest city).

Because I had no contacts, I wrote to the Argyll and Bute council before I left home, asking for an introduction to some of the Syrians. I was surprised by the council's negative response: the Syrian community on Bute has had a bad experience with the media, and has therefore made a collective decision not to engage with journalists or writers, whoever they are. I did a little research, and discovered that the bad media experience was related to that aforementioned standard Scottish question, usually asked by Scots themselves: is it (Bute, in this case) a terrible or a wonderful place?

Early media attention had stressed the happy aspect of the story. The Syrians had been warmly welcomed, and had fitted in well, and were happy on the island. But then a journalist found a couple of Syrians who dissented. Bute, they complained, was full of 'old people waiting to die.' The weather was miserable, there were hardly any jobs, and in the absence of a larger Arab or Muslim community, the Syrians felt isolated. This story wasn't much of a story. If a journalist were to stop 'native' Scots and ask them if their town or region or country was terrible or wonderful, about half would answer 'terrible', depending perhaps on the weather that day. But because a couple of incomers had answered 'terrible', the non-story was reprinted by several right-wing newspapers to make the implicit points that refugees are ungrateful, that they refuse to adapt, and that immigration is therefore a bad thing.

So the Syrians didn't want to talk, and I respected their desire. If I'd stayed longer I'm sure I would have met them anyway. I passed a Syrian barbershop, and a Syrian patisserie, but both were closed that evening.

In any case, I had another reason to spend the night in Bute. That is, it cut out the tedious part of my journey. In the morning I took a ferry from the northern tip of the island into Argyll, thus arriving immediately in the Highlands, and avoiding the traffic-packed trudge around Glasgow.

Back on the road. A long and wonderful day of driving ensues. I'm traveling alone. It's difficult to pick up the radio because of the mountains in the way. I prefer the noisiness of my thoughts anyway, or silence when I overcome them. Sometimes I listen to *Finnegans Wake*. Sometimes I sing.

And drive northwards, past Inverary, on the banks of Loch Fyne. I'm not stopping now but I've visited before with my wife, and I hope we visit again. The finest sea food is fished from Loch Fyne, and Inverary – home to the chiefs of Clan Campbell, now calling themselves the Dukes of Argyll – is a lovely place. The town is small but monumental, beneficiary of the royal favour that fell upon the Campbells once they'd defeated more unruly clans. Apparent from the road is the kind of well-tended castle that might decorate a shortbread box. Some miles further, on the edge of Loch Awe, is Kilchurn Castle. It's a dramatic ruin dating from an age when Clan Campbell needed strongholds more than frills.

I take a back road through the Glen of Orchy to avoid the traffic, and for half an hour the only other road users are two cyclists and three brown pigs. I wind on the river bank through Silver Birch and bracken. There are wading birds on the water, and no doubt salmon and plenty of trout beneath the surface. The water is copper-coloured over rocks, and black where it deepens. I have many more miles to go, but the glen makes me want to stop and make a fire, perhaps catch a fish for dinner. It reminds me of various mountain journeys and nights spent under the stars in this country and others – not least in the far north of Pakistan.

Most people wouldn't associate Scotland with Pakistan, but there are many connections, and not just those of empire. One such is the brown trout – an iconic Scottish fish which is also native to Afghanistan, and which the British introduced to northern Pakistan. Robin Ade's essay covers his adventures in Pakistan and Afghanistan, his fishing in lochs 'littered with rusting Soviet military ordinance', his brushes with the Taliban (and an angry eagle), and his friend Khalil's fishing visit to Scotland, in turn.

But there's no time now to catch a trout. I soon leave Glen Orchy to join the A82, the road stretching north of Loch Lomond which introduces most visitors to the Highlands. The route climbs onto Rannoch Moor. This is, for me, a dreamscape. There isn't anywhere suitable to stop, so I've only ever seen it properly in dreams. I know from sideway glances that the moor runs low and flat towards the mountains which surround it, that its colours pulse chameleon-like with the shifting of the clouds, and that it holds lochans of choppy cold water which in turn hold islands of wild fertility. Neither sheep nor deer can reach these isles, so trees can grow. The red trunks and high branches of Scots Pine make poses. Something in the scene reminds me of Chinese landscape painting. I recognise it, but don't know what it is I'm recognising. This is the same kind of recognition as when I listen and re-listen to *Finnegans Wake*. Some sense is made, though I don't know of what. I see, though I don't see at all.

Further on there are towering peaks and vast open valleys. I keep remembering Pakistan. The mountains here are small hills in comparison, though they used to be almost as high as the Hindu Kush or the Himalayas.

Millions upon millions of years of erosion, including various ice ages, have worn them down, but the geology and the far northern latitude makes them as wild as mountains anywhere. All this beauty has its effects on the human soul. A person of an earlier era would have called it 'sublime'.

Climbing again, until the road ascends to a higher plane. It's a spiritual experience; driving feels like flight. Set to the left is Buachaille Etive Mòr. What an astounding mountain it is. What an ur-mountain. If an alien were to ask you what a mountain was, you'd show him a picture of this one.

Now the road plunges in zigzags down to Glencoe. Where, in 1692, the MacDonalds were massacred, by Campbells and others, for refusing to pledge allegiance to the crown.

After that the road runs at sea level, and always beside water – Loch Leven, Loch Linnhe, Loch Lochy, Loch Oich, Loch Ness – through Fort William, and then Fort Augustus. Why are so many towns named after forts? Fort William was established as a garrison in 1690, Fort Augustus in 1730, and nearby Fort George in 1770. The purpose of each was to pacify the road-less and still independent people of the Highlands. The last major pitched battle in Scotland was at Culloden in 1746, when the Catholic and clan-backed Jacobites were defeated by the Protestant crown.

Once vanquished, the clans were repurposed. Clan warriors became the frontline troops of British imperialism as it spread overseas, converting in turn other defeated mountain men – the Gurkhas, for instance, or the Pathans – into crack cadres of empire. The clan chieftains, meanwhile, became lairds – lordly landowners who set about 'improving' their realms by exporting the native people. Some of the fighting men were retained at home in order to enforce these domestic 'clearances'.

The lairds were the same elites who had agreed to the 1707 Act of Union, joining Scotland to the English state. But before that, they, their landed Lowland peers, and the urban mercantile elites, had invested heavily in the disastrous Darien Scheme. This project was independent Scotland's attempt to build its own maritime empire. The only step taken towards this grandiose endeavour was the short-lived establishment of a colony in Panama. The first ship load of colonists left Scotland in 1698, with high hopes. Vast amounts of wealth were committed to the project; up to 40 percent of actual capital in Scotland was invested. Yet within a couple of years, everything had been lost.

Whatever could go wrong for the nascent imperialists did. They were ground down by local resistance, attacks by European competitors, and disease.

So Scotland's nobles were very nearly bankrupted. At this point, a plan was cooked up whereby the crown would reimburse them for their losses if they agreed to pass the powers of Scotland's parliament to Westminster. This was the context in which Scotland lost its independence and became another part of the United Kingdom. According to historian Thomas Martin Devine, 'the Act of Union was a legislative measure agreed in Scotland by a tiny patrician elite against some internal parliamentary opposition and much external popular hostility.'

Robert Burns famously called the patrician elite 'a parcel of rogues'. The novelist and critic, Neil M. Gunn drove the criticism home: 'with rare exceptions, the nobles and clan chiefs of Scotland, in the tragic hours of their people's need, showed themselves the sorriest and most treacherous crew that ever a decent land was damned by.'

As the lairds swung behind British expansion overseas, and as they cleared the people off their lands at home, poverty-stricken Scots either sailed for the Americas or populated the slums of the new industrial cities. Some eventually took pride in Scotland's industrial development, but the slums remained violent and cursed by alcoholism until the industrial decline – when heroin joined alcohol as refuge and curse of the alienated poor. According to Gunn: 'Altogether it is a disheartening story in a disheartened people, losing faith in themselves, growing ashamed of their Gaelic speech, of every characteristic that differentiated them from those born to the English tongue.'

I spend the night in a caravan, and the next day head westwards, where I might for the first time (other than on BBC Alba) hear the Gaelic speech spoken.

'Over the sea to Skye' goes the song, eternalising the flight of Bonny Prince Charlie, but these days a bridge at the Kyle of Lochalsh connects the mainland to the Inner Hebrides. So over the bridge I go.

Skye is a remarkable place, and the most remarkable part of it may be the Cuillin Hills. I park the car to take a photo, and end up stumbling upwards, awestruck, for an hour, past blue rocks, blue pools, white rapids, and rearing above them the most rugged mountains anywhere in the British Isles.

I return again the next day, to Glen Brittle, where I head uphill for 'the Fairy Pools' – so named in the nineteenth century for the first tourist craze. A broad white path snakes upward. Walking on it is like driving on the tourist-choked single-track roads: you have to stop frequently to allow oncoming traffic to pass.

It's the same further north at the Quirang – a dramatic set of rocky outcrops rising from smooth, ice-sculpted hills, with misty views of the sea and further wild isles beyond. Here too there's an onrush of vehicles and bodies. German, Dutch, Spanish, American. So many tourists. I can't complain because I am one of them, but still I'll complain… There are too many people, and in such a place that for almost all of its history would have been properly remote.

That evening in Portree I buy a map in a bookshop, and at the counter I hear a conversation conducted in Gaelic. The first and only. There seems to be less Gaelic spoken in Skye than German, at least at this time of year. (It's September – the last days of the tourist season. I suppose if I'd come in the winter the place would be less crowded.)

Even the small amount of Gaelic surviving is something of a miracle, following centuries of state and social Anglophone prejudice. The Statutes of Icolmkill, signed by the chiefs of the Outer Isles in 1609, were concerned that the 'Irishe language which is one of the chief and principall causis of the continewance of barbaritie and incivilitie amongis the inhabitants of the Isles and Heylandis may be abolisheit and removeit.' In the same Statutes, the chiefs were forced to agree to send their eldest sons to be educated in the lowlands, in English.

The tide may at last have turned. Local culture these days is something to be celebrated more than repressed. In her essay in these pages, Kirsty MacDougall examines the efforts to revive the Gaelic language since the 1970s, including the exponential growth in Gaelic-medium education. The Gaelic Language Act was passed by the Scottish Government in 2005. The Act, according to MacDougall, 'marked a historic milestone for the Gaelic language. This legislation meant that Gaelic was recognised officially as an "official language of Scotland, commanding equal respect to the English language".'

Up here in Skye, in any case, not just the place names but even the signs for 'hospital' (*ospadal*) and 'town centre' (*meadhan a bhaile*) are printed in Gaelic. And certainly the place and its people produce their own distinctive atmosphere. There's a particular soft lilt in the accent when the locals speak Scots. There's a general gentleness and air of cooperation which is common to all of Scotland, but here it may be still more intense. I tell the lady who manages the guest house that a light is flashing on my car dashboard. She sends me to her brother's garage, which does what's necessary at a discount price. Hostess and mechanic are Macraes. The biggest clan on the island is clan Macleod. The proportion of red-heads here is surely higher than on the mainland. Skye appears to be thriving, and one reason for that must be the tourism, which clogs the roads in the summer, sure, but provides the money to keep life going in the winter.

Next day I drive to Uig, then take the ferry for Harris and Lewis. I'm still heading for Stornoway, Lewis's capital, and for Scotland's most northerly mosque.

The ferry takes an hour and forty minutes, and it's a powerful vessel, moving fast. In the days before ferries, most people would never have left their islands. I wonder at how lonely their lives must have been, or perhaps how complete, perhaps embedded in community in ways we cannot today imagine. There's another island even further out to sea – St. Kilda, deserted by its last inhabitants in 1930. Now you can visit it only as a member of a work party. I have a friend who did just that. He says you can walk the island's entire perimeter in a few hours. A wind-swept rock inhabited by seabirds, and once by a few humans, whose neighbours for them were the entire world.

The ferry arrives at Tarbert, on Harris. I drive off the boat and turn southwards, to explore.

Harris and Lewis sound like two islands, but in fact are only one. The divide between them is made not of water but by a line of rugged hills. The landscape is treeless, and not tame enough for fields. Not much soil. There's more rock than anything, sometimes thinly covered with peat, and tough grass, and purple heather. Sheep wander the roads. The white sand beaches look almost tropical. The weather today is quite remarkable – hot, bright, dry. Later my landlady Margo will tell me that though she's come down dozens of times to visit relatives in Harris, she's never once seen the place free of cloud and mist, that she's never really known what it looks like.

Well, it looks beautiful. And wild and alien. It feels very distant from everything else, peripheral in an obvious way. But I know from my reading that these parts are also strangely central. It's as if events that start here build larger echoes as they reach out into the world.

Donald Trump's mother came from Lewis. The name Donald comes from the Gaelic Domhnall, meaning 'ruler of the world'.

Weird historical rhymes ricochet from rock to rock. The father of Arthur Balfour – he of the infamous Balfour Declaration, so an actor in the eviction of Palestinians from their land – once ordered the eviction of 27 families from Lewis. For the purposes of 'improvement'.

In ancient times, the island – low-lying Lewis more than high-humped Harris – was full of stone circles. It must have been some kind of ritual centre, but for a religion or a way of seeing that we now know nothing about. In early Christian times, it drew hermits and pilgrims, who settled in caves and beehive huts. It's not clear why they came. From the mediaeval Catholic culture, it retains *tobraichean*, or holy wells, and *teampaill*, or 'temple' chapels. From the Druidic religion (I assume) it inherits a rich folklore and a recently submerged belief in the *sith*, or fairies, and the *sithean*, the hollow hills which fairies inhabit. Harris and Lewis has been a spiritual site for all of its history, and still it is today.

Margo – my Stornoway guesthouse host – asks what I'm writing about.

'It's interesting that there's a mosque up here in Stornoway,' I say. 'And there's a strong Christian community too.'

'I know a lot about it,' says Margo. 'I was part of it for twenty years,' she exclaims disapprovingly, more or less rolling her eyes. There are at minimum three churches competing on the island. The Church of Scotland, the Free Church of Scotland that broke away from it, and then the church that broke away from the Free Church. The Free Church – or the 'Wee Free' as it's colloquially known – has the most adherents.

Once, of course, all the Christians here were Catholics. And once before that they were something else again. While exploring Harris I'd visited, at the island's southernmost tip, St. Clement's, a medieval church rebuilt in the sixteenth century by the Macleod chief, despite his Protestantism. Its tower is adorned by a *Sheila-na-Gig*, which is a stone-carved female figure found exclusively in mediaeval Irish and western Scottish church architecture. The sculpture displays exaggerated female genitalia. We can only speculate as to why – a warning against lust? a prayer for fertility? a survival from an earlier pantheon?

Bara and South Uist, the Hebridean islands to the south of Harris, still retain their Catholicism today, which in one sense at least has cut them off culturally from their nearest neighbours. Bara and South Uist are Scotland's only Catholic-majority areas, though most Scottish Catholics live in Glasgow. Many of the Glaswegian Catholics are the descendants of nineteenth century Irish immigrants. The human traffic went both ways – most of Northern Ireland's Protestant population descends from Scottish settlers.

The combination of power imbalances, political positioning, and religious identity, leads to sectarianism in north west Europe as surely as it does in the Middle East. And the Scottish example proves that religious belief is not a prerequisite for sectarian hatred. Most people in Glasgow are not believers these days, but many know which sect they belong to when Rangers and Celtic are playing football. Both teams have made efforts to diversify recently, so I'm oversimplifying, but: Rangers is a Protestant team, while Celtic is Catholic. Rangers supporters are more likely to wave the Union Jack, while Celtic fans tend to wave the Saltire – the Scottish flag. But the projection goes even further. In a complex metaphorical move, Rangers supporters sometimes raise the Israeli flag, because the Israeli settlement of Palestine seems to them to echo the Protestant British settlement of Ireland. In return, Celtic fans raise the Palestinian flag...

But back to Lewis, old-fashioned Lewis, where religion burns closer to the heart even than football.

Margo says: 'It's only the last fifteen years that the women haven't been obliged to wear hats. I was one of the first to go out without a hat. I had trouble for it. And you know, I once visited Morocco. And you might be surprised, but I found it quite familiar. There they were covering the women, and some of them trying to steal from you, but still they were worshipping Allah.'

'Hypocrisy lives everywhere,' I say.

'Well,' says Margo. 'You should look up the Lewis Revival. That was pretty bizarre. Led by a character named Duncan Campbell. You look at that and you think, how could that happen? And you should look up the Gaelic psalm singing. It's on YouTube. The singing sounds like the sound of the sea.'

I note this down, then ask: 'What are the other signs of religious life on the island?'

'That the Sabbath is observed. No work on Sundays. That's changing a bit now, but it was a good thing, I think it was. It meant even the non-religious people could spend the day at home with their families. But I'm talking too much...'

I assure her she isn't.

'It complicated really,' she says then. 'Religion can control people too much, and it's always ruined by corruption. Maybe it would be better to forget it. But then I think – what is all this? What's this life, and this universe? There must be something behind it all. And we're all so depressed and uncertain. We need something. And I'm still looking for it, I am still looking.'

In these last words she sums up a very common dilemma, and the last couple of hundred years of human history too.

Next morning, as she serves breakfast, Margo directs me to a stone circle which will be free of tourists. Except for me, of course. So I drive there, and park the car, and walk across sodden peaty ground, under cloud which the unseasonable sun is burning away. Each step seems to lead me a thousand paces further from human noise. I see a huge bird hovering. A Golden Eagle? Then I'm distracted by a ruined house, or church. Once a large structure, too complex for a sheep pen. A grey cat stares from between the stones. Another kind of consciousness.

The cat breaks its stare and darts down across the moor in the direction of the sea. I turn back towards the stone circle which stands against the clearing sky a little above me, up across heather. But on the way I find a miniature circle, a ring of boulders ankle-high, not big enough for ritual purposes, but too well and deliberately formed to be a random arrangement of nature. It must be a fairy *cnoc*, I think, a fortified *sithean*. Not seriously thinking it, but feeling it, out here on the moor.

I reach my destination. Five shapely upstanding stones forested thickly by lichen. The circle is a depression, boggier than its surrounds. No people there but me, it's just a place, so I feel it. The flap of the wind. The sun breaking through. There is presence here. Or my mind is making presence from absence.

On I drive to the standing stones at Calanais, or Callanish. Here there are tourists, and no surprise – these structures are a world wonder. They were built 5,000 years ago, at least five centuries before Stonehenge. Archeologists now believe that the circle-building culture or religion began here in the north and then spread slowly south, through Ireland, England, Brittany, to Portugal. The circles, like Mesopotamian ziggurats, probably reflected in some way the movements of sun, moon, and stars. Otherwise we know nothing. Did people sacrifice their victims here, or get drunk, or sing hymns, or just tell stories?

I drive on to an iron age broch – a defensive roundhouse a mere 2,500 years old, half the age of the circles. Then on again northwards. Sometimes here the signage is in Gaelic only. This tip of the island is a high, flat shelf above the sea. Thin fields stretch between the villages. There are more churches than shops. Every clump of grey houses is supplied with a church.

The houses are dirty grey pebbledash, sometimes dirty brown, or dirty cream. This ugliness (to be frank) feels deliberate. It feels more connected to Protestantism's suspicion of beauty than to poverty. Calvin, after all, called religious art 'brutish stupidity'.

I stop near the lighthouse at Nis Point. It's hot, and the sun is blazing. I'm delighted to spot a seal in the sea below, and then two more. I sit for a long time and watch. I think they're watching me too. Three young, very inquisitive siblings treading water, and then their mother comes and circles them, checking they're safe.

Cormorants perching on wave-spattered rocks, an elegant long-beaked white bird, thinner than a seagull. Birds diving into the water and swimming underneath.

I admire the rocks, which are Lewisian gneiss, the most ancient rocks in the British Isles. They contain lines of gold and black, and they fall to the sea in twisted blocks.

I go looking for stones to take home, wanting something for nothing.

I pick one up – black, with coloured bands and glittering flecks.

Then I hear something, like a hiss or a whistle or an exhalation, and glance up quickly to see whatever animal it is. But there's nothing, nor a bird above. Yet the sound continues as I look all around. A sound which comes from the earth itself. When eventually it stops, I put the stone I've stolen back in its place.

How easy it's becoming to believe in the fairies. Or something. Another consciousness.

Today is the peak of my spiritual tour. If that's what I'm doing...

I'm moving towards a destination. So back to the car, and to Stornoway.

Stornoway is the biggest town in the Western Isles, the biggest town I've seen since Fort William at least. It's a port containing a castle, a court, some council buildings, some thick-walled town houses, and some council houses. More trees in the gardens than anywhere else on the island. And plenty of churches – as well as the three Margo spoke of, there's the Episcopal church, and the Church of Jesus Christ of Latter Day Saints (that is, the Mormons).

And, at last, there's the Stornoway Mosque.

Which doesn't look a mosque. It looks like the white pebbledash child of a council house and an industrial estate unit. A sign on the pebbledash reads: 'Stornoway Masjid. Welcome/ Fáilte.'

I remove my shoes, open the door, and step in. I find myself in a kitchen. It's a little confusing. There's a sink, a cooker, a kettle, and some brothers at a table.

'Wa-alaykum assalaam, brother. Come in, welcome, sit down.'

I'm offered tea as introductions are made.

Four men. Pakistanis and British Pakistanis. Two living here, two visiting from Leeds. Of the two living here, one works as a handyman and one is the imam of the mosque.

'Pakistanis have come here to do business since the 1950s,' the imam tells me. (Later I find an article in the Stornoway Gazette which pushes the date back to the 1930s.) 'But most of them left as business declined.'

'So Stornoway used to be better for business?'

'Yes, it became worse. But now it is improving, insha'Allah.'

'How many Muslims do you have here now?'

He thinks about it. 'About 25 in total.'

'We have Syrian families living here too,' says the handyman. And he calls one up on the phone. Bilal, from Homs. He hands him over.

Bilal says he loves it here. The people are friendly and polite, you feel safe and at peace, and the place itself is truly lovely. 'Come and stay with me and see,' he says. 'You have a brother in Stornoway.'

When I put down the phone I find a plate of rice and curry has been placed before me. I ask between mouthfuls how the community gets on. Do they feel isolated up here?

'Not at all. These people are true Christians, you see, even the younger generation. It is really very good. On Sundays, no shops are open, only a petrol pump for an hour. And the churches are very busy!'

The imam beams at the attentive observance of his Christian brethren.

'As far as I'm concerned,' one of the Leeds brothers puts in. 'If everyone followed their own religion as best as they could, well, we wouldn't have all the problems we do have.'

The Stornoway mosque opened in 2018. Aihtsham Rashid, a builder from Leeds, drove the project. He organised the tradesmen to adapt the old building, and crowd funding raised the money. One local church expressed suspicions of the mosque, and of Islam in general. But most locals came round to the idea, and some even helped raise funds.

'O relations are very good, very good,' says the imam.

After our meal, we wash in the tiny ablutions room, then enter the hall to pray maghrib together.

And so I have done what I set out to do. I've arrived at the most northerly mosque in Scotland. And to reach this point I've gone beyond the Scotland I'm used to into something else.

For Muslims, at least for the religious sort that you find in a mosque, Lewis is wonderful because it's less secular than the rest of the country. Less alienating. In this respect, Lewis is like the past.

'In ruined Scottish castles and other remnants of the past,' writes Leila Aboulela in her essay, 'I felt connected to the believing Christians who had spent their days in worship and accepted Fate. They were more like me than modern Britons.'

Much of Aboulela's novel *Bird Summons* is set in a forest surrounding a ruined monastery. The forest, even more than the monastery, is cast as a magical realm. It represents spiritual freedom – and another kind of consciousness.

I want to talk more about trees. But before that, as the early morning ferry leaves Stornoway, let me talk once more about nationalism, the SNP, and their discontents.

The ferry's on time, and the trouble-free crossing is blessed by sun and dolphins. But the state-owned ferry company – Caledonian MacBrayne – is rarely free of trouble these days. Its fleet is ageing, and increasingly failing.

There have been so many cancellations that in some cases island shops have had to ration basic foods.

It's the Scottish government's responsibility to solve the problem, yet the problem persists. The economic and social life of the islands depends on these ferries – without a reliable and regular service, their populations will dwindle. Quite a few residents blame the SNP – who are in government, after all – accusing them of mismanagement and incompetence. And there are grumblings elsewhere in Scotland about other declining public services, particularly education.

The SNP might have been in power too long. Like any long-term incumbent, it has become sloppy – and this was highlighted recently by a damaging financial scandal. Some of the money the party had raised specifically to campaign for independence was spent on election campaigning and other party activities instead. Former leader Nicola Sturgeon and her husband were both arrested. Both were later released without charge. It isn't yet clear exactly what's happened. Sympathisers point out that the SNP relies solely on membership fees and small donations for its funding. It doesn't receive union contributions like Labour, nor benefit from the largesse of corporations and billionaires like the Conservatives. Its corruption, they argue, is a minor matter of juggling funds rather than theft. But in any case, perceptions of the SNP have changed for the worse. The bitter post-Sturgeon leadership contest didn't help either – it revealed how divided the SNP is, and that there's a socially-conservative right wing as well as a liberal left in the party.

The greatest irony, and one which bothers islanders in particular, is that the SNP – which opposes central control by Westminster – is itself too centralising. That is, it is too focused on the services and infrastructure of the central belt, where seventy percent of the population is clustered, and not enough on the rural peripheries. Yet it is still Scotland's most popular party, and support for independence remains at around fifty percent, wherever the SNP stands in the polls.

Around fifty percent is not really enough for a major constitutional change, at least not for a positive change which the whole society can accept. If only fifty one or fifty two percent were to vote for independence, the ramifications would be similar to those throughout Britain after the Brexit vote was won by fifty two percent – that is to say, half the country's population would feel embittered. At the same time, fifty percent is far too high a proportion to just dissolve. In the coming years, each side of the argument will continue to try to convince the other. And I personally will continue to argue for independence. This is in part because I am horrified by English, and therefore British, politics. But even more fundamentally, I think independence is necessary for democracy to work in Scotland. The Scots haven't voted Conservative since the 1950s, but – at the British level – they keep having Conservative governments foisted upon them. The Scots voted solidly against Brexit, but they had to have Brexit, because the English voted for it. Without democracy there can be no self-determination, and the Scots, with their very different political culture to the English, deserve self-determination.

But where was I? I was going beyond Scotland. And have I fallen off the edge? Not really. So – though I have already reached my conclusion – I will try once more, towards a different edge.

To this end, once arrived back on the mainland, I drive around the north west corner of the country, a rugged and wildly beautiful territory. This is Sutherland – so named, even though it's in the furthest north, because it was the southern land from the point of view of the Norwegian Vikings who once ruled here and in the Orkney Islands.

I stop to climb Ben Hope, the northernmost Munro (a Munro is a Scottish mountain over 3,000 feet high – there are 282 of them). The heat of the climb reminds me of mountaineering in Morocco or Oman. It is 27 degrees in the valley. In the far north of Scotland. In mid September. I like the heat, but this is depressing. There is no climate left, only crazy weather. What damage we have done…

The land has been cleared of trees as it's been cleared of people. I fall asleep thinking of that, and in the morning I drive onto the ferry for Stromness, in the Orkney Islands.

The Orkneys are worth visiting for their ancient remains, which are, again, older than Stonehenge, older than the Pyramids. The Standing Stones of Stenness and the Ring of Brodgar are particularly impressive.

And the Orkneys represent another kind of beyond – which is why I came. The people look more Norwegian than Scottish. They spoke Norn – a version of Old Norse – until the early eighteenth century, and today their accent still bears Scandinavian traces. The Orkney flag – similar to the Norwegian flag – is flown more often than the Saltire. Only a third of the people here voted for Scottish independence, and recently Orkney's council announced it was considering 'alternative forms of governance' to remaining in Scotland, including becoming a self-governing territory of Norway. That's very unlikely to happen, but the expression of discontent with centralising rule, whether from Westminster or Edinburgh, is significant.

So I'm glad I've come, but also slightly disappointed. After the high mountains and the rugged western isles, it's a bit of a let-down to come down to the lowlands. The Orkneys are flat, plain, windy, with no trees at all. At the Scara Brae visitors' centre I read that people were clearing and burning the woodland here six thousand years ago. This left them with no shelter from the raging wind, no easy building material, fewer birds and animals, less aesthetic pleasure. And I ask myself, so what is wrong with us? Not just in recent centuries, but since the very beginnings of civilisation. Why would we do that to ourselves?

It's a long journey home. I break it up with a night on Loch Ness and another in Aberfeldy, and two walks in Glen Affric.

The first walk is at Plodda Falls, among a mighty forest of Douglas Fir which gently diffuses the sunlight. These trees were planted in the nineteenth century by a Lord Tweedmouth. To me now they feel like ointment on sores, or like breathing after a suffocation. The air is perfumed. Insects buzz.

Next morning – before the final drive home – I walk around Loch Affric. Here most of the land surrounding the water has been protected by a deer-proof fence. The result is quite amazing – Scots Pine and Silver Birch grow thickly, interspersed with Rowan and Willow. And so everything is beautiful even when there is no view. The landscape feels homely, although the peaks that rise above are savage. It feels that if I were stuck here, I would still survive. There are comfortable places to sit and take shelter, and nuts on the hazel trees, and birds singing in the branches.

So is Scotland terrible or wonderful? With trees, without clearances, it's truly wonderful. When it's a natural environment, a home for people and other creatures – and not an industrial estate, a launch pad for empire or a site of internal colonisation – then it's as lovely as anywhere in creation. But the same could be said for many other countries too.

MY LOVE FOR SCOTLAND

Jeremy Henzell-Thomas

I have a soft spot for Bonnie Scotland, and not only because I was a lecturer on the MSc. course in Applied Linguistics in Buccleuch Place at Edinburgh University for a while in the 1980s. At that time my parents lived in Inverness where my father worked for the Highlands and Islands Development Board, and I loved to escape the rigours of academe by periodically driving there up the scenic A9 via Perth and Aviemore through the extensive Cairngorms National Park. It was also a joy to see my two children flourishing and benefitting hugely from the outstanding education offered by George Heriot's School in Edinburgh, where my son was very proud to be coached on the rugby field by Andy Irvine, the captain of the Scottish international rugby team and an ex-pupil of the school. I remember the children's blue blazers which sported the motto 'Distribute Chearfullie', reflecting the charitable foundation at the core of the school's ethos. I also remember the plaques on the walls of some of the houses in Buccleuch Place of famous graduates, including the influential historian, essayist and philosopher Thomas Carlyle and James Africanus Horton the first African to graduate from the university.

The weather certainly did not account for my affection for Scotland, for I well remember that on taking up my post at Edinburgh in 1985 after returning from a three-year contract in tropical Papua New Guinea the temperature in Braemar was minus 27 degrees Celsius, and I never saw the sun from my north-facing office in Edinburgh. Only a minor inconvenience nonetheless, especially when I was blessed every year by the exhilarating Edinburgh International Festival, founded in 1947 to transcend political and cultural boundaries through its arts programme which features the finest performers and ensembles from the world of music, opera, dance, and theatre. And then there was the thrill of the world-famous 45-minute display of fireworks from the castle which traditionally signalled the end of the festival and which usually attracted more than 250,000 spectators, but which did not run this summer for lack of a sponsor and may be replaced in the future by an alternative large-scale event.

It's worth noting here that the present Edinburgh Festival Fringe includes an annual celebration of Islam, hosted by Edinburgh Central Mosque, the doors of which are open to everyone, old or young, of any faith or none, so as to remove barriers and to teach about Islam through an exhibition, guided tours, talks, and workshops.

It was a great pleasure to return to Edinburgh in March 2010, over 20 years since I had resigned from my lectureship, to be present at the formal opening by the Duke of Edinburgh, Chancellor of the University of the Alwaleed Centre for the Study of Islam in the Contemporary World. I had been privileged to serve together with Dr Anas Al Shaikh-Ali and Professor Charles Butterworth as advisors to Prince Alwaleed Bin Talal on his proposed funding for the establishment of new Centres of Islamic Studies at two British universities. These were intended to complement the centres he had previously funded at Harvard and Georgetown Universities in the US, and at the American universities in Beirut and Cairo. On our recommendation, Cambridge and Edinburgh were duly endowed, and the Edinburgh Alwaleed Centre has become noted for ground-breaking interdisciplinary research, dynamic teaching and innovative outreach projects, working closely with local, national, and international partners and stakeholders to promote a better understanding of contemporary Islam and the Muslim world. Its founding director, Professor Hugh Goddard, a noted expert on Christian-Muslim relations, continues to serve the Centre as an Honorary Professorial Fellow.

A fine example of the work of the Edinburgh Alwaleed Centre is Khadijah Elshayyal's comprehensive survey of Scotland's Muslim population based on the 2011 census, and I will have recourse to refer to this in due course.

In unravelling *Brit-Myth: Who Do the British Think They Are?* Chris Rojek contends that in 'the high-water mark of empire' Britishness was regarded as 'the combination of the best and highest that nature and nurture could provide in the British Isles', with each nation within the Union providing 'crucial elements that the others lacked' – a composite identity representing a 'marriage between Scottish invention and discipline, Irish daring and imagination, Welsh decency and pluck, and English application and genius for compromise.' The distinctive contributions of each nation could, of course be amplified almost *ad infinitum*, with moral seriousness, for example, being identified as a characteristically Scottish Presbyterian virtue, or fiery eloquence (both in pulpit and on political platform) as distinctively Welsh.

The reputation of the Scots for inventiveness is certainly well deserved, even more so when it is realised that since census statistics became available in the nineteenth century the population of Scotland has rarely exceeded 10 percent of the population of the UK. As stated on the Scotland.org website, 'the world has been revolutionised time and time again by great Scottish inventors', fuelled by their 'boundless imagination', 'passion for innovation' and 'inspired creativity', qualities given practical realisation by virtue of the 'discipline' Rojek also identifies with the Scots. Many of us will already know that we owe it to the Scots for the invention of the steam engine (James Watt), the telephone (Alexander Graham Bell), and the television (John Logie Baird), as well as the discovery of penicillin (Alexander Fleming). To that list, we can also add many more Scottish inventions that have transformed modern life – the refrigerator (William Cullen), the vacuum flask (James Dewar), the flushing toilet, (Alexander Cumming), the pneumatic tyre, (John Boyd Dunlop), the colour photograph (James Clerk Maxwell), the hypodermic syringe (Alexander Wood), the MRI scanner (Aberdeen University team), fingerprinting in criminal investigation (Henry Faulds) and the ATM (James Goodfellow).

A very instructive parallel can be drawn here with the history of Muslim inventiveness during the 'golden age' of Islamic civilisation as described in the National Geographic publication *1001 Inventions: The Enduring Legacy of Muslim Civilization* and by Olivia Sterns in 'Muslim Inventions that shaped the modern world.' Salim al-Hassani, Chairman of the Foundation for Science, Technology and Civilisation, and editor of *1001 Inventions,* is surely right in drawing attention to the forgotten history of Muslim inventiveness: 'There's a hole in our knowledge, we leapfrog from the Renaissance to the Greeks.' Al-Hassani's top ten outstanding Muslim inventions dating from the ninth to the twelfth century include surgery (al-Zahrawi), hospitals (ninth century Egypt), the flying machine (Abbas ibn Firnas), the university (Fatima al-Firhi), algebra (al-Khwarizmi), optics (Ibn al-Haitham), the crank (al-Jazari), several musical instruments, and the coffee drink.

Taken together, the inventions of Muslims and Scots constitute a generous proportion of those inventions that have given rise to the modern world.

A more topical connection between Islam and Scotland has of course been brought into the public domain with the appointment in March 2023 of Humza Yousaf as First Minister of Scotland and Leader of the Scottish National Party (SNP) to succeed Nicola Sturgeon, making Scotland the first of the four nations of the UK to elect a Muslim to serve in such a high office. The 37-year-old Humza is the son of first-generation Pakistani immigrants, and his appointment says much about the character of Islam in Scotland. Habib Malik, a former Head of Islamic Relief, Scotland, with whom Yousaf worked as a volunteer from 2003-2011, initially in a charity shop and then as a fund-raiser, describes Yousaf as 'a strong believer, very passionate Scottish. He loves Scotland, born in Scotland. He strongly believes in an independent Scotland as part of Europe.' Malik also states that young Muslims in Scotland see Yousaf as 'a role model and a truly inspirational figure'.

According to Khadijah Elshayyal's detailed and comprehensive analysis of Scotland's Muslim population drawn from the 2011 Scottish census and published by the Alwaleed Centre, University of Edinburgh, roughly 77,000 people or about 1.4 percent of the total population in Scotland are Muslims. Of these, 71 percent consider their only national identity to be Scottish or British (or any combination of UK identities). The census concluded that 'Muslims have a strong sense of belonging to Scotland in particular and the UK more generally.'

Elshayyal's Executive Summary also notes that only 4.5 percent of Muslims in Scotland have weak or no English language skills. This sharply contrasts with the claim made by David Cameron in 2016 that 22 percent of Muslim women in England struggled with speaking English, a claim strongly disputed by the Muslim Council of Britain, whose 'British Muslims in Numbers' report estimated that this figure was closer to 6 percent. In referring to 'David Cameron's illiterate proposal to counter radicalisation by targeting Muslim women', British journalist Nafeez Ahmed points out that the large discrepancy between Cameron's and the

MCB's figures was 'due to the fact that they were measuring different variables.' The MCB estimate was based on the population aged three and over born in Pakistan or Bangladesh, whereas the Cameron government's estimate relied on a base population of Muslim women aged 17 and over. In response to this, Ahmed raises the legitimate question, 'if the 16 and underage band was excluded as irrelevant, then why was the 65+ age band retained?' Leaving aside the complexities of flawed or loaded figures ('lies, damned lies, and statistics') exploited to promote political advantage, I think we can rely on Elshayyal's balanced study of the Scottish census as a valid pointer to the English language skills possessed by Scottish Muslims.

Of particular interest is Elshayyal's finding that the percentage of highly educated Scottish Muslims holding degree level qualifications has markedly increased during the period 2001-2011, from 22.2 percent to 37.5 percent, compared to only 27.1 percent for the UK population as a whole. The summary concludes that Muslims in Scotland are 'somewhat socio-economically better off' than the Muslim population in England and Wales, and that 'viewed together with other findings in this report, the socio-economic profile of Muslims in Scotland suggests an aspirational population with a keen capacity for social mobility.'

According to articles in *The Scotsman* and *The Herald* in August 2018, Detective Chief Superintendent Gerry McLean, who leads Police Scotland's counterterrorism unit, said that as a result of better integration and a sense of inclusiveness north of the border, Scotland had avoided being a target of Islamist terrorism. 'Muslims perhaps feel more part of Scottish society and day-to-day life. They will have a wide range of political opinions, they will have views on global events, some of them will be very vocal, but at the same time they don't want to advance that in terms of hurting people or society.' Academic research also gives credibility to the picture of a Muslim population feeling at home in Scotland. Stefano Bonino, author of *Muslims in Scotland: The Making of Community in a Post-9/11 World* told the *Sunday Herald* that various factors have contributed to a Muslim sense of ease and wellbeing in Scotland, and the country's standing as being off the radar to Islamist terrorists. These include 'Scotland's fairly small Muslim population as compared with England, the limited levels of ethnic segregation and the all-embracing nature of Scottish nationalism, which, unlike English nationalism, has espoused civic values.' Mohammed Asif, who fled from the Taliban in Afghanistan and arrived in Glasgow in 2000, also told the *Sunday Herald* that he felt 'lucky to end up in Scotland.' Despite misinformation about asylum seekers from the right-wing media, he said that 'whichever Scottish government has been in power – especially the SNP government – has always been supportive of asylum seekers and refugees.'

It is important, however, not to idealise the situation for Muslims in Scotland and to label Islamophobia as a completely alien prejudice. Both Humza Yousaf and the Muslim leader of the Scottish Labour Party, Anas Sarwar, whose father was the first Muslim MP to be elected to the UK Parliament, have spoken of their experiences of Islamophobia. A Syrian refugee was also stabbed and nearly killed in Edinburgh in 2018. And any notion that Scotland's Muslims were immune from the fanaticism of ISIS was shattered in 2013 when it came to light that Aqsa Mahmood had left her Glasgow home at 19 to join the extremist group in Syria. Longstanding bigotry among Protestants and Catholics in Glasgow should also serve to remind us that Scotland is not immune from entrenched sectarianism.

That said, there is good reason to believe that the relative sense of wellbeing associated with most Scottish Muslims can be attributed to the sense of cohesion and integration, as opposed to assimilation, that they feel. This ensures that they retain a strong sense of being Muslim while simultaneously valuing their identity as Scottish citizens and the values they represent. The *Islamic Tartan* website agrees that 'recent studies show that Muslims in Scotland are more likely to identify themselves as Scottish than Muslims in England are to identify as English, suggesting that the Scottish education system and media are more fair-minded, egalitarian and enlightened than in England. This is something to celebrate and promote as communities with dual heritage seek to overcome religious intolerance and cultural discrimination. Scotland is thus in the vanguard for the creation of new citizens with a combined sensibility of nationality, religion and ethnicity.'

A fine exemplar of dual-heritage integration and community cohesion was the Pakistani-Scot Bashir Maan who was the first Muslim to be voted into public office in the UK when he won the Kingston ward of the City of Glasgow for Labour from the Conservatives in 1970 and found himself sharing front page news with the defeat of the Celtic football squad by

Feijenoord in the European Cup final on the same day. Over the next half-century, Maan became a prominent and highly respected figure in many areas of public life in the city, as judge and community leader, working tirelessly to build bridges of understanding between communities and inspiring subsequent generations. He was awarded the CBE in 2000 for services to race relations and the community in Scotland. Today, the Scots-Asian community plays a vital role in the enrichment of Scottish civic and cultural life which had been so amply encouraged and supported by Bashir Maan.

Bashir Maan describes some of the historical connections between Islam and Scotland on the Islamic Tartan website. He points out that Islam and Scotland have been connected as far back as the eighth and nineth centuries when pilgrims travelled to the Holy land and Scots traded with the expanding Islamic empire in Spain and North Africa. Maan mentions the 'discovery of silver coins from a hoard at Talnotrie, Glen of the Bar, Kirkcudbrigthshire, bearing the name of the mid-nineth century Abbasid Caliph al-Mutawakkal ala Allah. Other hoards discovered at Storr Rock in Skye and in Skail, Orkney (a Viking hoard) included a dozen coins from the eastern Islamic world dating from the tenth century.' Muhammad al-Idrisi, the twelfth century geographer and mapmaker, depicted Scotland on one of his maps which helped to inspire the explorers Christopher Columbus and Vasco Da Gama. Alan FitzWalter, High Steward of Scotland, and other Scottish knights (some of them Knights Templar) joined King Richard the Lionheart on the Third Crusade (1189-1192). Although Maan does not mention it, the fifteenth century Rosslyn Chapel in the village of Roslin, Midlothian, Scotland, has since the 1980s been associated with speculative theories connecting the chapel with the Knights Templar and the Holy Grail, and it featured prominently as such in Dan Brown's bestselling 2003 novel *The Da Vinci Code* and its film adaptation made in 2006. This has however been dismissed by historians as having no basis in fact, which is of course no reason to wholly discount it any more than we can safely dismiss the persistent legend of the Loch Ness monster as speculative illusion or fantasy.

As such an iconic inhabitant of Scottish folklore, Nessie surely deserves a digression at this point. According to Stephen Lyons, large aquatic beasties in Scottish folklore were first linked to Loch Ness by Saint

Columba, the man credited with introducing Christianity to Scotland. It is recorded in his biography that in 565 on his way along the shore of Loch Ness to visit a Pictish king, he saw a large beast about to attack a man who was swimming in the lake. In his 1974 book *The Loch Ness Story,* Nicholas Witchell referred to a number of twenty century references to large creatures in the loch, gradually shifting from such early mythical sightings to modern-day eyewitness descriptions. In 1933, a new road was completed along the shore, allowing a clear view from the northern side, and from this date the modern legend gained momentum as a media phenomenon inspired by an article in the *Inverness Courier* which described the sighting by a local couple of 'an enormous animal rolling and plunging on the surface'. Legions of monster hunters invaded the area after the actor, film director and big-game hunter Marmaduke Wetherell, having been hired by the *London Daily Mail* to track down the beastie, reported finding the fresh footprints of a large, four-toed animal which he estimated to be 20 feet long. Despite the fact that the footprints were identified by museum zoologists as those of a hippopotamus made with a stuffed hippo foot, and for the next three decades all further sightings were dismissed by scientists as optical illusions, Wetherell estimates that there have been more than 4,000 accounts of sightings by eyewitnesses since the hoax. Lyons concludes his article with the statement that 'what was most remarkable was that many of the eyewitnesses were sober, level-headed people: lawyers and priests, scientists and school teachers, policemen and fishermen – even a Nobel Prize Winner.'

I have inserted this digression about Nessie as a reminder (as much as to myself as to my readers) that in the midst of an essay replete with many 'facts' and statistics, it seems to me to be vitally important to keep our hearts and minds open to the mythical dimension that opens up more expansive vistas and keeps our imagination alive. This applies equally to the mysteries of the aforementioned Rosslyn Chapel which drew 181,500 visitors from across the world in 2019, and has featured along with Loch Ness, Edinburgh Castle, and Skara Brae (the best-preserved neolithic site in Europe), as one of Scotland's iconic destinations in the Channel 5 series 'Secret Scotland'.

To return to Scottish connections with the Muslim world, during the British Empire contacts increased markedly, with Scots travelling as merchants, members of the armed forces, engineers, missionaries, tea and indigo planters, teachers, and civil servants to many countries with Muslim populations, including India, Malaya, and Nigeria. A good example was George Turnbull, the Scottish engineer responsible from 1851 to 1863 for the construction of the first Indian long-distance railway line from Calcutta to Benares on the River Ganges. Scotland's landed families were a dominant force in the East India Company.

The first Muslims to settle in Scotland were seamen and servants brought over from India who worked from the late nineteenth century as pedlars selling drapery goods door to door in the rural areas around Glasgow. Their success in this endeavour encouraged their relatives and friends to join them so they could also improve their prospects by working in Scotland, and by the 1970s there were over 12,000 Muslims in Scotland working in a diverse range of trades and professions.

I readily confess to having an affinity with Scots, not because I have any known Scottish ancestry, but because of the Celtic roots I share with them in the Welsh dimension of my own family history. Historically, the Scots emerged in the early Middle Ages from an amalgamation of two Celtic-speaking peoples, the Picts and Gaels, who founded the Kingdom of Scotland (or Alba) in the nineth century. As we have seen, it was a Pictish king that Saint Columba was on his way to visit in the sixth century when he is reported as having seen that large beastie in Loch Ness.

So what is it about the Celts that draws me? Aware as I am of the risk of romanticising or stereotyping them, I think my impression of their courage on the field of battle and in the face of oppression is a major factor. Roman historians portrayed the Picts as barbarians and savages, kept at bay by the 80 miles of Hadrian's Wall, begun in 122, which marked the boundary between Roman Britannia and unconquered Caledonia to the north. The name Pict may be derived from Latin picti, 'painted', referring to their use of painting or possibly tattooing, something that horrified and intimidated the invading Romans. The Romans admitted that it was the ferocity and heroic courage of Celtic warriors that they feared the most, although it was the orderliness of the Romans that ultimately gave them the upper hand, in the same way as it was the stolid and orderly regimentation of mainly English troops that effectively countered the dreaded charge of the rampaging Highland Scots in the Jacobite rising in 1745, notably at the

Battle of Culloden. As for the 'dreaded charge', I'm reminded of 'Scotland Forever!', the celebrated 1881 oil painting and iconic representation of heroism by Lady Butler depicting the start of the charge of the Royal Scots Greys, a heavy cavalry regiment, at the Battle of Waterloo in 1815. Originally exhibited at the Egyptian Hall in Piccadilly in 1881, it is now in Leeds Art Gallery. The title of the painting comes from the battle cry of the Greys who called out 'Now, my boys, Scotland forever!' as they charged. So evocative is the image that during the First World War both the British and the Germans exploited it in their propaganda material, with the Scots Greys transfigured into Prussian cavalry by the Germans. When I lived in Malvern between 2008 and 2017 our house had a clear view of the iron age fort British Camp on Malvern Hills, the reputed location of the last stand of the Celtic chieftain Caractacus against the Roman invaders. Taken as a prisoner back to Rome, he so impressed the Emperor with his courage and eloquence that he was given his freedom and lived out the rest of his days in Rome. As already noted, Rojek identifies 'pluck' as a core virtue of the Welsh, but I would assign it equally to the Scots.

Two award-winning films, both made in 1995, also spring to mind when considering the valour of the Scots. The first, *Braveheart*, an epic historical drama directed by and starring Mel Gibson, portrays William Wallace, the Sottish knight and warrior who led the Scots in the First War of Scottish Independence against King Edward 1 ('Longshanks') of England. Despite being criticised for its many historical inaccuracies, the film has enhanced the legendary status of Wallace well beyond the shores of Scotland. Condemned to public torture and beheading for high treason, he resolutely refuses to submit to the king even whilst being disembowelled alive, and when the magistrate offers him one more chance if he were to ask for mercy, he shouts 'Freedom!' In 1314, Robert the Bruce, King of Scotland, led a Scottish army on the fields of Bannockburn against the army of King Edward II of England, invoking Wallace's memory so as to inspire his men to fight with him as they had done so courageously with Wallace. Chanting Wallace's name, they achieved a decisive victory on the battlefield, one of the most celebrated victories in Scottish history.

The second film, *Rob Roy*, starring Liam Neeson, and shot entirely on location in the Scottish Highlands, depicts the eighteenth century Scottish clan chief and folk hero Rob Roy MacGregor, declared an outlaw after a dispute with a nobleman, the Marquess of Montrose, who also seizes his land. The publication of *Rob Roy* by Sir Walter Scott in 1817, ensured his fame, although its depiction of its hero bore little relation to the historical figure. Hector Berlioz, an avid reader of the novels of Scott, was inspired by the book to compose an overture, *Rob Roy*.

The particular virtues Rojek attributed to each of the four nations might usefully be expanded. For example, to add to the distinctively English virtues of application and genius for compromise, we might also include modesty and reserve, as well as a respect for the creative amateur as opposed to making an idol of so-called professionalism. In the same way, to complement the Scottish virtue of disciplined inventiveness we might add moral seriousness. This has unfortunately been grossly distorted and stereotyped in depicting the Scots as staunch puritanical Calvinists, represented perhaps most starkly by the Protestant Reformation preacher John Knox, notorious for his polemical 1558 work *The First Blast of the Trumpet Against the Monstrous Regiment of Women* which attacked female monarchs, claiming that gynarchy or rule by women was contrary to Biblical teachings.

Daniel MacLeod, however, in his study of Calvinism in Scotland maintains that the belief that until very recently Scotland was a Calvinist nation is 'pure myth', since 'there have been very few periods when anything resembling Calvinism was the dominant influence in Scottish life and culture.' 'Part of the reason', he claims, is that Scotland amplifies its remaining Calvinist bodies through magnifying-glasses. 'We cannot shake off our fascination with the Free Church and the Free Presbyterian Church. They are part bogeymen, part scarecrow, part dinosaur and part Super Ego.' Yet, as he points out, the total male membership of the Free Presbyterian Church is probably less than a hundred and that of the Free Church only a fraction of the population of Inverness. 'Calvinism' has become a term 'used to disparage anything in Scotland... blamed for depression and alcoholism, the Highland Clearances, the disappearance of Gaelic folklore, the absence of great Scottish drama and prevalent underfunding for the arts.' It is what the Gaelic poet, Derek Thomson, called 'The Scarecrow', otherwise a Presbyterian clergyman: 'A tall, thin, black-haired man wearing black clothes' taking the heart out of music and 'lighting the searing bonfire of guilt in our breasts.'

In the same way as we might appreciate the positive convergence between Scottish and Muslim inventiveness, we might also detect a less positive convergence between the austere and puritanical religious stereotypes often projected onto Scots and Muslims. Just as puritanical 'Calvinism' has been misguidedly projected onto the Scots so puritanical fundamentalism is often disproportionately attributed to Muslims.

To see Scotland through the right lens, we surely need to bring to light the achievements of the Scottish Enlightenment during the eighteenth and early nineteenth centuries, although this is a topic that needs a major essay in itself. To be brief, let me simply refer to some key comments by Alistair MacDonald, a senior policy analyst based at the British Council office in Edinburgh, made in the run-up to the Edinburgh Festival of 2016. 'The origins of modern economics, sociology and linguistics can all be traced to the Scottish Enlightenment', he said, and 'Scotland has long been an incubator of radical thinking with influence far beyond its borders.' To all that we can of course add the flourishing of moral and natural philosophy, empiricism, science, engineering, architecture and medicine. This is all the more remarkable given the fact that at the time Scotland was a nation of barely one million people, compared to under six million in England, 25 million in France and 15 million across what is Germany today. At the time when eighteenth century England only had two universities (Oxford and Cambridge) Scotland had five (St Andrews, Glasgow, Edinburgh, and King's College and Marischal College, both in Aberdeen) and international students as well as Scots were attracted by the tolerant and expansive outlook of Scottish liberal education. In his study of Scottish literacy between 1600 and 1800, R.A. Houston points to the greater social mobility in Scotland that fostered a broader, more socially mixed and intellectually vibrant student body. The resultant openness to new ideas from Europe and the colonies was greatly admired by international scholars, scientists, and politicians. MacDonald quotes the plaudits of three of them: 'So far as science is concerned, no place in the world can pretend to competition with Edinburgh' (Thomas Jefferson); 'The University of Edinburgh possessed a set of truly great men, Professors of Several Branches of Knowledge, as have ever appeared in any age or country' (Benjamin Franklin); 'We look to Scotland for all our ideas of civilisation'

(Voltaire). In view of that, it is hardly surprising that the *Encyclopaedia Britannica* was first published between 1768 and 1771 in Edinburgh.

Many of us will probably be aware of key figures associated with the Scottish Enlightenment. An article in *The Scotsman* identifies several 'who helped shape the world', the most famous of whom are probably Adam Smith, the 'father of capitalism', whose text *The Wealth of Nations* set out the guiding principles of free-market economics, and the philosopher David Hume, whose major philosophical works – *A Treatise of Human Nature* (1739–1740), *Enquiries concerning Human Understanding* (1748) and *Concerning the Principles of Morals* (1751), as well as his posthumously published *Dialogues concerning Natural Religion* (1779) – remain highly influential. His boldly sceptical and empirical approach, disentangling philosophy from religion, and his 'science of human nature' based on observation and careful argument, grounding morality in human emotions, led Kant to affirm that Hume's works aroused him from his 'dogmatic slumbers', and Jeremy Bentham, the founder of modern utilitarianism, admitted that reading Hume 'caused the scales to fall' from his eyes. Hume concluded that no theory of reality based on reason is feasible and that only experience can be the basis of true knowledge.

That profound affirmation of the centrality of direct experience is somewhat reminiscent of al-Ghazali's contention that the way to certainty (*yaqin*) is through 'tasting' or direct experience (*dhawq*), although clearly al-Ghazali writes from a very different perspective, given the fact that Hume was reproached as 'the great infidel' by his pious adversaries. With that focus on direct experience, I am brought back to Edinburgh, where Hume spent most of his life, and in particular to the university, which, incidentally, Hume attended at the age of 11, and which formed the background to a life-changing experience of my own in 1988. This was a dream, one of several that had a direct bearing on my journey to Islam. In this dream, I had been asked to give the oration or eulogy at the funeral of a Saudi princess before a large audience at a public stadium. I recalled at the time that the Saudi Princess Mishaal had been publicly executed for adultery in 1977 at the age of 19, an event covered in the British 1980 documentary *Death of a Princess*. I have no doubt that my dream was reflecting this and pointing to my own passion for championing the soul of the feminine which became so important to me in my persistent critiques of the patriarchy over the years. I had another dream at the time in which I saw a young woman dressed in a white shroud being stoned to death by jeering young men in a pit in the centre of a mosque.

In the dream about the princess, I had arrived at the stadium to deliver my eulogy, but there was a gatekeeper, the brother of the late princess. To gain entry, I needed to show my credentials, so I reached into my pocket to take out the text of my address, but on looking at it I saw that it was the text of a lecture I had actually just given on the MSc course in Applied Linguistics at Edinburgh University. It was a rigorous and comprehensive lecture about the cognitive processes involved in the comprehension of words and texts, and had been rated by the graduate students as the best lecture on the MSc course. But I immediately realised of course that an academic lecture on psycholinguistics was not something I could deliver as a eulogy for the princess. At that moment the gatekeeper looked up and his eyes met mine in one of those striking moments when something profoundly meaningful is communicated. He said: 'Only speak from the heart'. At that point I realised I was not ready for the task, and I turned round and walked away. Within a few months of the dream, however, I had abandoned my fully tenured lectureship and a promising academic career and left Edinburgh for a new life in Glastonbury. And so it was that Edinburgh became for me not the place of the fulfilment of academic ambition but a place where a window opened in my heart to reveal the psychological and spiritual journey that lay ahead.

THE ARTIST, THE GENERAL
AND THE HAJJAH

Leila Aboulela

Three Scottish historical figures have fascinated me and entered my fiction: David Roberts (1786-1864), Charles Gordon (1833-1885), and Lady Evelyn Cobbold (1867-1963). They were born well after the Acts of Union in which the Scottish and English Parliaments united to become the Parliament of Great Britain. All three travelled to the Middle East and Africa at the height of the British Empire. Talented, adventurous, and ambitious, they set out with a sense of entitlement. By writing about them, I was able to explore, at the individual level, Scotland's extensive engagement with the British Empire. Through a literary response, it is possible to gain understanding of a distinctive Scottish imperialism that existed side by side with Scotland's progressive, liberal tradition.

David Roberts was an artist whose lithographs of Egypt were hugely popular and are, even today, instantly recognisable. Charles Gordon was a Victorian military hero and one of the earliest examples of a media sensation. Gordon's luck ran out in Sudan when, while he was Governor General, Khartoum was put under siege by the Mahdist rebels, and he was assassinated. Lady Evelyn Cobbold was an aristocrat and a traveller. She converted to Islam and was the first European woman, on record, to undertake the Hajj.

Lady Evelyn was the only one of the three whose connection to the Scottish Highlands was clear in my mind. I had studied about Gordon in school in Sudan but thought of him as English. This was because the Sudanese refer to the British, who ruled Sudan from 1898 to 1956, as the *Ingeleez*. They did so not out of ignorance but because, officially, the British Empire was 'English', and all the Scots engaged in empire-building and administration presented themselves as English. When it came to international affairs, even the Scottish press of the time used 'England' in reference to the state. Similarly, I had known David Roberts's paintings but did not know that he was born in Edinburgh. I am always seeking connections between Sudan and Scotland – the country I came from and the one I am living in now. Through fiction, I bring them closer to give meaning to my own personal trajectory.

In my 2019 novel *Bird Summons*, three Muslim women embark on a road trip to the Highlands to visit the grave of Zainab/ Lady Evelyn Cobbold. Their leader, Salma, says, '*We might never understand what it's like to be the eldest daughter of the seventh Earl of Dunmore or to have a townhouse in Mayfair and a 15,000-acre estate in the Highlands, but Lady Evelyn was a woman like us, a wife and a grandmother. She worshipped as we worshipped though she kept her own culture, wore Edwardian fashion, shot deer and left instructions for bagpipes to be played at her funeral. She is the mother of Scottish Islam and we need her as our role model.*'

During the drive across Scotland, the women bicker and banter, field phone calls from family and ex-suitors from 'back home', and navigate the obstacles to getting to that grave on the Glencarron estate. Outsiders in Britain, hesitant in their interactions and feeling unsettled, the women seek in Lady Evelyn a connection that would make them more comfortable and grounded in the Scottish landscape. Transcending race, they seize on Lady Evelyn as someone 'like us', someone who had prayed as they pray, who had read the Qur'an and believed as they believe. Despite the huge gulf between her and them, the women's journey is an insistence on the sisterhood of Islam.

Salma, Moni, and Iman are united in that they are Muslim, Arab, and they moved to live in Scotland at some point in their lives. They see themselves as good, observant Muslims, but even within their conventional lives there is a danger of wandering astray. Salma has no intention of having an affair with Amir and feels safe flirting with him long-distance but, still, she is cheating on her husband and taking the first steps in ruining her marriage, and by extension her successful life. Moni believes she is a wonderful mother, sacrificing all for her disabled son, but in doing so she is neglecting everything else, and ultimately being unfair to herself. Iman feels justified in rebelling against the constraints of her femininity, but it is maturity that she needs more than freedom.

On the shores of Loch Ness, the women stay at a monastery which has been converted into a resort. Can they connect to the Christian monks who once worshipped here? '*They would have understood each other, asked forgiveness from the same God, followed the ten commandments, experienced the trajectory of weakness, sin, regret, then redemption.*'

Many impulses and observations go into making a novel. I had been struck once and truly dismayed by a television programme in which inner-city Muslim youth were taken to visit a cathedral in the English countryside. The programme was made during the years of the War on Terror, when it was deemed necessary for the media to wring its hands over the 'Muslim problem'. In that climate, the youngsters were filmed saying that they felt no connection whatsoever to either the cathedral or the countryside, that neither meant anything to them, though they were born and grew up nearby. I was dismayed because I often felt the exact opposite. In ruined Scottish castles and other remnants of the past, I felt connected to the believing Christians who had spent their days in worship and accepted Fate. They were more like me than modern Britons.

In *Bird Summons*, magic realism made it possible for me to link the present to the past and convey a sense of the unseen aspects of the religious experience. In their attempt to visit Lady Evelyn's grave, the women experience surreal manifestations of the spiritual dangers they are facing. The consequences of their life choices take tangible shapes that pose a threat and issue a warning. Away from the city (which represents restrictions, formality, and rituals both religious and secular), the spiritual freedom that the women encounter is vast and beyond control. As Lady Evelyn was able to transform her life, undertaking the pilgrimage to Mecca as a lone European woman to become the first British hajjah, so do the Arab women in Scotland traverse a spiritual expanse and gain a better understanding of their roles and the truths of their existence. Outdoors, the women feel that their worship is witnessed by nature. '*In the back of her mind [Moni] wondered if she was making history. Perhaps for the first time ever, the words of the Qur'an were reaching this particular part of the earth. Perhaps one day, to her credit, coastline, machair and sandstone would bear witness to what they had heard her recite.*' And in another chapter, '*The grass was [Salma's] prayer mat, the wind a protector, her knees felt grounded to this particular piece of earth. She* spoke to it and said, "Bear witness for me on the day I will need you to. On the day you will be able to speak and I will not.'"

I first encountered Lady Evelyn Cobbald in Michael Wolfe's wonderful 1997 classic anthology *One Thousand Roads to Mecca: Ten Centuries of Travelers Writing about the Muslim Pilgrimage.* Only a handful of the entries were written by women and so hers made an impact. It was taken from her book *Pilgrimage to Mecca*, which was first published in 1934. The book was reissued in 2009 by Arabian Publishing with an excellent and long introduction by William Facey. The introduction serves as a biography as well as a critical assessment of Lady Evelyn Cobbald as a worldly writer who moved in circles that included T.E Lawrence and Marmaduke Pickthall. She had spent her childhood in Algiers and Cairo and, as was typical of the Victorian aristocracy, spent most of her time with the household staff. These nannies were Muslim, and with them she visited mosques, where the call of the azan made a deep impression on her. As an adult, visiting the Vatican with friends, she was asked by the Pope if she were a Catholic. In the introduction to *Pilgrimage to Mecca* she writes, 'I was taken aback for a moment and then I replied that I was a Moslem. What possessed me I don't pretend to know as I had not given a thought to Islam for many years. A match was lit and I then and there determined to read up and study the Faith. The more I read and the more I studied, the more convinced I became that Islam was the most practical religion'.

My admiration for Lady Evelyn, which verged on awe, killed my ability to fictionalise her. I rendered her as she was and not as an imaginary character. I could not put words in her mouth nor place her in situations that I contrived. As a result, in *Bird Summons* she is a figure revered by the women who are visiting her grave. The novel is about them and not about her. She is an inspiration to them; her book accompanies them on the journey and they are impressed by her story of conversion. I personally found myself moved by the account of her burial. Reading about it brought tears to my eyes; writing about it in the last chapter of the novel felt like reaching a destination. '*In January 1963, when Lady Evelyn died in a nursing home in Inverness, a telephone call was made to the mosque in Woking. The story the imam heard was strange. An aristocratic Scottish woman, over ninety years old, had laid down the terms of her funeral in a will. She wished to be interned according to the rules of her faith, a faith that was not that of her family or the people around her. She wanted an imam to read the prayers in Arabic. She wanted bagpipes to be played and no Christian minister must be present. She wanted to lie facing Mecca in a place where the red stags could run over her grave. The imam took the overnight train to Inverness, far away, he later said, like the distance between Lahore and Karachi…'*

I found it easier to fictionalise Charles Gordon in my 2023 novel *River Spirit*. The novel charts Sudan's pivotal move from Ottoman rule to becoming forcibly part of the British empire. The novel is narrated from the viewpoints of several characters, most of them Sudanese and women. Each character passes on the baton of the story to the next. One of the characters is Gordon himself, Governor General of Sudan, who was killed in Khartoum in 1895 by revolutionary forces. These had put Khartoum under a tough siege for several months while Gordon held out, standing on the roof of his palace, looking out with his telescope over the Blue Nile, desperately waiting for the British relief expedition. When it did arrive, it was too late.

Gordon was the archetypical Victorian hero. He had supressed the Taiping rebellion in China and was dubbed by the adoring British press as 'Chinese Gordon'. His death at the hands of a rogue assassin, and the hacking of his head, just two days before the relief expedition arrived, was a national trauma for Britain. Queen Victoria wept, his journals were published widely, and countless books were written about him. In the 1960s, Hollywood glamorised him with the epic war film *Khartoum*, in which his character was played by Charlton Heston, and Laurence Olivier, in blackface, played his Sudanese enemy!

Attending school in Sudan, I had studied a different version of history, the Sudanese version, in which Gordon was himself his own worst enemy. Gordon believed himself to be exceptional. Delusional, stressed, he defied authority and forced the British government to send in an army to rescue him. His stance resulted in the death of many Sudanese. If he had surrendered Khartoum instead of holding out at all costs, its inhabitants would have been spared much bloodshed.

In my novel, Gordon does not speak until the start of the last quarter. He comes late into the story because from the Sudanese perspective, the story had started long before his arrival. In the nineteenth century, Sudan was part of the Ottoman Empire, and was ruled through Egypt. The

Sudanese lived on the frayed edge of an empire that was in decline. Years of harsh rule, excessive taxation, and cruel exploitation had taken their toll. People started anticipating the prophecy that the Mahdi – the Guided One – would surely appear to rescue them from the awfulness of their lives. When a man named Muhammed Ahmed claimed that the Prophet Muhammed had told him in a dream that he was the Mahdi, the Sudanese took heed. Muhammed Ahmed announced that people didn't need to pay taxes and that they should revolt against what he pronounced as the 'infidel' government.

In my research I found it fascinating that the ulema of Khartoum, themselves government employees and loyal to the Ottoman Caliphate, did not immediately reject Muhammad Ahmed's claim to being the Mahdi. Educated in the prestigious Azhar University, well versed in the characteristics of the Expected Madhi as described in the hadith, the ulema's initial response was to hear him out and give him the benefit of the doubt. When they found that he did not fulfil the characteristics of the Mahdi, they (and later the Azhar) issued fatwas and proclamations against him. The northern Sudanese tribes adhered to these fatwas and supported the government. So did the Sufi tariqas which Muhammad Ahmed had abolished along with the four schools of Islamic law!

The Mahdist rebellion started as a religious movement that denounced a world which was coming to an end. Its adherents wore patches on their clothes and lived frugally. Armed only with spears and farming utensils, they were able to defeat, against the odds, the government soldiers that were sent against them. The news spread throughout Sudan of these miraculous victories as proof of Muhammed Ahmed's authentic Mahdism. When one success led to the other and more tribes joined in, the movement became a nationwide revolution against foreign rule. Worldly gains and political power became part of the impetus. The Mahdi also began to fight the Sudanese tribes who refused to join him. Every Sudanese was compelled to pay allegiance to his cause. If they did not, they were regarded as a *kaffir*. At one point, even marriages were annulled between women living in territories under the Mahdi's rule and their husbands who fought on the side of the government.

In the meantime, Britain had invaded Egypt, and was ruling Sudan as a subsidiary territory. This was when Gordon stepped into the picture. He was appointed by the Khedive of Egypt, but he was getting his orders from London. When he arrived in Khartoum, the Mahdi had already taken over the west of the country. Gordon's orders were to evacuate the Egyptian garrisons in Khartoum; the roused British press wanted their hero to 'smash' the Mahdi. Instead, the Mahdi put Khartoum under siege and Gordon started calling out for a rescue expedition. This again was supported by British public opinion and, after pressure, an expedition was gathered and sent out. It arrived too late, exactly two days after the Mahdists had taken over Khartoum and assassinated Gordon.

The Prime Minister, William Ewart Gladstone, was blamed for delaying the relief expedition, and the Liberal government fell as a consequence. Gordon had certainly captured the public imagination. For the next fourteen years, as Sudan remained an independent state under Mahdist rule (a rule comparable to those of ISIS or Boko Haram), the desire to avenge Gordon bubbled. His death was used to extend British influence in Africa. He was lauded as a hero, and many young men were inspired to fight to 'regain' the Sudan. It was conveniently forgotten that Gordon had disobeyed orders. Instead of evacuating as he was instructed to, he had dug in. Many Sudanese lives would have been saved if he had surrendered Khartoum to the Mahdi.

I hesitated to write about Gordon, let alone from his point of view. He was an imperialist and a racist, opining in his journals that all black women were sluts. Researching his life was wading into propaganda. There was so much material that I did not want to be influenced by! So, I began my novel with the Sudanese characters, telling the Sudanese perspective before allowing Gordon to speak in chapter nineteen. As I had used first names with the other characters, I also entitled his chapter 'Charles' rather than Gordon. This was a simple change but it freed something within me. The name 'Gordon' was so loaded, so much talked about. 'Charles' was more humble; I could write about a Charles. Also, for the first time in my writing life, I used the second person. I began the chapter with, *'You like how they say your name, changing the 'g' to the guttural 'gh', elongating the second syllable so that it sounds Scots. Ghur-doun. Ghur-doun Basha, they say. The title 'Pasha' is Ottoman as are the decorations of the Order of the Osmanieh and the Order of the Medjidie. You do not mind honours, they sit well with your nature, they do justice to your achievements. Major-General, Companion of the Order of the*

Bath, Companion of the Order of the Dragon, Chevalier of the Legion of Honour,
the Imperial Yellow Jacket. It is monetary prizes that you shun. You detest the
acquisition of wealth, the constant wrangling over salaries and benefits. It is
pedantic and you do admire spirit.You admire your enemies, the fanatics led by the
Mahdi, the dervishes who throw themselves into battle as if death will not touch
them.You wish you were leading them.'

The conquest of the Sudan took place in 1898. The decisive Battle of
Umdurman (in which a young Winston Churchill served) was particularly
brutal, with thousands of Sudanese killed. Using the latest, most powerful
artillery, the British destroyed the Mahdi's tomb. To avenge Gordon, the
Mahdi's body was dug out and dismembered. To copy Gordon's death, his
skull was detached and preserved while his bones were thrown in the Nile.
And Gordon continued to be a symbol of what was right about
imperialism. He inspired soldiers and school children, missionaries and
colonial settlers. There are statues of him in London at the Embankment,
in Chatham, in Gravesham, and a memorial in Southampton.

If I get up from my desk now and drive for ten minutes, I will find a huge
bronze statue of Gordon right in the middle of Aberdeen city centre. My
own local Gordon statue! It was a shock when I first came across it, soon
after I first arrived in the 1990s. The word 'Khartoum' chiselled in the
inscription. I could not help but be thrilled by the connection to the city
where I spent the first twenty-three years of my life. Here, somehow, was
an assertion of my identify, proof of a shared history. Gordon had been
there, and I was now here. The university I had graduated from, the
University of Khartoum, was once Gordon Memorial College. The palace
where he died was only a few miles from where I had grown up. The Blue
Nile he gazed at every day was what had watered my ancestors for
generations. I knew his history, I knew his story, and this knowledge,
despite all the obstacles, enabled me to write about him. *'Every single day,*
you look north through your telescope, waiting for the sight of the red uniforms, the
flutter of the Union Jack. End of November was your calculation. Food wise and
ammunition, Khartoum could only hold out until the end of November otherwise 'the
game is up and Rule Britannia.'Yet here you are weeks later, just about. Soldiers
reduced to skin and bones, snoozing on their feet, people dying of malnutrition, so
many corpses in the streets that you pay twenty piastres to anyone who would bury
one. The city is shelled day and night. Shells fall in the Nile, scar buildings, kill

children and horses. Shells shatter the windows of the palace which you insist on lighting up through the night. Lanterns and candles, lots of candles, to ward off the beat of the war drums. Ghur-doun. Doun. Doom. They are beating for you and no one else. Every night, murdering your sleep, raiding your nerves, turning your hair white.

It is white now – all of it. You notice it when you shave. You notice too that your hand does not tremble. You are not afraid. It is others who are afraid of you. The Mahdi now encamped across the river, hesitating to attack, even though he knows the appalling condition of the city. Your officers who in your presence cannot hold their hands steady to light a cigarette. Grown men reduced to stammering because they face Ghur-doun. Ghur-doun who is not afraid of death.'

Gordon was not the only Scottish character in *River Spirit*. A disproportionate number of Scots played a part in Britain's colonial administration. I therefore had no reservation in including another man, Robert, the engineer whose true vocation is art. My initial idea for the novel was of a young man from Edinburgh who becomes fascinated by the vernacular architecture of colonial Sudan. He paints the Nile and starts to dress like a native. When he sketches the wife of a tribal chief and the drawing is discovered, his career and safety are in jeopardy. But I ended up deviating quite far from this original idea. The Sudanese woman in the drawing took centre stage, and the artist was no longer the main character.

As my writing progressed, Robert became more ruthlessly ambitious, enslaving a young woman in order to paint her. '*He saw her again. The girl he had seen six months ago, the one he had almost purchased and then at the end didn't, feeling it was beneath him to do so. He had often looked at the sketches he made of her that day. Her special beauty, only oil could do justice to her blue-black skin, the contrast of the white cloth against it, not only white, but any colour would sing. Her brooding eyes – the longing in them when she turned away to look at the river. On returning home that day, he was struck by a brilliant idea – he could free her once he was done with her. This would assuage his troubled conscience.'*

In constructing Robert's character, I researched Scottish artists and settled on David Roberts, the renowned Orientalist painter. So, from the inception, I was not fictionalising David Roberts but using his life to build a character that was already part of my imagination. I had known David Roberts's work for years. When my husband was a university student in 1980s Cairo, he bought a calendar of Ancient Egypt lithographs by David Roberts. He kept the calendar long afterwards and I was enthralled by the images. Bulky temples in the desert with a few tiny people next to them. The sunny, sandy pyramids of Giza. Romantic visions of boats sailing on the Nile at sunset. When my mother-in-law passed away, we found among her belongings a coffee table book entitled *Egypt-Yesterday and Today* by David Roberts. In it were page after page of gorgeous paintings of the Nile Valley, all in his distinctive, unmistakable style inspired by his travels in Egypt in the mid-nineteenth century. I also learnt that Roberts had been born in Edinburgh. One of the most famous Scottish artists of his time had painted my part of the world. I was excited by the connection.

David Roberts not only painted archaeological sites, among his best works were also lavish crowded street scenes, majestic mosques, souqs and slave girls. This of course was the exotic East – the Temple of Karnak, obelisk and Sphinx – and though I knew that it was idealised and not altogether 'real', I succumbed to the charms of his Orientalist vision. Now, in my hallway in Aberdeen, there are four framed lithographs by David Roberts. Minarets and the facades of mosques are rendered in extraordinary architectural detail. Women wear veils like the ones my great-grandmother wore. In *The Silk Merchants' Bazaar*, piles of merchandise and shoppers mingle under intricate woodwork and lattice windows.

In his biography by Katharine Sim, Roberts's childhood is described in Dickensian terms. Born in 1796 in West Kirk, his family lived in the cramped, downstairs rooms of a tenement. Two of his siblings died at a young age. Robert's father was a shoemaker, and his mother took in washing to supplement the family's income. They could not afford to keep their son at school, and at the age of ten, David was apprenticed to a housepainter. In his teens he worked for a circus as a scene-painter, and then joined a company of strolling players. He continued to design and paint stage scenery in the Edinburgh Theatre Royal, the Glasgow Theatre Royal and, in his late twenties, in the Drury Lane Theatre London. Painting full-scale scenery and stage sets had a big influence on his later paintings of the Middle East.

David Roberts, though, never did travel as far south as Sudan. Instead, after Egypt, he went to Syria and Palestine, and accomplished his most popular work *The Holy Land, Syria, Idumea, Arabia*. During his long tours, he produced vast amounts of drawings and watercolours. On his return to Scotland, he used these as a basis for paintings and lithographs. These lithographic prints were produced in mass quantities and sold to the public through a system of subscription. Appearing before the advent of widespread photography, and at a time when there was huge interest in the lands of the Bible, Roberts quickly garnered subscribers, among them the young Queen Victoria. The Royal Collection today includes her complete set.

In David Roberts's work I was often struck by how disproportionally small people were in relation to the buildings. That he was more fascinated by landscapes and monuments was also evident in his journals. The sun setting over the hills, the white sails of the boats on the Nile, fascinated him more than the people with whom he did not have the language skills to communicate. An exception to this were the Nubian woman, graceful dancing girls and those filling their water jugs at the river. After his death, such enthusiastic passages were censored by his 'prudish' daughter Christine and regarded as too 'licentious' to be made public.

Christine's mother, Margaret, had been an alcoholic. His wife's behaviour was a constant source of distress for David as she quarrelled with his parents and pressured him with requests for more money. Keeping Margaret at a distance and his beloved, Christine, close, was a life-long struggle. Even after being separated for years, he was constantly dodging his wife by travelling, and calling her 'the brazen faced monster' as time and again he had to settle her debts.

Despite these difficulties, Roberts rose to become one of the most prominent Orientalist painters of his time, counting the artist Turner and the novelist Thackeray among his admirers. He was talented, hardworking and ambitious — and these qualities I borrowed for my fictional Robert labouring on his art in Sudan. I also dropped the name of David Roberts into this paragraph. '*He was satisfied with his work, intoxicated by what he could further achieve. A body of work that would possess more than charm. As good as anything by the Glasgow Boys — those children of shipping magnates who could afford to study in Paris, enrol in ateliers; sons of the manse propped up by financial support. All the formal education Robert ever had was from the School of Art, especially set up for working men unable to study full-time. Every day except Sunday, he would rise before dawn to attend lessons before putting in a full day at the shipbrokers. An oil portrait of the girl ... could end up as masterful as Jean-Leon Gerome's Bashi-Bazouk. Not as lavish, certainly starker but still in its own way gorgeous. His conception of it was so strong it was palpable; he was confident that he could pull it off once he got back home and had the space and materials for a large oil canvas. In the meantime, his technique and subject matter were on a par with David Roberts's, his watercolours comparable to Arthur Melville's, dare he say, work that Owen Jones, had he still been alive, would have approved of. In a year, he could make his mark in the world of Scottish Art. His name listed among the artists in a catalogue. His name linked to the painters who depicted the Orient. His own atelier. Each painting selling for thirty pounds, fourty, sixty. He would never have to work with ships again.'*

David Roberts achieved the dream of the outsider joining the inner circle. In 1841, he was elected as a Royal Academician, was awarded a prize at the Paris International Exposition, and later received the Freedom of the City of Edinburgh. The child with little prospects had become one of Scotland's establishment figures. And history will count him as one of the first British professional artists to interpret the Middle East. His vision of the Middle East became the quintessential one.

The regions David Roberts travelled through and sketched were part of an ageing Ottoman Empire. In only a few decades, these places would fall into Britain's hands. The explorers, missionaries, soldiers, and administrators who came to play a role in the British Empire very likely travelled there with expectations built around the images portrayed in his art. Among these travellers were Gordon, and among them was Lady Evelyn Cobbald. They would most likely have been familiar with Roberts's work.

David Roberts (1786-1864), Charles Gordon (1833-1885), and Lady Evelyn Cobbold (1867-1963). Three Scottish figures who spent considerable time in the Muslim world, took and gave in varying portions. Roberts and Lady Evelynn were secure in their Scottish identity but completely divergent in class. Gordon, descended from generations of British military men, was born in England and hardly ever lived in Scotland. His public image was that of an English army officer. As men, Gordon and Roberts enjoyed more freedom and agency than Lady Evelyn who, despite being adventurous, was held back by social conventions and motherhood. It was through conversion that she penetrated deeper into the Muslim world and saw what they never did – the Ka'ba and the Prophet Muhammad's mosque in Medina. Lady Evelyn and Gordon were closer in social grouping but, as a writer, she might have connected more intellectually with the artist, David Roberts. The lives of the three overlapped but, as far as I know, they never met. Roberts in the last years of his life would have read in the newspapers about the young Gordon's outstanding success in China. Gordon as a practising Christian would have been interested in Roberts's lithographs of the Holy Lands. Lady Evelyn was eighteen when Gordon was assassinated. In Cairo with her father, moving in British colonial circles, entranced by the azan, she would have been following the dramatic news of the Khartoum siege and Gordon's last days. Visiting the Giza pyramids and the Sphinx for the first time, I imagine her comparing the reality with David Roberts's lithograph of the same scene.

I believe that Scotland, the nation which produced these three exceptional individuals, endowed them with gravitas and awareness of the marginal perspective, the desire to understand (if not always fully) and the will to see (if not always clearly). Roberts, Gordon, and Cobbold were not simple opportunists. They shared a sense of integrity and depth; the desire to excel in their chosen field and the urge to engage fully with their surroundings.

Scotland is a nation that is familiar with resistance and opposition. Its political culture has always been one of enlightenment and anti-imperialism. This, however, did not prevent it from playing an active role in the British Empire. Roberts, Gordon, and Cobbold arrived in North Africa as privileged, white members of a colonial class, shaped by Victorian values and prejudices. Lady Evelyn was steeped in aristocracy. David Roberts's orientalist paintings paved the way for European dominance and hegemony. Gordon, in his diaries, railed bitterly against the Liberal Prime Minister, Gladstone, when the latter stood up in parliament and declared that the Sudanese had a right to freedom. The extent of the legacy of the three travellers illustrates the involvement of Scotland in the British Empire, a complicit relationship that cannot be denied.

SAVING THE ENVIRONMENT

Nayab Khalid

During the past few years, the global environmental movement has been undergoing a period of reflection and reckoning, much like other social justice movements. The whiteness, privilege and colonial origins of the environment movement are being questioned. The discourse is de-centring the 'climate anxiety' and 'climate grief' felt by the privileged denizens of the 'Global North', and focusing instead on the displacement, violence, and threats to lives and livelihoods faced by the people of the 'majority world' due to environmental breakdown. Work is finally being done to understand the intersections of the climate and ecological crisis with racism, economic disparity, and other social justice issues.

In Scotland, where I live, a lot of this work has been focused and shaped around communities – communities of place, communities of practice, communities of interest, and communities of faith – including, of course, the Muslim community.

But how much of this work is real? Are the powers that be – the Scottish Government, environmental organisations, and other third sector initiatives – committed to a real change in practice? Has the Muslim community properly integrated and internalised this discourse? Has there been a lasting change in people's daily lives? Has there been any inkling of an Islamic environmentalist pedagogy? Or has this just been a case of pandering on one side and a funding opportunity on the other?

Let me being with my own estrangement and alienation from spaces dedicated to environmentalism and sustainability when I first moved to Scotland.

I grew up in Islamabad, Pakistan. My parents were academics and public servants, my education was private and western-liberal, and my family background is Punjabi and Sunni – it has taken me some time to unpick my own majoritarian privilege. Growing up, there was always a sense of stewardship towards the environment and towards people less fortunate. It was never something I was explicitly taught, but it speaks volumes about my parents that I can't perceive being any different way. Moving to Scotland then, moving to an 'elite' university in a tiny town on the picturesque east coast, was jarring for many reasons. But mostly, it was jarring because – suddenly an ethnic minority – I had lost this sense of ownership and stewardship. It wasn't that I found myself in predominantly white spaces, be it community gardens, skill shares, workshops, and so on. It was my perceived role in these spaces – I was the person that needed to be looked after and catered to, a 'service user' and not someone with skills and capabilities of my own. It has taken me many years to regain the sense of ownership, and in some ways this essay is a chronicle of that journey.

It is true that the University of St Andrews is very much a microcosm, under-representative of most of Scotland as well as unrepresentative of me. Most students are American, English, or middle European (German, French, Dutch), financially very comfortable, naive, upbeat and very, very privileged. I remember my friend, a Dutch fellow student, for example, who would fly his recycling back to the Netherlands with him on breaks because he was convinced that the Dutch recycling system was far superior to the UK's own. He was otherwise a very passionate and committed activist and campaigner who was always front and centre in any protest or initiative. He may well have been right about the recycling system, but I remember this particular idiosyncrasy of his because it struck me as particularly representative of exactly the kind of middle-class environmentalism, I have a problem with, more a performative gesture or artistic intervention and not a step towards coherent behavioural change.

In her article 'Indigenizing the Anthropocene', Métis scholar, Zoe Todd, talks about the 'white public space'. The term originates in criticisms of academia, which is and continues to be patriarchal, Eurocentric, and white. However, according to Todd, the academy is not the only 'white public space'. She utilises the term when critiquing the current engagement with environmental causes and crises, especially centred around the narrative frame of the Anthropocene – a term which is gaining traction in academic and environmentalist spaces, and which describes the current epoch in which humans are the dominant drivers of global geological change. As A PhD candidate at the University of Aberdeen in the early 2010s, I imagine Todd encountered similar attitudes to those I found at St Andrews. Scotland is, after all, a country with a long and bloody history of enclosure, clearances, and deindustrialisation, the complex nexus of class, power, and land reform. Nevertheless, the Scottish environmental movement as a whole is well grounded and rooted in working class and communities-led activism as exemplified in coal miners and factory workers setting the agenda for class-conscious environmentalism as far back as the Scottish Trades Union Congress of 1972, the community land buyout by the people of the island of Eigg in 1997, and in Glasgow, Colin MacLeod's Pollok Free State anti-motorway protests in the early 1990s. These were certainly well-rooted instances of activism. But the same cannot be said of the current sector – the intersection of the academy, the arts and a certain type of climate activism.

Activist and Quaker academic, Alastair McIntosh argues in *Riders on the Storm*, that the current mainstream climate activism movements, such as Extinction Rebellion or Deep Adaptation, lack scientific rigour in their publications and manifestos. But his real concern comes from what he perceives as 'alarmism' – a fetishisation of the climate crisis, and a projection of people's personal anxieties. 'When I listen to frightened people talk about global warming', he says, 'it can seem as if the climate can become what psychotherapists call a 'chosen trauma' – a focus of meaning that objectifies and seems to make sense of wider constellations of anxiety in their life'. McIntosh presents a rather terrifying picture of the extremes of such attitudes – such panic can lead to activists advocating potentially disastrous ideologies such as ecofascism, and there is already a growing alt-right fringe in the environmental movement. Both the 'Unabomber' in the US and the Christchurch mosque gunman included a 'green' narrative in their manifestos.

While these extreme attitudes are few and far between, this anxiety, coupled with a disconnect from working class or ethnic minority communities, can manifest in strange ways. One example is the Remembrance Day for Lost Species (RDLS), whose founders have since conclusively reflected on and critiqued their own privilege and the exclusionary nature. They pointed out that their approach lacked an analysis of structural racism and classism. RDLS was an environmental project and an artistic intervention which grieved the loss of biodiversity and extinct species in rituals, vigils, and other artist-led projects. However, an artistic project of this kind is largely irrelevant to people who are culturally, economically, or otherwise marginalised. As the RDLS founders said, 'rather late in life, we realised that our brand of environmentalism was a product of racial and class privilege – and worse, that its "colour blindness" colluded in the ongoingness of white supremacy. Privilege had led us to assume it was acceptable to focus on biodiversity loss without building this work on a foundation of solidarity and anti-racist practice.'

In Scotland, the shift in attitude was signalled by the Government's Climate Challenge Fund – the CCF, which ran from 2008 to 2022. It was designed to support community-led projects towards reductions in carbon emissions, as well as develop a sustainable legacy of low-carbon behaviour. CCF grants supported a range of projects in areas such as energy efficiency, sustainable and active travel, reducing and recycling waste, and food growing.

When it was first launched, the CCF struggled with engagement from 'ethnic minority' communities. So did the CCF, and the shift in attitudes and culture, had any impact on the Scottish Muslim communities? I put the question to Zarina Ahmad, formerly a Climate Change and Environment Officer at the Council for Ethnic Minority Voluntary Organisations, Scotland (CEMVO Scotland) and currently a PhD candidate at the University of Manchester. CEMVO Scotland's position as an intermediary and partner organisation for the Scottish Government on issues of race and equality made it uniquely well-suited to advise the government on the CCF and related projects. Ahmad worked extensively with many ethnic minority communities and organisations in Scotland – in particular Muslim community groups, acting as a liaison between them and the Scottish Government, as well as providing training, support, and development.

At the time, the Scottish Government's attitude towards ethnic minority communities was that they were 'hard to reach' communities – communities that weren't engaging on climate change, communities that didn't want to prioritise environmental issues, or had other priorities such as racism and discrimination. Ahmad said that, when she was brought in to engage with these communities, she had expected her work to be difficult but 'it was the easiest job I've ever done!' This was for two reasons: First, climate change was not an abstract concept for most of the communities she worked with – many of the people involved had experienced droughts, floods and other hostile conditions first-hand. Second, most of the communities she was working with were faith-based communities, and their faith already provided them a strong grounding in environmentalism.

In her role as liaison with the Scottish Government, Ahmad's first step was to collect data. She referenced a conference she had organised in 2012. This provided a platform for community organisations to meet with the Scottish Government and the administrators of the fund. She was able to 'prove to the Scottish Government that if these communities knew about the funding, they would apply for the funding.' She said that the conference provided evidence to the Scottish Government that 'targeted work with ethnic minorities was needed,' and opened up the space for this work.

Some tangible results which followed from this included being able to put into place targeted outcomes pertaining to ethnic minority communities which the CCF administrators had to meet, as well as setting up a grant to enable communities to develop their projects. Ahmad realised that, since the communities she was working with had a very different starting point than the groups which were already applying for the fund, work needed to be done in order to make the fund more equitable. The development grant enabled community groups to undertake feasibility studies, do consultations, develop organisational capacity, and carry out community engagement around climate change and climate action. According to Ahmad, 'this meant that when they were doing their funding applications, that they were in a stronger place.

Ahmad also provided help and support towards writing the funding applications. She acknowledges that this went a long way towards developing trust and building strong relationships with the community groups she was working with. It meant a lot for people to know that this wasn't just a fly by night thing. Like, 'Zarina's not just come in, told us about funding, and disappeared. She's actually here to help us work'.

In terms of community engagement, what really worked was shifting the conversation from CO_2 emissions and net-zero targets towards stewardship and responsibility. Many community leaders initially did not understand how climate action linked to Islam – for example, what do solar panels or recycling have to do with Islam? But when Ahmad started speaking about the relationship with the soil and the land, and the loss of biodiversity, bringing the conversation to values and ethics, attitudes began to change and things began happening.

Ahmad made the point that faith communities are in a unique position to bridge the global and local aspects of climate change. Mainstream activists, when they talk about climate justice, approach it from the point of view of 'somewhere else'. But there are also climate and environmental injustices within the UK that need to be linked up. There can't be a conversation about climate change without talking about things like poverty, racism, and other structural social injustices that are interlinked with climate change. Ethnic minority communities are able to provide both local and global perspectives which are needed in this conversation. For example, Ahmad says, 'if you've got somebody who's lived in the north of Pakistan or Nepal, their families have probably already been impacted by the glaciers melting.'

Environmental organisations in Scotland can be divided into two categories. In the first category, we find public sector organisations and NGOs which operate at the national level in conservation or land management such as NatureScot, The Forestry Commission, the RSPB, and the Scottish Wildlife Trust. In the second category, we have environmental activists such as Extinction Rebellion, Friends of the Earth, and others. For people of colour, and Muslims in particular, it is difficult to fit into either of these spaces. The activist space is difficult because a lot of the activism centres around direct action, which is not seen as a safe space for ethnic minorities, who are already marginalised and targeted. They just do not feel comfortable putting their bodies on the line in a similar way to white 'arrestable' activists. And then there was the NGO or public sector space, where there was a certain jargon in vogue, along with elitism, racism, and all the other 'isms'. These organisations are very white, and very nepotistic, and seldom open to insiders. However, as Ahmad points out, there has been a change in attitudes here too, over the last few years. Black Lives Matter was a turning point that made these organisations start to look inwards and confront their structural racism.

The CCF grants also changed things on the ground, albeit on a smaller scale. This was made clear by Javed Ali, managing director at the Andalus Mosque and Community Centre in Glasgow. Like its namesake, the emirate of al-Andalus in the Iberian peninsula, the Centre tries to evoke a feeling of 'Islam in the West'. It was set up in the year 2000 by Muslims who were born and raised in Glasgow and saw their cultural identity as being Scottish more than anything else, but who desired a place which reflected their Muslim religion and values. Ali envisions Andalus as a place for young people and for families, without the conservative, segregated – and frankly, closed off and inward looking – culture of the more mainstream mosques.

However – much like anyone else who's attempting to build something different – Ali finds that Andalus is somehow stuck in the middle. It is too 'radical' for the more conservative Muslims and yet too conservative theologically for the more secular or culturally Muslim. It tends to attract a more middle-class crowd, whereas Ali hopes to get more grassroots or working-class people involved. At the moment, the most frequent use of the Centre is for children's Quran classes. Rather wryly, Ali reflected that despite how otherwise indifferent they might be towards community initiatives, children's Quran classes are something almost all Muslim parents will support.

The Andalus Centre's Climate Challenge Funded project, called 'Living Active and Going Green', included a community garden space, an eco-cooking club, and an urban cycling club. As well as the quantitative targets required of any CCF project, such as CO_2 emissions reduction, the project aimed to inculcate a change in attitudes and culture, particularly around food and being active. Ali was fairly circumspect about the long-term success of the project. He criticised its short-term nature, pointing out that the momentum almost always dies when the funding runs out. He says that this is true for grant funding in general – the focus is on outcomes and results, and there is a tendency to get lost in technicalities. Now this was definitely true for CCF grants, where the focus on measurable or quantifiable targets often took away from the more community-led or behavioural-change aspects of the projects.

Despite his reticence, Ali acknowledged that the CCF grant gave Andalus the ability to build good infrastructure which could be used for future projects. It enabled his team to retrofit their building with LED lighting and double-glazed windows, as well as to set up their community garden and bike hub, and the beehives on their roof. But while the beehives have flourished, both the community garden and bike hub have fallen into disuse and disrepair. The community garden suffered when student flats were built next door, blocking off most of the light and creating a wind tunnel. Ali was also unhappy with his community members' approach to the garden – most people would just come to the garden to harvest or take, rather than volunteering their time towards growing for everyone. He complained that this attitude persists. Even though many Muslim and/or Asian people in Glasgow keep allotments or grow food in other spaces, there is little communality when it comes to people's attitudes towards food growing. On the other hand, Ali feels the bike hub is hampered by excessive health and safety requirements. He says that twenty years ago they could do what they wanted to, and weren't held back by risk assessments. Their bikes are currently in storage, waiting for the next big impetus – but the infrastructure is there!

Andalus's CCF project encountered the same issues that the Centre itself faces. Ali envisions the Centre as a space for developing people and ideas. In this respect, he'd prefer a more cohesive approach towards building for the future, rather than getting bogged down by short-term-ism or pursuing individual projects. He would like to bring people in who are interested in and support the vision of the Centre, rather than just bringing in people for a project and watching them leave when the project ends. He sees Andalus as a space for training volunteers, with paid (sessional) work available for those who are committed. He does struggle with finding enough volunteers though, since his approach towards volunteering is about inspiring people and inculcating leadership skills, rather than providing set tasks and guidelines.

Ali admitted that at the moment Andalus doesn't have enough capacity or structure to launch the types of projects we have been talking about, and that it needs to be more developed as an organisation. And a major reason for that is that there are not enough like-minded individuals and community members taking the vision forward. Like he says, at the end of the day the onus lies on the individual.

Of course, Andalus is just one organisation in a myriad of other Muslim community initiatives and organisations, all of which approach faith and environmentalism in different ways. Women on Wheels founder Shgufta Anwar says, 'in terms of what we're doing to the climate, with our cars, polluting it, not worrying about future generations, destroying the earth – that goes completely against our faith. Working on your faith and taking action against climate change, in my opinion, are kind of one and the same.' And Zahrah Mahmood, the president of Ramblers Scotland, says of hillwalking, 'I've managed to enhance my spiritual health through the outdoors. The Prophet Muhammad (peace and blessings be upon him) used to frequently escape the hustle and bustle of the city to enjoy the solitude of the hills, using it as a means to reconnect and reflect with God. I now strive to have this intention when escaping to the mountains.'

What ties all of these threads together is the understanding that there needs to be a depth to environmental activism. To build a lasting movement, our approach needs to be values-led and relatable. For Scottish Muslim communities, this means approaching environmentalism from a sense of stewardship and responsibility, not just responding to funding opportunities or jumping from one project to another. For outside actors seeking to lend their support and their expertise, this means understanding the unique and valuable perspectives brought to the struggle by communities and faith groups.

THE MUSLIM CONNECTION

Saqib Razzaq

According to the 2021 Census, 1.4 percent of Scots are Muslim. Most live in Glasgow and other big cities, but they are present in the countryside too, and in the islands and Highlands. And they've been here for a long time – at least since 1504. There is evidence that King James IV of Scotland and his successors employed 'black moors' (Moorish) musicians and entertainers at that time. Mores or Moors was what Europeans called the people of North Africa, especially Morocco.

The message of Islam had a particular resonance for Victorian Britain, and particularly on Scots. A number of Scottish Muslims converted to Islam. One such was Lady Zainab Evelyn Cobbold – a Scottish diarist, traveller, and noblewoman who converted to Islam in 1915. She went on to become the first British Muslim woman to perform Hajj in 1933. She was buried according to her wishes on a remote hillside on her Glencarron estate in the Highlands, where she had lived during her last years. An imam conducted her funeral whilst a lone piper played the 'Macrimmon's Lament' at her graveside. It was a ceremony in keeping with her dual identity as a Muslim and a Scottish aristocratic lady. Her graveside is marked with an inscription from Sura Noor of the Quran: 'Allah is the Light of the Heavens and the Earth'.

Yahya (John) Parkinson from Kilwhinning, Ayrshire, also accepted Islam at the turn of the twentieth century. He maintained contact with Abdullah Quilliam in Liverpool, and later produced articles, a collection of poems titled 'Lays of Love and War', and books on Islamic philosophy. He was considered the Muslim equivalent of Robert Burns. A more recent well-known convert is Ian Dallas, now known as Sheikh Abdul Qadir. A scion of a Highland family, he accepted Islam in Morocco in 1968, and founded the world-wide Murabateen movement.

Aside from a small number of converts, the majority of Scotland's
Muslims are South Asians. Initially, before the 1947 partition, they came
from India, but the majority of Muslims that settled in Scotland after 1947
came from the Pakistani side of the new border. One of the first reported
Muslims in Glasgow was Sundhi Din, from a village called Balanda. He came
to Scotland some time before World War I as a valet to a retiring Scottish
Army Officer in whose service he had been for many years in India. Another
was N.M. Tanda, joint owner of the warehouse 'Tanda and Ashrif', who
came in 1916. Yet another was Nathoo Mohammed from Kot Badal Khan,
who arrived in 1919. It is narrated that he went to Bombay around 1917 and
signed on as a Lascar on a British Merchant ship. It is not known if Nathoo
had a contact from the Lascar colony in the Anderston area or whether he
had another contact already in Glasgow, someone such as Sundhi Din, who
came from a village only seven miles from his own home village.

'Lascar' was a broad term that Europeans used over several centuries to
describe sailors from the Indian Ocean whom they employed aboard their
ships. They were not a single ethnic or religious group but were drawn from
cultures as diverse as the Malay and the Yemeni. Some settled in Glasgow
and other Scottish ports, as they did, for example, in Liverpool, Bristol, and
Swansea. The Lascar community's links with Glasgow were further proven
by the discovery of a metal plaque from the Stobcross Quay in Glasgow,
now stored by Glasgow Museums. This was recovered during renovation
work at Stobcross Quay in Glasgow Harbour, close to the site of Scotland's
largest exhibition centre the Scottish Event Campus Centre (SECC), next
to the River Clyde. In 1992, Glasgow Museums was given this cast iron
plaque, which had 'LASCARS ONLY' written on it in both English and
Bengali. The sign also read, 'washroom area/ toilets'. It is believed to have
been made in Glasgow, and shows that once there was a sizeable number of
Bangla-speaking people in Glasgow. These people were mostly Muslims
from Sylhet. Many ship captains saw a distinct advantage in employing
Muslim Lascars as they were unlikely to drink alcohol at work.

During both World Wars, four million soldiers of the British Indian Army
(BIA) fought to protect Britain. Scotland had a unique connection with the
BIA through a special, mainly Muslim, Punjabi Indian contingent called
Force K6. They were part of a mule transport corps that made its way to
France during World War Two. Many of these fighters escaped from Dunkirk

to England as German troops closed in. From England they made their way to Wales, and then nearly 1700 of them were stationed in the Highlands of Scotland. Here 13 Muslim soldiers are buried, with the largest concentration buried at Kingussie Cemetery near Aviemore. An inspirational story of selfless care and humanity connected to Force K6 is that of the late centenarian Isobel Harling, who lovingly tended to these graves for nearly 70 years. She always referred to the buried men as 'my boys'.

But most of Scotland's Muslim community arrived here after World War II and the partition of India and Pakistan in 1947. They came as 'economic migrants', and the majority had a 'five-year plan' to work, save money, and return to Pakistan. However, as their families grew in the late 1950s and the 1960s, they ended up settling in Scotland accepting it as their home.

Scotland's Muslim community – certainly Glasgow's – mainly consists of Pakistanis from the Punjab area, and these people have some unique characteristics. Most families originate from Faisalabad, Lahore, and the neighbouring satellite villages. In Scotland, they have been thought of as well organised, forward looking, and somewhat better integrated into the host society than the English Muslim community.

The early Muslim settlers mainly arrived in Glasgow, settling first in the Port Dundas area where housing was derelict and cheap. Then, following in the footsteps of the Jewish community, they moved into the Gorbals area. Here they lived in groups of five to twelve men, sharing accommodation and the household chores such as buying provisions and cooking for one another. They also shared facilities such as 'hot beds', with one in and one out to work. This helped build camaraderie amongst men in an alien country as they sought security and companionship in numbers. They faced a number of problems in this foreign land, mainly the weather, the language barrier, and of course their clothing. They quickly adapted to wearing Western attire such as suits, shirts, ties, jackets, trench coats, and hats, so that visually they would blend in with the Scots.

They took up jobs that were rejected by the native workforce, working often as hawkers and streetlamp lighters. They did not compete for jobs with the indigenous community and so became innovative, creating their own jobs as peddlers, with many becoming known as 'Johnny the peddler'. As peddlers, they called on door after door to sell their goods from a suitcase, thus providing a convenient and much needed mobile shopping service for the locals. Most of them were illiterate men from Punjabi villages, so they resorted to using symbols in their logbooks. They were given training in a few words and phrases they could use, and they picked up the rest through interaction with their customers. This helped them gain valuable communication skills, and of course the confidence to travel further afield for work.

They would travel far and wide out of Glasgow, often on buses and boats to the north of Scotland and to the Hebridean Islands such as Harris and Lewis. Their work helped to expose them to a variety of people from the Scottish indigenous community, thus improving the linguistic and social skills which were key to better integration. The lack of ethno-religious clustering (except in Pollokshields & Govanhill) also facilitated contact between Muslims and non-Muslims.

From the 1960s onwards, many in the South Asian community became the backbone of the Glasgow Transport Corporation. They became bus conductors, drivers, and inspectors. This in turn gave them the confidence to set up their own businesses, including restaurants and takeaways. In comparison, their English counterparts, who worked mainly in mills and factories in the Midlands and Yorkshire, did not integrate to the same extent, as they were not exposed to anybody other than their fellow workers. The wives and children of these working men arrived in greater numbers in the late 1950s and 1960s and settled in the Gorbals area. Living away from their extended families was a lonely experience for them. Very often they formed their own networks of friends so they could socialise and learn life skills such as sewing clothes for themselves and their children. They also taught each other to cook various dishes.

In later years, once more families started to arrive in Glasgow, the community moved from the Gorbals to the Pollokshields area. Once again they were following in the footsteps of the Jewish community, and several old synagogues became mosques. One example is the Madrassah Taleem-ul-Islam in the heart of Pollokshields, which was a synagogue from 1929 until 1984. It was converted to a mosque in 1988.

The community achieved great things in Scotland's unique socio-political environment. In 1970, for instance, Bashir Maan became the first Muslim to be elected as a councillor in Scotland and therefore in Britain. Then in 1997, Britain's first Muslim Member of Parliament was elected in

Scotland. This was Mohammed Sarwar, founder of a cash-and-carry grocery business, who became Labour MP for Glasgow Govan. Later he gave up his British citizenship in order to serve as the Governor of Punjab, but his son Anas Sarwar became not only a Labour MP but in 2021 the first Muslim leader of a major political party in Scotland. In 2023, Humza Yousaf made history once again by securing the highest office in the land by becoming the first Pakistani Muslim First Minister of Scotland. That makes him the first Muslim politician ever elected to lead a non-Muslim Western democracy. He, along with a select few others, are the political trailblazers shaping our time.

In terms of business, Yaqub Ali built the largest cash-and-carry operation in Europe. It was called Castle, and it used to be located near the Gorbals in Glasgow. The nation's favourite curry, the chicken tikka masala, was invented by Ali Mohammed, owner of the Scottish restaurant Shish Mahal. He claims to have invented the dish by using a tin of tomato soup to make the gravy! Our South Asian elders, such as Yaqub Ali and Ali Mohammed, made huge sacrifices. Many were displaced during partition and then experienced the trauma of migration and loss of loved ones again when they came to Scotland. Yet their resilient and determined nature allowed them to deal with the challenges of staying put and building their future in a foreign land. They paved the way for those who followed by creating faith schools, mosques, and cemeteries as well as South Asian grocery stores and restaurants.

But many of our South Asian and Muslim elders were passing away, and so much history and experience was passing with them. Nobody was documenting their lives. So, in 2010, a group of Scottish Muslims sat down informally to discuss the loss we were experiencing. We wanted our history told in our own words by the protagonists themselves. That's why we established Colourful Heritage, a resource for Scots of all backgrounds, and particularly for Muslim Scots. In the words of the organisation's founder, Omar Shaikh, 'we may not have changed the course of history, but we have most certainly gone a long way to documenting it, and to addressing the archival silence. This is our history, told by our community.'

Colourful Heritage has curated numerous resources. These include over 130 video testimonies in which people of various backgrounds tell their stories. The best represented are people of Pakistani Muslim background. They recount their experiences of the 1947 partition, of the journey to

Scotland, then of the work they did in the new country, and how they raised a family there. The interviewees come from Glasgow, Edinburgh, and Dundee. Amongst the resources are a 'Digital Schools Resource Pack' for teachers and parents, and a digital timeline spanning from 1855, when Maharaja Duleep Singh arrived to live in Perthshire, to 2023, when Humza Yousaf became Scotland's First Minister. There are exhibitions, podcasts, heritage trails, and British Indian Army (BIA) resources. We have also put together the Bashir Maan archive, now located within the majestic Mitchell Library in Glasgow. The archive contains photographs, newspaper cuttings and documents telling the story of our first Muslim councillor.

Bashir Maan was born a subject of the British empire. In the year 2000, he was made a Commander of the British Empire, CBE, for services to race relations, community affairs, and politics. He lived in Scotland for 66 years, and held various prominent positions in Scottish public life as well as councillor. In his spare time, he authored three well-received books: *The New Scots: The Story of Asians in Scotland* (1992), *The Thistle and The Crescent: A Study of Scottish-Islam Relations* (2008), and *Muslims in Scotland* (2015). He held two fellowships and three honorary doctorates – from the University of Strathclyde, Glasgow University, and Glasgow Caledonian University. In his video interviews for the Colourful Heritage project, he says, 'it's only ignorance that breeds prejudice or hatred. Once you get to know a thing you might start loving it.'

Bashir Maan was the first publicly elected Muslim Councillor in the UK. One might have expected this prize to have been won first in England, considering the much greater number of Muslims there – but the combination of Scotland's welcoming culture and Maan's hard work meant that Scotland led the way. His other civic offices included district court judge, Deputy Lieutenant of Glasgow, Convenor of the Strathclyde Joint Police Board, and Scotland's first South Asian Justice of the Peace. He was also the founding chair of the Scottish Pakistani Association (1984–1998), and spokesperson and chair of the Glasgow Central Mosque Committee (1984–1992). He was involved in the planning and development of the mosque for over 17 years.

Another key figure in the establishment of the Glasgow Central Mosque, and in Scotland's Muslim life in general, was Atta Ashrif, who arrived in Glasgow as an economic migrant in 1926. He had started his journey in a village in undivided India called Mardarpur. In the new country, he set up business in the Gorbals area, where he was joint owner, in partnership with N M Tanda, of a warehouse at 23 Nicholson Street – 'Tanda and Ashrif'. The building was a space where Pakistanis could socialise, play cards, and discuss their concerns about work and housing. Ashrif lived in the flat upstairs, and at four o'clock every afternoon his wife would send down tea and homemade snacks for everyone to enjoy. The warehouse also acted as a 'bank' for many of the peddlers. This was because the items they sold were usually given on credit.

Atta Ashrif realised that the Muslim men working in and around Glasgow needed a space where they could gather for prayer. In 1933, he established the first Muslim Association in Glasgow. It was only the third in the UK outside London. At first it was called Jamiat ul Muslimin. Later, after merging with another group in 1945, it became known as the Jamiat Ittehad ul Muslimin, and also as the Muslim Mission. This was the humble beginning of the organised Muslim community in Glasgow and in Scotland.

The aim of the association was to fundraise in order to establish Glasgow's first mosque. With the help of seven people, each of whom contributed £100, it managed in late 1944 or early 1945 to convert a building at 27/29 Oxford Street, at the heart of the Gorbals where most of the community lived. The Muslim Mission had purchased the entire three-story tenement building, which also housed the 'Seamen's Club' for Indian sailors arriving in the docks.

The mosque itself was located on the first floor. Residential flats on the other floors were rented out to raise income. In later years, the mosque was also used as an Urdu and Islamic school. When families with young children arrived, they sent them here to learn the Quran. In that sense, it was a social space where parents as well as children could meet each other to talk and learn about both their culture and religion. The National Library of Scotland's Moving Image Archive has some amazing footage of the tenement mosque building and the Muslim School from the mid-1960s. It shows the large number of boys and girls that attended classes. This was the start of the community expressing their faith identity in Scotland.

Sadly, the building was demolished during slum clearance and regeneration in the Gorbals. This is when the love and care for the Muslim community of another early pioneer, Mohammed Tufail Shaheen, came into play. He allowed the use of one of his buildings at Carlton Place to be used as a Glasgow's second mosque.

Meanwhile, in the mid 1950s, around the same time that Glasgow's first mosque was established, Sandymount Cemetery became the city's first Muslim burial site. The nearly 350 graves are now in the process of restoration by a local Glasgow Muslim. The work includes fixing the headstones and repainting the elaborate text in Urdu, Arabic, and English.

The community continued to pool resources through the decades, and by 1983 it had raised three million pounds to construct Scotland's first – and still the largest – purpose-built mosque: the Glasgow Central Mosque. The entire community contributed to the effort, including many of the Pakistani women, who organised door-to-door collections and several 'meena bazaars'. Today the mosque takes pride of place in the Gorbals, and is visible from afar. It's beautiful gold and green glass dome glistens like a treasured jewel beside the River Clyde. Signs outside welcome everyone with the Gaelic word *failte*.

There are now over eighty mosques and Islamic associations across Scotland. They stretch from the largest cities and towns to many of the more remote villages and islands, and still they continue to expand. In his book *Muslims in Scotland*, Bashir Maan wrote of Atta Ashrif, 'the seed sowed by him has now grown into a large strong tree with many branches. What a legacy to leave behind!'

The children of that first generation built a great academic legacy. In 1936, for example, Atta Ashrif's son Ibrahim began studying at the fee-paying Allan Glen school in Glasgow. In 1948, Ibrahim Ashrif enrolled for a doctorate in Agricultural Sciences at Edinburgh University, and in the mid 1950s he went on to work for the British Foreign Service in Gambia. In 1964, he was awarded the Order of the British Empire (OBE) for his work in writing a dictionary of the Mandingo language to help his colleagues in Gambia. The Colourful Heritage archive contains testimony by Ibrahim's son Zahid, the grandson of Atta Ashrif, who tells his father's story.

Another Scottish Muslim who excelled in learning was Ihsan Ullah Khand, who made a significant contribution to global science. He came from Lahore to study for his PhD in Chemistry at Strathclyde University in 1965. In subsequent years, he published over 30 papers. His most important discovery was the 'Pauson Khand Reaction'. His family remained in Glasgow and are now into their third Scottish generation. Aother success story of our contemporary generation is Osama Saeed. A communications professional and politician, he has been a parliamentary candidate for the Scottish National Party (SNP) and head of media and public relations at al-Jazeera in Qatar. Yet another is the high-profile activist lawyer Aamer Anwar, who made history when he won his case against the Scottish Police in 1995 after a racially motivated attack in Ashton Lane.

The women of the community also excelled. After arriving as a young bride from Pakistan in 1969, Bushra Iqbal held various posts in her 50-year inspirational career. She worked for Strathclyde Regional Council and then as Equality Advisor and Head of Strategy at the West of Scotland Regional Equality Council. In 1994, she founded the North Lanarkshire Muslim Women's Alliance. Also in 1994, Farkhanda Chaudhary was the first Scottish Muslim woman to become a Justice of the Peace. The late Salma Sheikh instigated women's Islamic education circles in the 1990s, and campaigned to fundraise for the women only Almeezan building in Glasgow. This was finally purchased in 2005 to provide further Islamic education to women. In more recent times, Baroness Nosheena Mobarik became an MEP (Member of European Parliament) in 2017 and now sits in the House of Lords. And since 2021, Kaukab Stewart MSP has been the first Muslim woman to serve as a Minister in the Scottish Parliament. Both Bushra Iqbal and Farkhanda Chaudhary were awarded MBE, while Nosheena Mobarik was made a CBE.

While Pakistanis make up by far the largest component of Glasgow's Muslim community, the communities in Edinburgh and Dundee include a much larger proportion of Arabs. Their countries of origin include Algeria, Iraq, and of course Syria. Aberdeen, which attracts workers to the North Sea oil industry, has a Muslim community made up of five 'national' groups – Pakistani, Arab, Bangladeshi, African, and other Asian – in roughly equal numbers. In most of Scotland's towns and many of its villages, Muslims run shops, tend to patients, serve food, and drive taxis. And there are Muslim students in all of Scotland's universities.

Of course, not everything is rosy. Systemic barriers of racism, Islamophobia, and socio-economic deprivation continue to hold Scottish Muslims back. We are not generally an affluent community. According to a Scottish Government report of March 2023, 63 percent of all Muslim adults (40,000) live in poverty. And a 2021 report on Islamophobia by the Cross Party Group of the Scottish Government found that 75 percent of Muslims said Islamophobia was a regular or everyday issue in Scottish society. Muslim women were more likely to encounter Islamophobia than men. Worryingly, 78 percent of respondents believed Islamophobia was getting worse in Scotland.

Nevertheless, for most Muslims, Scotland has become a comparatively welcoming home.

In 2017, Colourful Heritage produced a book called *Scotland's Muslims: Society, Politics and Identity*. One chapter of the book is entitled 'Feeling Scottish and Being Muslim'. This was based on our video archive in which a number of elderly Pakistani-origin Muslim participants were asked about their identity. Surprisingly 68 percent of them used a multifaceted hybrid identity which included the word 'Scottish'. Considering that they were not born in Scotland and that they came from Pakistan originally, many of these individuals would have initially identified as Pakistani or Muslim. The fact that they identify now as Scottish Pakistanis or a Scottish Muslims is evidence that they have integrated well and feel welcomed in Scotland. This is a very different story to the Muslims in England who generally prefer to be known as British Muslims rather than as English Muslims.

The 2011 Census showed that Scottish Muslims feel more Scottish (24 percent) than English Muslims feel English (14 percent) and that Pakistani Muslims tend to prioritise their Scottish or British identities more than their ethnic one. Glasgow & Dundee Muslims record higher feelings of belonging to Scotland and lower affiliations to their non-UK ethnic identities compared with Muslims in Edinburgh and Aberdeen.

So why do Muslims seem to have integrated more happily in Scotland than they have in England? The experiences of Scottish Muslims are often quite different to the experiences of English Muslims, and for several reasons. There are far fewer Muslims in Scotland than in England. Coupled with the welcoming nature and sociability of Scots (which is similar to that of Punjabis), this has made Muslim integration into society easier. In addition, sectarian tensions between Catholics and Protestants existed before the arrival of South Asians, and they have to some extent protected other religious minorities from serious prejudice. The governing Scottish National Party's welcoming attitudes towards refugees, minorities, and asylum seekers, meanwhile, explain the community's gradual shift from the Labour Party towards the SNP. The SNP has also released statements that speak to the hearts of many Muslims in Scotland. Its vocal resistance to the Iraq War is a prime example. After the 30 June 2007 al-Qaida attack on Glasgow Airport, SNP officials stood shoulder to shoulder with the Muslim community at the Glasgow Central Mosque. This helped to reassure both Muslim and non-Muslim communities that friendly coexistence would continue between them.

In marked contrast to Westminster, Scotland's parliament voted for a ceasefire in the 2023 Gaza war. The Scottish Government has also hosted around a fifth of the Syrian refugees in Britain. It has implemented special settlement programmes to help them adjust and integrate into the wider community. Successful inclusive policies mean that Scotland can serve as a model for integration in other European countries. While English politics over the last years have taken an increasingly anti-immigrant tone, the same has not been the case in Scotland. One recent incident illustrates the difference. On 13 May 2021, a large crowd of local people halted a UK government immigration raid on Kenmure Street in Glasgow's Pollokshields. The immigration officers tried to remove two Indian Sikh men from a flat for alleged immigration violations, but had to give up the attempt after an eight-hour sit-in around their van. This was seen as a significant victory for community resistance, and – because so many of the protestors were white – for community cohesion.

Despite the problems, Scotland's Muslims feel so much at home here that they have designed and created their very own Islamic tartan! This is the brainchild of Azeem Ibrahim, a political scientist, entrepreneur, and author, currently a professor at the Strategic Studies Institute at the US Army War College, and a director at the Newlines Institute for Strategy and Policy.

The tartan serves as a timely and powerful symbol of the recognition by Scotland's Islamic communities of their national identity. The visual weaving together of Scottish and Islamic cultural heritages produces a profound sense of historical continuity for future generations. It is a fitting symbol and a celebration of the contributions made to civilisation by these two great cultures and intellectual traditions.

IT STARTED WITH THE VIOLIN

Arusa Qureshi

Can you remember the first time you held a melody? Maybe it was on one of those tiny baby keyboards, where you bashed out some notes that inadvertently led to a semi-familiar tune. Or maybe it was in primary school, where you were forced to play the recorder, the assertive screeching of you and your classmates enough to drive anyone in your immediate vicinity mad. For a lot of young Muslims, their first introduction to something resembling melody would have likely been the Islamic call to prayer – the melodious chant, calling Muslim worshippers to each of the five daily prayers. To call the adhan a piece of music, however, is incorrect. Some would even consider it deeply offensive. But it's also impossible not to recognise the significance of euphonic recitation when it comes to Islam. The adhan is based on the Middle Eastern maqam melodic system and the elongation of vowels, incorporation of scales, and emphasis on tone all contribute to evoking a myriad of emotions. It's not music, but there's something inescapably musical about it – and as a child growing up in a Muslim household, it was something I couldn't ignore.

I think I've always been pulled in by sound and melody. As melodramatic as it might be to write down or say out loud, music is that one thread that has weaved its way through every major moment, memory, and emotion in my 30 years. As a child, I immersed myself in as many music-based activities as I could get my hands on, and in my early teens, I was adamant that I was going to be a musician. This was, of course, somewhat complicated by my familial background and the fact that for many Muslims, there was a perception that music was a generally forbidden territory. The permissibility of music remains a subject of debate within the Muslim community and among many scholars, all of whom have varying views on the matter relating to how Islamic scriptures have been and continue to be interpreted. For my parents, it proved to be the cause of many internal conflicts (which I believe continue to this day) because they were blessed (or cursed, depending on how you see it) with children that seemingly possessed natural skill in music and an environment that undeniably sought to nurture this talent. It started with my older sister, who took piano lessons at school, which my parents encouraged in a bid to add colour and variety to her academic life. Then I came along and took it to a whole other level.

It started with the violin.

When I was around five years old, my family and I travelled down to London for the wedding of a distant relative. It was my first time in the city and admittedly, it was terrifying – the rush of people, the incessant noise and the general sense of overwhelm compared to my much smaller home city of Edinburgh. Though I don't remember a great deal about the trip or the wedding itself, the distinct memory of feeling out of place always seems to linger.

A few days before the wedding, we made a shopping trip to gather last minute supplies (most likely *mehndi* (hanna), new sets of bangles that we didn't need, and yet more treats like *mithai* (sweets) to hand out en masse – all the staples of an Asian wedding). In between visits to jewelry emporiums and impressive lehenga boutiques, we popped into a charity shop. This offered an easy way for my mother to keep me occupied and suppress the boredom of being carted around shop after shop. It was a fairly standard, unassuming outlet, but in the window, I spotted magic – a second-hand, minimally shabby, but clearly well-kept violin.

A good amount of begging later and my mother relented. She bought me this violin, which was 4/4 size, or in other words, suitable for an adult – neither of us having any idea about appropriate sizing for a beginner. Balancing this giant violin on my tiny chin, I felt powerful and valued.

When we returned to Edinburgh, my parents reluctantly agreed to a few violin lessons – more than anything, to stop my relentless pleading – thinking I'd quickly get bored and move onto the next thing. But lo and behold, I stuck with it and in time, it became my whole world.

I went on to play the piano and the guitar too and was successful in applying for a music scholarship that meant my parents (much to their relief) didn't have to pay for any more lessons. Gradually, music became the basis of my entire identity – it made sense to me and crucially, it made me feel like I belonged and had worth as a brown person in what was a predominantly white environment. It was around this time that I found myself actively rebelling against the tenets of my Muslim upbringing. This was the point at which my faith began to diminish. Because behind every achievement, every music exam passed with flying colours, and every concert performance executed with finesse, there was this underlying feeling that what I was doing was inherently wrong or 'bad'. My parents were always incredibly supportive because they knew how much music meant to me, but even they found themselves conflicted in terms of their support of my talent and their own individual belief systems. But they didn't stand in my way, even when I proudly proclaimed I was going to study music at university and become a world-class touring musician. So many of my friends of similar Asian backgrounds were being gently nudged towards careers in science but I never had that pressure and I'm extremely grateful for that. Maybe in some strange way, my parents subconsciously knew that there was more to come; that I wasn't meant to be a musician and that I'd figure it out eventually on my own.

This is where hip hop enters the picture.

As well as playing music, much of my early teens were dominated by writing – mostly long, meandering essays about and reviews of music. It was a way to try to explain to others, and to myself, why this art form and creative outlet meant so much in the grand scheme of things. After all, how could something that had such a profound impact on my soul and my being be considered forbidden or shameful? I loved to dismantle lyrics to find meaning and magic in the mundane, and there was one genre that really stood out in this regard. I found comfort in hip hop – in the rhythmic heart, lyrical playfulness and profound politics in the genre, which drew me in like no other form of music had done before. All these years later, I can credit that initial fascination for not only a substantial portion of the career I have today, but also for how I view certain elements of our life and our world, such as injustices, principles and societal issues in the everyday.

I went on to study English Literature at university, where I wrote my dissertation on the theme of defiance within the poetry of hip hop. And from here, I forged a path into the worlds of journalism and publishing, which is where I still am today. I'm passionate about telling stories that centre around marginalised experience, be that shining a spotlight on people doing incredible things with their own creativity or groups innovating and changing the landscape for the better. This extends to arts and culture more generally, but within hip hop, I seem to have found a niche and a sense of refuge that I want to share with as many people as possible.

In 2020, I wrote a book called *Flip the Script: How Women Came to Rule Hip Hop*. It was published by 404 Ink the following year. It's not a history or a deep analysis; it's basically a love letter to the genre, telling the stories of some of the really important women of UK hip hop in their own words. I chose to focus on the UK because my own interest in the genre started with American hip hop and I wanted to dig further into how the movement's beginnings in the Bronx allowed it to morph and evolve as it travelled the world. It was my way of celebrating where we are right now, but also acknowledging the women that came first, many of whom have been erased from the canon of hip hop, and the work that is still needed.

I considered hip hop a kind of safe haven, which I always returned to when I desperately needed a boost. It was thanks to hip hop that I realised my passion for music extended beyond playing it; it lay too in the analysis and in the sharing of that passion with others, who perhaps don't see or understand its value as an art form. Hip hop is such an important and interesting part of popular culture that (I believe) it reveals a lot about wider society. It's not just music – it's poetry, its criticism, it's protest and activism. We're in an incredible place in hip hop as far as creativity goes, but especially when it comes to the women involved in the scene. I expanded upon this theme in my book.

In the introduction, I also wrote about the influence of my older sister on my taste in music, and why this was so significant: 'I was lucky in that I was exposed to everyone from Salt-N-Pepa and Left Eye to Queen Latifah and Missy Elliott early on thanks to my older sister. Women were very much a big part of everything I knew about hip hop. In many ways they were the reason I started falling for hip hop in the first place. Seeing not only people of colour but women of colour on screen – powerful, confident, and completely in control – contributed to what I believed was possible for us growing up. It contributed to my idea of this safe haven. It was obvious, though, in terms of the videos that were being played on loop on MTV and the rappers that were climbing the charts, who was ruling the roost. I didn't care though, before I knew anything about misogyny or stereotypes, hip hop was female empowerment epitomised to my clueless self.'

Returning to those early days as a music-obsessed child playing the violin, I could see connections between how music itself was viewed as 'bad' or forbidden in an Islamic context, and how hip hop was so often coloured in a harsh light by the wider music scene. I wasn't supposed to like hip hop, especially as a woman, just as I wasn't supposed to excel in and enjoy music.

It's true that there were and still are many negative connotations that follow the genre, especially when we look at the Golden Age of the 1990s and onwards. Gang culture, drugs, death, violence, and sexism were all closely associated with hip hop via artists that placed such behaviour front and centre. And it wouldn't be fair to ignore this or say that there isn't some truth in how this manifested in the music. But ultimately, women have always been present in hip hop and contributed to shaping the culture, and it was predominantly these women that I grew up listening to and watching on TV, whose words I clung to and whose rebellion and resistance I appreciated. As the marketability and commercial value of hip hop increased, the role of women gradually shifted to something more cynical, where their contributions were diminished while their image and sexuality became the ruling factor above all else. I don't absolve hip hop of its sins, but I don't entirely blame it either – I place much of the responsibility on capitalism, marketing and the commodification of Black culture.

In some strange roundabout way, I've made it my mission to prove the value of hip hop as an art form and as a movement with the same gusto that I sought to reject the labelling of music as illicit in my family home. The arguments of high versus low culture pervade when we discuss art – opera is 'real' art and worthy of discussion and funding but hip hop cannot be seen as legitimate, and thus should not be taken seriously. There are, of course, other factors at play here, namely that hip hop began life as a predominantly African American art form, adopted by inner city Black youth as a means of expression. If you wanted to rap, you didn't need equipment or money or for someone to let you in – in theory, anyone could do it. Accessibility shouldn't lower the value of an art form, but in the case of hip hop and in its lack of barriers to entry, there has indeed been an effort to devalue it.

The US is perhaps further ahead than the UK when it comes to hip hop being taken seriously and held up alongside other types of art and poetry. Kendrick Lamar winning the Pulitzer Prize in 2018 for his album *Damn*, for example, was a huge step forward, emphasising how the genre should be viewed, instead of simply by stereotypes or preconceived judgements. There is still work to be done in the UK, and this is especially true in Scotland, where the hip hop scene is smaller in comparison to its counterpart in England. But there are artists, organisers, and projects that are operating successfully and highlighting the breadth of talent that exists in all corners. We can see this in the existence and popularity of artists like Bemz, collectives like Glasgow's Peach, and initiatives such as the Scottish Hip Hop Bursary, which was launched as a partnership between Sunny G Radio, UP2STNDRD, 644 Studios, and Creative Scotland, to assist hip hop artists with the development of their practice.

And I firmly believe that it's women who are leading the charge by innovating, experimenting, and collaborating across borders and art forms. What initially kicked off the thinking around my book was the fact that the winners of both the Scottish Album of the Year Award and the Welsh Music Prize in 2020 were women rappers – Nova and Deyah respectively. And beyond the UK, Denise Chaila was announced as the winner of the Choice Music Prize Irish Album of the Year 2020. Perhaps it was a coincidence, but at the time, and even now, it felt like so much more.

I currently work as a freelancer across the Scottish creative industries, but my specific roles in music vary from journalist and editor to programmer, board member, DJ, and more. Hip hop has always been at the heart of my work in music though, and I'll forever feel connected to it, whether it's to the defiance of its content, the raw emotion of its lyricism or the incredible power of the women, and in particular, the Black women, that have pioneered while battling gendered social expectations.

I think my sister and I were the first generation of immigrant kids that naturally rebelled against our parents' desire to assimilate us into their South Asian heritage. We looked to music and TV instead for a different cultural fix. We brushed off Bollywood in favour of American hip hop and shunned our parents' Asian sitcoms and soaps for the Fresh Prince of Bel Air and Sister Sister. Black American culture spoke to us and, growing up in Scotland with very few brown people around, it was our only immediate bridge to other people of colour. Sure, it wasn't our culture and it wasn't about our experiences, but there was something in hip hop in particular that made me feel like it was okay, and kind of cool, to be the only brown person in the room.

To paraphrase author and professor of English Mickey Hess, I understand that I am a guest in the house of hip hop, but I hope that I can use my love, appreciation, and respect for this genre and its immense levels of creativity to simultaneously fight for it and to give the pioneers the credit they deserve. I'm glad I didn't pursue a career as a musician; in all honesty, I would have been terrible at it. But I am glad I rebelled against judgement and feelings of immorality or wrong-doing, and that my parents didn't hinder my self-expression, despite their own commitment to their faith and their hopes for my future.

Whether or not music is haram is not for me to say. I don't consider myself a person of faith these days for a myriad of reasons, some simple and some far more complex and personal, and therefore I feel that it's not my place to have an opinion. But many of my elders hold onto the idea that music is forbidden. For that reason, I try to respect the idea even if I don't necessarily understand or agree. I also respect people who don't appreciate hip hop, even if, in a similar way, I don't understand or agree. Growing up in a Muslim household, I was taught that having this level of respect and compassion was of utmost importance in everything we do as human beings. I was lucky to find solace in music and in hip hop early on. And I can categorically say that my work in music is centred around lifting others up and pushing them forward – with that same respect, compassion, and just a little bit of defiance.

GAELIC

Kirsty MacDougall

Is mise Kirsty NicDhùghaill, 's ann às an Eilean Sgitheanach a tha mi agus chaidh mo thogail a' bruidhinn Gàidhlig na h-Alba.

My name is Kirsty MacDougall, I was born and raised in the Isle of Skye, and I am native speaker of Scottish Gaelic.

The Isle of Skye, situated off the west coast of Scotland, is the largest island of the Inner Hebrides. It is inhabited by approximately 13,000 people. Often referred to as Eilean a' Cheò (the Misty Isle, in Gaelic), Skye is iconic on the global stage as a world class tourist destination. Home to some of Scotland's most dramatic scenery, Skye's rugged coastline attracts thousands of tourists annually. Key features include the Cuillin Range, the Fairy Pools, the Old Man of Storr, the Quiraing, and much more. Skye boasts a vibrant history steeped in legends, along with a wealth of musical and poetic traditions. It is little wonder that our population almost triples in the summer. To me, Skye is not just a tourist destination; it's home, and has been home to my family for generations. I feel very privileged to live and work on such a beautiful island that boasts such a wealth of history and culture. My first language is Scottish Gaelic, and it is the language I work and communicate in daily.

Scottish Gaelic, known as 'Gàidhlig', is autochthonous to Scotland and belongs to the Q-Celtic, Goidelic Celtic language family. This linguistic affiliation means that it shares more similarities with Irish and Manx than with the other Celtic languages such as Welsh, Breton, and Cornish. During the eleventh century, Gaelic was widely spoken around most of Scotland. At this time, Gaelic became the language of the medieval kingdom of Alba (Gaelic for Scotland) and was spoken throughout Scotland. However, due to a range of economic and political factors, from the fourteenth century onwards Gaelic became predominantly confined to the North-West of Scotland, particularly to the Highlands and the Western Isles. Gaelic belongs to the whole of Scotland and forms an integral part of Scottish history. The language and its culture have played a crucial part in shaping Scotland today, influencing various aspects of its history, music, literature, and identity.

The 2011 Scottish Census reported 57,375 speakers of Scottish Gaelic, which comprises 1.1 percent of the population of Scotland. Therefore, the situation of Gaelic is precarious, and despite considerable efforts, there are concerns as to whether Gaelic will survive as a community language in the next decade. The socioeconomic structure of Scotland is critical to understanding the decline of the Scottish Gaelic language today. The factors contributing to the decline of Gaelic in Scotland are multifaceted, and several key periods and events played a significant role. Factors such as the anti-Gaelic Statutes of Iona in the seventeenth century, the Jacobite uprisings in the eighteenth century, and the aftermath of the Battle of Culloden in 1746, marked a turning point in Gaelic history, leading to an introduction of harsh measures in the Highlands. The Highland Clearances, which primarily occurred during the eighteenth and nineteenth centuries, involved the eviction and displacement of Highlanders from their homes and communities by landlords. This was done to make way for large-scale crofting, particularly farming sheep, which was deemed more profitable. The number of people living in the Highlands fell sharply throughout the twentieth century, resulting in the transformation of many formerly Gaelic-speaking regions in the Gàidhealtachd into predominately English-speaking areas. Population displacement through migration has had a profound and lasting impact on Scottish Gaelic, where many Gaels emigrated, and villages throughout the Highlands now remain as deserted settlements. I am always reminded of the impact of the Clearances when visiting the villages of Boreraig and Suisnish in Skye and Hallaig in the Isle of Raasay. In these coastal villages, all that remains are ruined houses, many of whose walls still stand at head height, but with no roof. They are a stark reminder of the harshness and challenges faced by the Gaels who once called these empty villages home.

It is important to note that migration wasn't always caused by eviction, but by the bleak socio-economic situation at home. Many left the Highlands for a variety of complex reasons. Today the Gaelic diaspora is spread around the world, particularly in North America, Australia, and New Zealand. Scottish Gaelic, for example, has a historical and cultural presence in Cape Breton, Nova Scotia. Cape Breton has its own Gaelic College, Colaisde na Gàidhlig, dedicated to the promotion and preservation of traditional Gaelic culture in the community of St Ann's, Nova Scotia. And the impact of Scottish immigration is evident in place names globally. For instance, the Scottish Highlands' capital, known as Inverness, or Inbhir Nis in Gaelic, shares its name with cities in Australia, Canada, and the United States. Similarly, the capital Edinburgh, called Dùn Èideann in Gaelic, has inspired the naming of Dunedin, the second-largest city in the South Island of New Zealand.

Tens of thousands of people were affected by the Clearances, and their impact on Gaelic communities was significant for the generations that followed. While the Highland Clearances cannot be held solely responsible for the decline of Gaelic, their effects continue to be felt in the Highlands even in the present day.

Today Gaelic is an endangered language, and features in UNESCO's Atlas of the World's Languages in Danger. UNESCO warns that unless prompt action is taken by governments and communities, half of the world's languages currently in use may face the risk of extinction before the end of the century. As stated by UNESCO's director-general, Koichiro Matsuura, in 2009 when launching the Atlas, 'the death of a language leads to the disappearance of many forms of intangible cultural heritage, especially the invaluable heritage of traditions and oral expressions of the community that spoke it – from poems and legends to proverbs and jokes.' We have a phrase in Gaelic that reflects this sentiment 'Tìr gun chànan, Tìr gun anam' – a land without a language is a land without a soul.

All Gaelic speakers nowadays are bilingual in English, and whilst many older speakers are Gaelic-dominant, increasingly younger people are learning the language within the realms of education, and are strongly English dominant. The 2011 census showed a decline of speakers in the core 'heartland' areas, with na h-Eileanan Siar (the Western Isles) reporting just over half (52 percent) of the population as Gaelic speakers. The census also showed us that 48 percent of Gaelic speakers now live in the Lowlands, concentrated mainly in the cities of Glasgow and

Edinburgh. In these Lowland areas, however, the proportion of Gaelic speakers in the population is low, around 1 percent or below.

Since the 1970s, there have been substantial efforts to revitalise Gaelic in Scotland, particularly in the fields of education and broadcasting. Gaelic medium education has played a significant role in the revitalisation of the language and has experienced exponential growth in the last 38 years. But Gaelic did not always have its place in the Scottish education system. The Education Act (1872) was a significant piece of legislation that profoundly affected the Scottish education system, aiming to ensure that all children in Scotland had access to schooling. While this Act introduced compulsory education for children between five and 13, it made no mention of Gaelic. Although Gaelic wasn't explicitly banned, the needs of Gaelic speakers were not recognised. It can be said that the Education Act impacted the way that the Gaels valued their language. Gaelic was viewed as the language of the croft, while English was the language of officialdom. Therefore, despite the Act not specifically prohibiting Gaelic, the exclusion of the language in the curriculum had a damaging impact on its perception.

Gaelic medium education began in 1985, driven by substantial efforts and initiatives from Gaelic speakers and grassroots organisations dedicated to reversing the language shift. Currently available in 15 out of 32 Scottish local authorities, approximately 5,000 pupils currently receive Gaelic medium education at both primary and secondary levels. Over the years, Gaelic medium education has evolved, initially with the establishment of Gaelic medium units within existing schools, and in recent years we have welcomed the creation of stand-alone Gaelic schools. The curriculum in Gaelic medium education (GME) aligns with the Scottish curriculum. However, it is delivered through the medium of Gaelic. In Gaelic medium education, pupils are taught entirely in Gaelic for the first three years in primary school. Studies have demonstrated the benefits of bilingualism, showing that pupils can acquire or develop Gaelic without compromising their attainment in other areas.

I am a former GME pupil, and I have incredibly fond memories of my Gaelic medium education in Skye. I attended playgroup (cròileagan), pre-school (sgoil-àraich), was in a Gaelic medium unit in an English school, studied as many subjects as possible available to me in High School through the medium of Gaelic, undertook a degree in Gaelic, and I am now a lecturer at the National Centre for Gaelic Language and Culture, Sabhal Mòr Ostaig in Skye.

Skye is at the forefront of Gaelic development nationally, particularly in the field of education. Apart from the Gaelic college Sabhal Mòr Ostaig, which offers degrees taught entirely through the medium of Gaelic, there is also Bun-sgoil Ghàidhlig Phort-Rìgh, the first dedicated Gaelic school in a traditional Gaelic-speaking area, opened in 2018. I consider myself fortunate to have had access to Gaelic medium education, which is available from early years to university level in Skye. I relished the opportunities to take part in our local and national Mòd, a Gaelic festival which invites people of all ages to perform a range of competitive disciplines related to Gaelic music and culture, I loved learning about our culture through songs and drama with organisations such as Fèisean nan Gàidheal, and I have so much respect for teachers supporting and teaching our language to the next generation.

However, given that only 15 out of 32 local authorities in Scotland offer Gaelic medium education, Gaelic medium education is not an option for the majority of children in Scotland.

The majority of the Gaelic schools are in the Highland Council and in Comhairle nan Eilean Siar (the Western Isles). Glasgow has three Gaelic primary schools and Scotland's only Gaelic secondary school, while Edinburgh has one primary and one secondary school providing Gaelic education. Gaelic is offered in one primary and one high school in the north-east of the country, in Aberdeen city. We are facing a crisis with a lack of Gaelic teachers, and there is a lack of resources in Gaelic. Schools in the central belt are full to the brim, with some children, particularly in Glasgow, being refused entry to primary schools because of pupil numbers being capped. I find this situation to be unfair, and believe there should be greater access to Gaelic medium education across the country. It is clear that we should not rely solely on schools to combat the decline in speakers, though it is evident that education is fundamental to the future of the language, and greater support is needed in order to build on the success of Gaelic medium education.

Alongside education, governmental and community initiatives have been key in efforts to reverse language shift. The Gaelic Language Act was passed by the Scottish Government in 2005. The Act, which received cross-party support, marked a historic milestone for the Gaelic language. This legislation meant that Gaelic was recognised officially as an 'official language of Scotland, commanding equal respect to the English language'. The formation of the Gaelic language development body, Bòrd na Gàidhlig, was a direct result of this Act. Bòrd na Gàidhlig are responsible for promoting Gaelic development, including providing advice to Scottish Ministers on Gaelic issues. The Act mandates that the Bòrd prepares a National Gaelic Language plan every five years, and other public bodies can also be requested by the Bòrd to formulate and implement a Gaelic language plan. The functions of Bòrd na Gàidhlig were discussed as part of the Scottish Languages Bill 2023, prompted by concerns regarding the substance of the Act and the potential need for further measures.

There are two important media outlets: BBC ALBA and Radio nan Gàidheal. Launched in 2008, BBC ALBA was initially only available via satellite, then later on Freeview, Gaelic speakers and learners alike were thrilled with this dedicated channel for the language. The channel offers a varied schedule of programmes including news and current affairs, documentaries, music, entertainment, sport and children's programs. It can be said that BBC ALBA struggles with providing an adequate service due to budget constrictions, and as a result broadcasts for around seven hours a day only. Despite budget constraints and broadcasting limitations, BBC ALBA continues to play a vital role in bringing Gaelic language and culture to a wider audience, perhaps to those who may have never come across the language before, and to Gaelic speakers who are able to watch some television through the language.

Radio nan Gàidheal also broadcasts Gaelic-language programmes covering a range of topics on a daily basis, and is available worldwide via the internet. These platforms play a crucial role in promoting the language and providing opportunities to its speakers, offering a range of content that reflects the language's diverse and rich traditions. From playing traditional Gaelic music to promoting new Gaelic artists, Radio nan Gàidheal has been pivotal.

As I was brought up in a Gaelic speaking home, I used Gaelic with my maternal family. My maternal grandparents lived half a mile up the road from us and we spent a lot of time at their house. When I think about my relationship with Gaelic, I often think of my late grandfather. My maternal grandfather was brought up in the northwest of the Isle of Skye in 1941, and Gaelic was the language of his home and village. Throughout his childhood, Gaelic was widely spoken in his local crofting village on the north end of the island. My grandfather grew up in a world that was paradoxically very different from the environment and learning experienced by those now attending GME. Gaelic was spoken at home; English was the language of the classroom. In his 1984 study, *Gaelic Scotland*, Charles Withers pointed out that 'there is evidence not only of different use of Gaelic or English by generations within the family but also of differences in the use of one language or another for given social purposes: English was used for schooling and commerce as a symbol for culture and individual social progress; Gaelic for religious worship, the heart and the hearth but with no contemporary value attached to it by outsiders (and some Gaels) as the language of social advancement.'

My grandfather told me that, unlike his forebearers, he was not punished for using Gaelic in school. However, his education was conducted solely through the medium of English, and he was expected to communicate with teaching staff in that language. Outside the classroom, though, the children played together in Gaelic. Gaelic served as the language for social interactions with peers, family and within the community. Meanwhile, English was the language seen on road signs, used in authoritative and formal situations, and considered the language advantageous for economic benefits.

In 1962, my grandfather met my grandmother, another Sgitheanach (someone from Skye) who lived five miles down the road from him. They married in 1963 and had three daughters. At this time Gaelic was declining as a vernacular language in communities around the north end of Skye, and increasingly, families in the village, for the first time, stopped speaking Gaelic to their children. Notably, even my grandparents' siblings, despite having Gaelic-speaking spouses, did not pass the language on to their children. This decline in intergenerational transmission was commonplace in the 1960/1970s Skye, as parents believed that English would provide greater advantages for children's progress in the world. Despite this, my mother and her sisters grew up with Gaelic as their first language, and the eldest didn't learn English until she went to school. The majority of children attending my Mum and Aunties' local school had Gaelic-speaking parents, yet many of them did not speak Gaelic themselves. My mother recounts stories of being in the village or at friends' houses, where she would speak Gaelic to her friends' parents and English to her friends. Regardless of the fact that English was spoken at school and with friends, Gaelic remained the language of their family home and was respected by all within the family.

Twenty years later, my grandparents welcomed nine grandchildren, including myself, and Gaelic was very much still the language of Granny and Grandad's house. I often think of my grandfather when I read the poem 'Cisteachan laighe' (Coffins) by Ruairidh MacThòmais, a well-known Gaelic poet. In this poem, MacThòmais discusses the death of his grandfather, a carpenter, who made coffins. He associates the death of his grandfather with the death of his language and culture. Whilst I don't believe Gaelic is 'dead' as such, I empathised with his sentiment where he is grieving the loss of a tradition bearer, and at the same time keenly aware of how fragile our existing culture, traditions and customs are.

It wasn't until now, as I'm ten years older and studying a PhD in intergenerational transmission of Gaelic, that I have understood how difficult this must have been for my grandparents, facilitating a Gaelic environment in an area becoming increasingly monoglot. When I recently asked my granny about it she said, 'It wasn't difficult, it was just the language we used and we didn't see an alternative.' It is understandable that other families in the community did not make a conscious decision to keep the language alive within their homes as there had been a gradual erosion of its usage as a vernacular language resulting from neglect and persecution over several centuries.

As we look forwards, I believe that the future of the language lies firmly in the hands of Gaelic speakers. The formal status of the language should continue to be protected and promoted at government and community level, but I believe there is a huge amount that we as individuals can do to secure a stable future for our threatened minority languages. My grandparents' insistence on the family using Gaelic within the home in the early 1960s is an important example of perseverance within intergenerational transmission. At that time, Gaelic was declining considerably in the community, there was no language Act, no Gaelic medium education, or policies supporting their decision to make Gaelic the language of the home for my mother and her sisters. They (along with many others) went against the status quo and fought against the perception that our language and culture wasn't valuable. They saw that there was no alternative to speaking our native tongue; it wasn't so much a decision as it was a natural choice.

There are thousands, if not millions, of versions of my grandfather out there – these forebears who saw value in their own language and culture and wanted to preserve it. Sociolinguistics emphasise the importance of intergenerational transmission, and the role of individuals, families, and communities in language revitalisation. The impact of globalisation, and how global forces influence our daily lives has never been greater. Despite the decline in speakers, and the persistent headlines from a few online claiming that 'Gaelic is a dying language' and a 'waste of money', I personally am optimistic for the future. In March 2023, Young Scot conducted a survey on how young people engage with Gaelic. The survey found that 83.9 percent of young people believed that Gaelic culture and heritage were valuable. The enthusiastic backing for Gaelic among the younger generation is a very positive sign, given that young people play a crucial role in influencing and shaping tomorrow's society. However, the young need the help of the older generations. I know that politics always has its part to play, but I believe it is crucial that speakers realise the value of their languages so as to resist the sway of monolingualism.

For centuries, British and Scottish elites have done their best to evict people from their lands and to silence their language. They have not yet fully succeeded. The attitudes of Scotland's younger generation suggest that they never will. The slogan of the nineteenth century Crofters' Party comes to mind: *Is Treasa tuath na tighearan* – 'the People are mightier than a lord'.

A FISHERMAN'S TALE

Robin Ade

Since 1966, a regular part of my travels from Scotland to Afghanistan and Pakistan has been the study and enhancement of brown trout, a fish which is native to cold waters from Iceland eastwards to the borders of China. It also thrives as a popular immigrant outwith its native range, and Scottish brown trout are now naturalised in many other parts of the world, including the mountains of the old Northwest Frontier of Pakistan, a forgotten trout fishing region which the Western media tells us is populated mostly by terrorists and madmen. Our story begins on the Indus tributaries of Swat, Chitral, and Gilgit.

The subcontinent lacks native trout, a fact which was keenly felt by British anglers during the time of the British Raj. Great efforts were made to introduce them. Scottish brown trout were taken on a truly epic journey, firstly as eggs sailed by ship to Bombay in 1899, and then up to the cool streams of the Nilgiri Hills, where they were successfully reared. When railway travel started, some were taken north to Kashmir, where they became naturalised, then westwards by mule across the Himalayan passes as far as Gilgit, and finally, in the 1950s, to the old princely state of Chitral on the Afghan border. Interestingly they could have been brought from only a few miles away in Afghanistan, where they are native, avoiding those thousands of miles of rail, sea, and mule journeys from Scotland. This option probably didn't occur to anyone since, in the days of the British Raj, their presence may not have been well known, and anyway Afghanistan was forbidden territory.

Trout are sight hunters and need clear water, which in Northern Pakistan is restricted mainly to a handful of small streams and lochs in the Hindu Kush, Hindu Raj, and Karakorum mountains. The first one I visited was in 1970. This was in Bomberet Valley, where a fast mountain stream runs down from the Afghan border to the main Chitral River. In those days I only carried a spool of line and some hooks so, after walking 10 miles upstream through a dramatic gorge, I found a 10 foot willow branch for a rod, dug up a few worms, and caught a beautiful 12-inch brown trout which I spotted lying in a clear pool. My friend Ralph and I were then approached by a shepherd boy who milked a nearby goat and gave us a bowl to drink. It was the second day of Ramadan, the fasting month, but he was a member of the Kalash, the local pagan tribe, and was clearly delighted to share a drink with fellow 'unbelievers'.

An older Muslim boy then appeared, and on seeing the trout became very excited and began talking about thousands of rupees. It seemed very strange that trout fishing should be regulated in this remote place; in nearby Afghanistan, where we were living at the time, fishing permits were unheard of. Not having thousands of rupees, we immediately took off several miles down the valley and turned up into Rumbur, the remotest of the three Kalash glens, where we were received by women in the first village we came to, who placed garlands round our necks.

Back in Bomberet a couple of years later, we learnt more about those fishing regulations when we came across a Pathan gentleman, Matsee Babu – or Fish Baba – who issued me an old British-style permit, complete with beat numbers and size limits, for the grand price of five rupees. He spent the next two days walking over a major pass to Chitral village and back to deliver the five rupees to the government fisheries officer. I felt like I was the first person to have bought a fishing permit since the British left.

Matsee Babu also ran a trout hatchery in Bomberet which the government may have located here because the Kalash tribe have a taboo against eating birds and fish and so were unlikely to poach the trout. Or perhaps it was because the Kalash are Chitral's only real tourist attraction, and they had hopes of selling tickets to the disappointingly small number of foreign tourists and occasional anthropologists who visit the Kalash valleys to observe their pre-Islamic, pre-Vedic, Shamanistic culture.

At that time the Kalash had wooden idols in the fields, sacred groves, and temples decorated with fresh drawings of markhor and ibex, the huge wild goats which still thrive in the mountains above. Their sacred mountain, to which their spirits are said to return after death, they call the Throne of the Golden King. This is Tirich Mir, which dominates the 200-mile long Chitral valley; at over 25,000 feet, it is the highest peak in the

Hindu Kush and the highest in the world outwith the Himalayas. Seasonal festivals include Chowmas, at the winter solstice, which the Kalash associate with the Christian Christmas. They say that when they are finally pushed out by the neighbouring Muslims, they will go to Germany or Britain, and that Gish, their great war god, had already migrated to London a century before.

I also visited the Lutkoh, a larger stream running down from the Afghan border some 40 miles north of Bomberet and the only other significant trout water in Chitral. The trout here are said to have been introduced from Gilgit by a Scot in the early 1960s, and they bred in huge numbers; a friend caught many while spinning from horseback, and Matsee Babu, visiting from Bomberet, caught a six pounder while fishing with a willow stick. By the time I visited there in 1973, they were coming under fishing pressure from local people, although I managed to catch nine trout of up to 15 inches in an afternoon.

The Lutkoh is prone to damage from floods, and in 1995, when I fished there after a major flood event with three British visitors, we caught only one eight-inch fish. The Bomberet stream, in spite of the best efforts of Matsee Babu, had also become effectively unfishable thanks to catastrophic floods caused by the felling of the magnificent cedar forests which in the 1970s still covered the adjoining mountains. Meanwhile, the increasingly rare trout had become a must-have item for visiting VIPs, and no effort was spared to obtain them. One year, when tobacco magnate Lord Wills visited, I suggested substituting the local so-called snow trout, an unrelated fish which is tasty enough, though extremely bony.

By the 1990s, the popularity of trout had even extended to the Kalash valleys, where they probably accounted for a decline in the fish-eating taboo. My Kalash friend Abdul Khaliq, being somewhat of an entrepreneur, even tried to start a small trout farm, but the idea never took off. He also tried to establish a chicken farm in a house he owned but was voted down by the Community Council who still felt strongly about the traditional taboo against eating birds. He then rented the house out to a group of Pakistani Christians who had come up to try to convert the Kalash. They turned the house into a church. One year Abdul Khaliq was somewhat embarrassed when they turned up without warning and found some of his relatives living in it; after that they were good enough to contact him well before their annual visit so he could put his relatives elsewhere.

In the 1990s, I made several visits to Chitral with my nephew Tom and a group of fishing friends from Scotland. One of our aims was to establish trout ponds in some of the villages, a venture in which we were for various reasons almost completely unsuccessful. It was suggested that rainbow trout, which do better in fast water than browns, could be used for restocking the torrential rivers but local people objected to the introduction of this 'foreign' fish; for them the Scottish brown trout had by now become the Chitrali trout.

We heard recently that there was one village pond where our stocked trout had survived but had then been washed out by yet another flood and established themselves in the nearby Laspur River, which runs down from the Shandur Pass on the Gilgit border. Not only that, but they were reaching huge weights – approaching 20 pounds. They had also run up a tributary to occupy a small loch where they now form a stable population. From here they can restock the stream naturally when trout are washed out by the inevitable floods. The Laspur River now joins the Lutkoh as the only sustainable trout water in the 200-mile long valley of Chitral.

Scottish trout had also been successfully introduced to two larger rivers, the Utrot and Ushu, in the upper reaches of the Swat Valley southeast of Chitral. When I first fished there, in 1973, I took care to obtain a government permit at Kalam Village, although this did not impress a local Pathan I met by the river. He made it clear that the fish belonged to his tribal community. In any case, I cut a willow stick rod and caught twenty-three nice trout to over a pound behind boulders. I could not reach the main stream where I knew much bigger trout were present. I had a similar catch when I returned there in 1976.

My main fishing memory of those visits is the daily change in the river which in the mornings ran low and clear, but in the afternoons became swollen and turbid due to snowmelt upstream. I have since been caught out by snowmelt in Gilgit, and also in Scotland, by leaving live trout in riverside puddles only to find, when I returned an hour or two later, that the water had risen, and they had escaped back into the river.

I returned to the Utrot in June 1994 with a couple of local friends and found that, as in Chitral, it had been heavily overfished and was not worth trying except perhaps in the distant upper reaches. However, we heard that the neighbouring Ushu still had very good fishing some 20 miles upstream, so we took a jeep from Kalam up to Matiltan Village, and covered the last 12 miles on foot, a walk which took us up over 10,000 feet across some precipitous snowfields to the fishing grounds of Mahadon, the 'Fish Lake', an exotically beautiful area set about with great deodar cedars and fields of red primulas. I found a huge dead eagle owl among the trees there, and tied a trout fly from a wing feather, a large version of the old Scottish hoolet fly which imitates a moth.

We started catching trout immediately on flies and spinners although we had to take regular sleep breaks due to fits of nausea caused by coming up too fast from the lowlands. The fish were not particularly large, but we caught plenty, despite the water being a mere five degrees Celsius, well below a normal feeding temperature. Their food though was clearly abundant, with enormous rafts of chironomid flies circling in the eddies. I later learnt that chironomid larvae can thrive in glaciers up to 12 degrees below zero, colder than anything in Antarctica, by living off the layers of organic pollution which rise up from the sub-continent below and settle on the high mountains.

We did not catch any big fish, but were interested to learn from our guide Mohammad that there were large trout in a small, nameless, and equally remote loch in Gilgit, about 30 miles north of Mahadon. He had walked up there a few weeks before and showed us a photo of one he had caught on a Mepps spinner and handline; it weighed 16 pounds and Mohammad's right hand had a deep scar where the heavy line had bitten into it.

The problem for us was that the trek to the loch involved climbing a 16,000-foot snowbound pass, which we were in no fit state to do. So, we decided to take the 200-mile scenic route which involved a walk back down to Matiltan, a jeep to Kalam, tribal buses and jeeps southwest down the main Swat valley, north into Dir State, up over the 10,000-foot Lowari Pass into Chitral and then south again over the 12,000-foot Shandur Pass into Gilgit. The final leg consisted of an eight-mile uphill walk along a small, uninhabited tributary of the upper Ghizar River to the loch, a shallow oxbow of a few acres.

The fishing was well worth the six-day journey. As we approached the water we saw a group of nice trout chasing tadpoles in the gin-clear margins, and immediately put up our fly rods. I attached a Black Pennel fly and cast to the nearest fish; it sunk behind it, but the trout spotted it, turned around, sucked it off the bottom, and made a 40-yard dash across the loch. It weighed nearly three pounds and was in excellent condition. We soon discovered that the trout here were not only large, averaging two pounds, but also very numerous. They made excellent eating, which was nice because we were relying on them to avoid having to carry several days' worth of food up in our rucksacks.

After a couple of days our trout diet, however delicious, became a little repetitive. We were relieved when an old man arrived together with a lad carrying a small live sheep across his shoulders. These small mountain sheep are very tasty, and we were happy to join them in a dinner of lamb kebabs. The old man was a prince from lower Gilgit who had fished here many times; the largest trout he knew of had been caught from the adjoining stream by his father, and weighed 26 pounds. The nearest we came to catching a really big one was when one of our party, spinning in the stream, had a double figure trout follow his lure in to the bank. Tom caught a four pounder, the biggest we had from the loch that year.

The reason why trout grow so big here is something of a mystery. We saw no sign of small forage fish; their stomachs contained only invertebrates, tadpoles and one large freshwater shrimp, the so-called Tibetan shrimp which is apparently the basis for seafood restaurants in Tibet. It appeared that the trout here fed mainly on invertebrates which, as in Swat, were very numerous.

Another feature of the trout was that since their arrival, probably less than a hundred years before, they had separated into two types, a silver one like a sea trout and one with normal brown trout colouration. The same phenomenon can be seen among trout in many Scottish lochs, including some which have become isolated since hydro dams were built. In natural lochs they have been separated for millennia, and are probably quite distinct genetically.

Trout samples from the Gilgit loch were examined by my friend Andy Ferguson, Professor of Genetics at the Queens University in Belfast, who found that the original fish introduced to the sub-Continent in the 1800s were not in fact Loch Leven trout, as stated in the textbooks, but were descended from the standard Howietoun fish farm stock consisting of mixed Scottish east coast and west coast races.

My favourite fishing spot was the huge boulder from which Mohammed had caught his 16 pounder and from where I could watch dozens of trout lying across the shallows. They did not respond to my lure until around three in the afternoon each day. Then they suddenly became active and I had a hit almost every cast. This behaviour confirmed that loch trout, here as in Scotland, have regular mealtimes when they will begin feeding in unison without the stimulus of a fly hatch.

When four of us went up in September the following year, we hired three donkeys to carry our bags and food for several days. Unfortunately, the donkeys turned out be geriatrics and could not even manage walking pace, so we ended up carrying most of the gear ourselves. We also took a paraffin stove to avoid cutting into the depleted birch wood coppices which were the main fuel source for the nearest village, eight miles downstream. This time the trout were finishing their breakfast by seven in the morning and did not seriously come on to feed again until five in the afternoon; over the next few days we caught forty, averaging well over a pound in weight.

The wildlife at the Gilgit loch was impressive. The previous year the old prince had pointed out flocks of markhor and ibex goats grazing on the slopes of the 16,000-foot mountain above us, and there were many species of birds. On the way up, we had watched a family of saker falcons catching dragonflies by a roadside pool, and at the loch itself there were flocks of migratory birds resting up on their autumn flight from Siberia to the Sub-continent. Our driver Latif, who had brought a shotgun up with him, had already bagged three species of dove outside villages on our way up through Chitral, and at the loch he got a stint, a pretty wading bird I recognised only from bird guides. He also shot a heron, a rare and almost mythological bird in north Pakistan. The Chitrali word for heron translates as 'top chicken', and he said he would be a hero in his village when he took it home. He intended to eat it, but I imagine he would have needed a lot of chillies to disguise its flavour.

On our return, Latif and I met a man with a donkey which we hired to carry our gear. This one turned out to be a much better donkey which had no trouble carrying not only our rucksacks, but a heavy bag of trout destined for friends in Chitral.

While we headed for Chitral, Tom and his friend explored the upper reaches of the main Ghizar River which rises out of Khokush, a large fishless loch, not far from the Shandur Pass, which looked like it had only quite recently formed below the glacier at its head. Khokush is probably the largest of the handful of lochs in northern Pakistan, and the following year I decided to try and carry some trout up from the Ghizar River below, and up over the rocky, porous moraine which was preventing them from accessing the loch. I reached the Shandur Pass in late September, and spent the night in a big tent with a group of Pathan tribals who had spent the summer trying to catch shaheen – or peregrine falcons. They had with them a captive bird which they were using to attract wild ones, but without success. A few years later, an Arab donor introduced seven peregrines to the area to boost numbers.

The Pathans said they had previously been to neighbouring China where there were plenty of peregrines, but where they not only had to pay large bribes but were also unable to make any friends. I said they should come to Scotland, where there were also plenty of peregrines, but they somehow knew that would be impossible. I imagined the outrage when a group of Taliban types were caught poaching peregrines in the Highlands – the Royal Society for the Protection of Birds would demand the death penalty! The main entertainment that evening was peregrine feeding time. Everyone retired to their sleeping bags to watch with rapt attention the magnificent captive bird devouring its dinner.

The next morning, I set off for Khokush across a gravel plain dotted with clumps of wild roses, miniature honeysuckle, and wild black currant bushes; the only notable creature I met on the way was a large and impassive bull yak. There were no pools as such on the river, only a continuous stony cataract filled with very small trout which had eroded fins from being battered against the stones, making them look like fish farm trout.

I camped below the moraine that evening and constructed a holding device using a piece of netting wrapped around a frame of willow branches. The campsite was absolute luxury. I would fill my teapot with water at night so that in the morning I could reach out from my bivouac and grab a handful of bark from an aptly named paper birch, lay it in the fireplace with some twigs and put the teapot on while I said good morning to the friendly seven-inch trout which lived in a tiny clear backwater a few feet away. All without getting out of my sleeping bag.

The following day I fished hard and got 21 trout including a 12-inch 'monster' which I had for dinner. I have a vivid memory of a trout dashing through a big green standing wave after my fly. The next morning, I put 17 in a plastic jerrycan with just enough water to cover their backs, and carried them up the moraine to the loch; I knew that if I kept moving, the water would stay well oxygenated.

One glance into the loch and I could tell there were no fish in it; the bed was thickly covered in caddis and mayfly larvae while red and brown chironomid worms hung suspended in the freezing water. If trout succeeded in breeding here this invertebrate zoo would be decimated. I let loch water slowly into the jerrycan to let the fish acclimatise to the temperature before they slowly swam out, right side up, and sat quietly on the bottom to recover from their rough journey before swimming steadily off into the depths. Just as they did when I introduced 16 small trout into a fishless loch on the island of Eigg in western Scotland a few years later.

The following morning, it was snowing gently and the snowline, which had crept lower down the mountains every day, had almost reached the valley floor. I had no warm clothes so decided to head back, stopping to catch 17 more trout to add to a dozen I had the evening before, enough for a meal for my Pathan friends. They were beginning to worry about me as I had only planned to be away for two days. They had been trying unsuccessfully to catch trout on a heavy hand line with big hooks, so the next day I left them with some trout flies which they were most impressed with.

I returned to Khokush five years later, in mid-May 2001, with a party of six, three from Scotland and three locals. We camped near the peregrine hunter's site and caught around 60 very small trout for dinner. We deep fried them, but at that elevation they seemed to take forever to brown; a pan of potatoes took over an hour before it even thought about being ready to eat. Up at Khokush, there was still snow lying under the birches and a hard freezing wind. I wouldn't expect to catch trout in Scotland in such conditions, and sure enough we fished for a few hours without a sign of a fish. So, I still didn't know if any of the 17 trout had survived to find a suitable burn in which to spawn and reproduce.

The answer came several years later when I read an article in *Trout & Salmon* magazine by a British fisherman who had gone up to Khokush with a Pakistani tourist guide and made a big catch of good-sized trout. The area around Shandur has now been turned into a national park and I imagine the trout are an important attraction. It seems that our efforts had led to the establishment of two large and sustainable Scottish brown trout fisheries in northern Pakistan.

Trout fishing is not an occupation usually associated with Afghanistan. Yet the brown trout is in fact a native of rivers running north from the Hindu Kush Mountains, which run across the centre of the country, to join the Amu Darya or Oxus, the historic waterway which forms the border with the so-called Stans – Turkmenistan, Uzbekistan, and Tajikistan. Trout are highly prized by local people who catch them with yak hair throwing nets or handlines. In the Kokcha, the 200-mile river in the north-eastern province of Badakhshan, they grow to over 20 pounds.

The first trout I caught in Afghanistan came from Karga lake outside Kabul in the summer of 1970. It was not a brown trout but my first rainbow trout, the progeny of fish gifted to the country by the Bulgarian government. It was memorable for its bright rainbow colours, which matched those of the dawn sky over the nearby peaks of the Hindu Kush.

The closest brown trout to Kabul inhabit a headwater stream of the Kunduz River 50 miles north across the 12,000 foot Salang Pass over the Hindu Kush. One September morning in 1972, my neighbour Dick and I set off to fish there in a VW bus armed with a nicely balanced fly-fishing outfit, a lucky find in the bazaar which probably came from the house of a diplomat, probably British, the only foreign nationality which seemed to know much about Afghan trout.

It took all day to reach the stream. Our vehicle broke near the summit of the pass, and we freewheeled 19 kilometres back down to the village of Jebal Siraj, where Dick used our only money to take a bus to Kabul to collect another vehicle, while I remained at a loose end in the village. Not for long, though, for I came across the Salang Malang, a local dervish I knew from a previous journey north, when I had given him a lift from the top of the pass down to the village. He took me into the nearest tea house and ordered a welcome meal. Payment was not required since nobody would think of asking a respected dervish or his guest for money.

Dick finally arrived with another vehicle, and we set off again up the pass and a few miles beyond, where the precipitous burn looked large enough to be worth fishing. We camped overnight and took turns with the beautifully balanced fly outfit to catch some 20 fish, typical small mountain trout which provided dinner for our households back in Kabul the following evening.

At that time, Afghanistan had enjoyed peace for 50 years, including what older Afghans call the Golden Age of the 1960s and 70s, the so-called hippie era when foreigners came in their thousands, with peaceful agendas quite unlike the other foreign invasions before and after. By the time I fished there again, the Russians had come and gone, killing a million and a half people in their ten-year occupation, and leaving the country in a state of chaos which persists to this day.

The first record I have of a Scottish connection with Afghan fish is from 1839, during the first Anglo-Afghan War, when one Lt. John McClelland seems to have spent much of the war fishing. His descriptions and illustrations comprised the first scientific work on the subject and still form the basis of Afghan fish studies today.

There were some high-level Scottish connections during the 1800s. William Campbell became the only foreigner to head the Afghan army during the reign of Dost Mohammed Shah and for many years thereafter, including the reign of Abdur Rahman, the 'Iron Amir' who re-united the country after a long spell of chaos (he referred to Afghanistan as Yagistan, the Land of Rebellion). The Amir also had a Scottish lady doctor, who was instrumental in having his biography published in London.

There was also the remarkable case of a Scottish girl who was captured on the Frontier and taken to north Afghanistan. When General Sale offered to rescue her during the second Anglo-Afghan War, she refused, saying she had many fine sons now, and had no interest in returning to British India.

In 1997, I fished two lochs on the headwaters of the Kokcha river in Badakhshan, one of the few provinces still outside Taliban control. It was October, too late I thought for fly hatches, especially at 12,000 feet, although as it turned out there were big hatches of chironomid flies between the frequent snow showers. Natural bait was unobtainable in the bone-dry ground, so I caught a couple of trout on spinners which provided four trout eyes, the strange but effective bait used by local fishers. My Afghan companion Khalil reminded me recently that we caught over a hundred trout one day at the smaller of the lochs. The catch provided plenty of samples for a biological study on Afghan trout, the main reason for our visit. The fish were small, although I met a commercial fisherman there whose precious hand line had been broken by a massive 'cannibal' trout; he was most grateful when I was able to replace it with a spare spool of strong nylon.

The upper loch was a mile long and had a great reputation. On the bank there was once the remains of a boat used by its most famous visiting angler, the Afghan King Zahir Shah, in the 1970s, while the depths held the carcasses of two Russian helicopter gunships shot down by Stinger missiles in the 1980s. The banks of both lochs were littered with rusting Soviet military ordinance.

The biggest trout were said to be caught alongside the inaccessible boulder fields at the far shore, but since we had no boat, we fished our Mepps spinners and trout eyes around the inlet stream at the head of the loch. The trout were larger here than in the wee loch, though less numerous; we caught enough of these prized fish to pay for our food and accommodation at the nearby Northern Alliance military camp, where we were staying.

It was at the head of the loch that I had one of my most alarming moments in Afghanistan. This had nothing to do with difficult humans, but with the golden eagle which flew high over the camp every morning, high enough to avoid the enthusiastic bursts of Kalashnikov rounds which trigger-happy soldiers fired up at it. Afghan eagles are in the habit of knocking wild sheep and goats off mountain ledges and this one had decided to get its own back on the human race by targeting me. The first time it tried I happened to look round and it veered away but a few days later I was fishing from a large boulder when the sky went black and there was a huge blast of wind as the bird came down within inches of my head. I felt fortunate that it had not knocked me off the boulder or put a talon down and taken my scalp off.

There were also less threatening birds, with daily arrivals of ducks and waders from Siberia *en route* to their South Asian wintering grounds. We came across a pretty young water rail which had not yet learnt to fly.

Our trips to the head of the loch had attracted attention from the camp and we soon had a daily entourage of Northern Alliance fighters wanting to try their hand at trout fishing. I had with me three small telescopic rods bought from a now defunct fishing shop in Glasgow, and these proved useful, especially to Khalil who later set up a lucrative business selling trout at the camp until the commander forbade him, in the name, he claimed, of conservation. Some weeks later Khalil was fishing some 200 miles downstream at the provincial capital of Faizabad when he was approached by Burhanuddin Rabbani, then the internationally recognised president of Afghanistan, who also asked to try his hand at trout fishing. He hooked a fish on a spinner but lost it. Rather appropriately, I thought, because he was then in the process of losing his entire country to the all-conquering Taliban.

On his journey down the Kokcha, Khalil visited a riverside teahouse and saw the carcase of a 20 pound trout from the main river. The name for trout in Dari means 'spotted fish', as it does in Gaelic and in Turkish, and he met a qalandar by the river, a travelling dervish, who had a charming explanation for these famous spots; they signify a hierarchy, the big, heavily spotted fish being the kings and queens, the lesser spotted ones the prime ministers, and so forth down the social scale.

Our fishing came to an end late one afternoon when a heavy snowfall began. Khalil decided we should leave before the 15,000-foot pass into Pakistan became blocked. I wanted to stay on, but Khalil was adamant, fortunately as it turned out, since his decision saved both our lives. He took a photo of me near the top of the pass, looking down on the loch during a break in the snowstorm, only minutes before a series of events combined to turn our jaunt into a nightmare. A line of wild looking horsemen suddenly appeared on the skyline above us, but before we could decide who they were, the snow blew in again, dusk turned to darkness, and I developed my first case of elevation sickness. The rest of the journey became a blur as I fell into a broken sleep while my horse negotiated its way down several miles of steep screes. At one point it lost its footing and Khalil caught it, and me, as it stumbled over a rocky incline.

We managed to avoid the main dangers of the pass where several people were dying each week, mainly from hypothermia, after coming up to 15,000 feet from the lowlands without warm clothing. Even at the level of the loch, the daytime temperature plummeted from 10 degrees Celsius to below zero every time the sun went in. The other danger was wolves, which knew that men did not carry firearms over the pass, and were not shy of attacking travellers, especially at night.

As we reached the low ground, we met a group of teenage boys setting off up the pass in the dark, with ponies heavily laden with fuel cans. No one had climbed the pass since before sunset; we were concerned for their welfare, but they were in a frenzy of excitement and could not be persuaded to wait until daylight. One of their ponies stumbled and fell; Khalil, always helpful, put it on its feet again. We learnt later that they had all died on the pass that night, their bodies partly eaten by wolves; one of them had an entire leg missing. We also learnt that the horsemen we had seen on the skyline were part of a Taliban invasion force *en route* to attacking the Northern Alliance camp. That night they rocketed the camp, resulting in many deaths. The big tent in which we had been staying was particularly hard hit, and everyone in it was killed.

Khalil had heard that the wolves on this particular pass attack by approaching backwards and kicking snow into the faces of the ponies before moving in for the kill. This seemed to us a little strange, but not long after Khalil was returning near dusk and alone over the pass when he experienced it himself. A pack of wolves moved in, kicking snow up and panicking his horse; just as they were moving in for the kill a group of travellers appeared from down the hill and the wolves retreated.

Khalil's home is in the high mountains of Nuristan, in the northeast of the country, which we visited in 2002 while organising the building of the first primary schools there on behalf of our local Scottish charity, the Afghan Schools Trust. We visited many villages and walked many miles along emerald, green rivers which looked as though they must contain trout, although unfortunately, being on the Indus catchment, they didn't. Naturally we thought of introducing some, either farmed Scottish trout from Chitral, a two-day trek over a major pass to the west, or native Afghan trout from our familiar lochs in Badakhshan, which lie beyond another high pass into the Oxus catchment to the north.

We decided on the Afghan trout option and the following year we had the project organised using containers on ponies, much the same method used to transport trout across the Himalayas in the days of the British Raj. We were almost ready to go when we heard that a local man had just had his leg blown off on the northern pass in a new minefield planted by the Taliban, so we cancelled our plans. But local people are keen on the idea of introducing trout, and now that the Taliban have brought security to the country, we may yet succeed.

The last brown trout I caught in Afghanistan was in 2005. It came from the Salang stream, where I had caught my first one over 30 years before. Our travelling party included our late friend Godfrey Smith, Chairman of the Afghan Schools Trust, together with my daughter, baby Hana, and her mother Alexandra. We had stopped to wait for a traffic jam to clear on the northern side of the Salang pass while returning from a school's project in Mazar-i-Sharif. We had about twenty minutes to wait, so I told Alexandra to stay put while I grabbed my rod and headed for the stream. I then noticed that the roadside was lined with red and white painted stones marking a live minefield, a fact we had learnt only an hour before when we stopped at an office of the Halo Trust, the famous mine clearing organisation based at Thornhill in Scotland. While I hesitated, three young men appeared and told me it was fine to cross over by leaping from stone to stone down to the stream, which we quickly did. One of them was carrying a knife and a silver plate to prepare our catch, while another dug a worm for bait, took away my rod, and proceeded to fish, while the third waited with the baby's changing bucket to put the catch in. The boy with the rod did not look like he was going to catch anything, so I took the rod back, dropped the worm behind a boulder and pulled out an eight-inch trout.

At that point the traffic started moving again, so we put the trout in the bucket and headed back to the road, only to find that Alexandra, carrying baby Hana, was making her way steadily towards the stream closely accompanied by a worried looking old man who was trying to stop her from stepping between the boulders, which of course was where the mines were. By the time we reached her, she was happily collecting hips from a wild rose bush. I wondered if I had made the wrong choice a few days before when I declined the offer of a cheeky old Uzbek on the streets of Balkh. He had offered me 30 sheep for her.

There are several beautiful and varied wild rose species in Afghanistan, but that one from the Salang pass, whose offspring are now thriving in Scotland, on the bank of the River Ken, looks just like the familiar Scottish dog rose.

We got back to the road safely, and before setting off again I had a quick word with Latif, the man with the changing bucket, who was clearly a trout enthusiast. He pointed out various aspects of the fish we had caught, including its prominent spots, a feature lacking in the native shirmaye, or sweetfish, from his home river in the nearby Panjshir Valley. The valley became famous by holding out through the whole Russian occupation, in spite of regular carpet bombing and attacks from the main Russian base only a few miles away. When I visited the Panjshir in 2002, it was still littered with dead Russian tanks; at the mouth of the valley a small boy was selling sweetfish by the road.

After 2005, I made several more trips to Afghanistan with Godfrey on behalf of the Afghan Schools Trust, but I had to restrict most of my fishing to Friday outings with students. The security situation made travel for trout fishing difficult. Now the Taliban are in control and no longer fighting, the roads have become safe for the first time since the 1970s, and trout waters are once again becoming accessible. In 2013, two years before Godfrey's death, we had a good day out on the Lal River, not far from our women's centre in the Hazarajat Mountains. Here we caught a bag of the local sweetfish, enough to make a good evening meal for the staff at the Afghan medical clinic where we were staying.

Khalil, with whom I fished many times in Afghanistan and northern Pakistan, was able to visit Scotland in 2018, and to enjoy fishing our local waters. He caught some fine wild brown trout of up to three pounds while loch fishing, as well as making some good catches on the rivers; he hooked a very big trout and climbed the Cairnsmore of Carsphairn on the same day. He also had the experience of playing a fresh-run salmon on our River Urr. We are still working with the Afghan Schools Trust to re-open the six primary schools we initiated in Nuristan back in 2001 but which have been closed for the last 15 years due to the wars.

As well as establishing primary schools in remote parts of Afghanistan, our adventures in the Hindu Kush had some practical results in terms of trout enhancement and research. In northern Pakistan our Scottish group succeeded, eventually, in establishing sustainable trout populations in Khokush Lake in what is now the Shandur National Park in Gilgit, as well as in the Laspur River in Chitral. In Badakhshan, Khalil and I caught enough trout not only to pay for our stay but also to provide a large number of samples for the first genetic and biological studies of Afghan trout by two of the world's leading trout biologists, the late Robert Behnke of the University of Colorado, and Andy Ferguson, formerly professor emeritus at Queens University Belfast, and now resident near Castle Douglas in Scotland. I was also able to provide information, photos, and cover artwork for the first book on Afghan fish by professor Brian Coad of the National Museum of Ottawa.

Should I take up a recent offer by the Taliban education department to come over and discuss our schools programme, I may yet have the opportunity to visit some of the fine trout waters in Afghanistan which I know only by reputation. In the meantime, I continue fishing the burns of Galloway and the Highlands, in stirring landscapes which remind me so much of the Hindu Kush.

~~TRIGGER NOTEBOOK:~~
THE COASTLINE OF MY MEMORY

Alycia Pirmohamed

During the first lockdown in 2020, I lived in an old tenement building on Easter Road in Edinburgh, Scotland. One day, I looked up the distance between my flat and Lochend Park, the nearest green space. 1.126 kilometres. I could gaze out my kitchen window in its direction while washing dishes or making coffee. Although I couldn't see the loch itself, nor its abundance of waterfowl, something in my body eased knowing that it was close by. In ten minutes or less, I could arrive at Lochend Butterfly Way and be surrounded, almost as if suddenly, by trees and swans.

I found that number online. I am obsessed with the distance between spaces. By that, I mean not only geographical distances but temporal and inherited distances too. In this context, a number as concrete as 1.126 kilometres can, at times, feel meaningless. When I slide into memory, the distance between my old flat and Lochend Park might as well be infinite. At the loch, I might look over its edge and feel myself transported to the Bow River, the body of water that bisects the city of Calgary. I could lean against the strong trunk of an oak tree, thriving with spring blossoms, and instead find myself under the shade of the half-blossomed crab-apple tree in the backyard of one of my several childhood homes. Simply put, places remind me of other places and I am less bothered – more intrigued – that these remembrances swell between the boundaries of real and unreal.

If I am honest, wild waters did not always mean so much to me. I grew up in Edmonton, a midwestern city, landlocked and far away from the ocean. Even within that city, I lived in the opposite direction from one of its watery landmarks, the North Saskatchewan River. And later, my time living in a small town in rural Alberta, overwhelmed with farmlands and rolling prairies, also instilled within me a craving for busy cities rather than wide open natural spaces. Perhaps every young girl is always looking elsewhere, facing the direction of something she desires, and in that process, turns away from all that she has.

~~You are hiding something here. You know that in rural Alberta, the natural world, those wide open spaces, did not always feel welcoming. Near the town you lived in, there might have been grasslands and birch trees, neighbouring lakes, mesmeric gardens, and long stretches canola fields, but amidst all that space, there was not even one single mosque.~~

That spring, during lockdown, I walked to Lochend Park almost every day. I had just completed my PhD thesis at the University of Edinburgh – my studies were what had first brought me to Scotland – and my mind was conditioned to analysis, to notetaking. I had amassed fieldnotes upon fieldnotes in my notebooks. *The swans are a nostalgic tracing on the water* says one section, and it sits next to a quote from Leanne Betasamosake Simpson writing about Nishnaabeg pedagogy: '"Theory" isn't just an intellectual pursuit–it is woven with kinetics, spiritual presence and emotion, it is contextual and relational'.

I walked the loop around the loch and read poetry out loud to the water birds. Sometimes they stuck around for the whole piece. Other times they disappeared beneath the permeable surface of the glittering loch. Or, like the swans, they threaded the near-bare trees around the water the whole time, their bodies disappearing and reappearing like a poetic refrain.

*

Memory itself is a vast, deep ocean. It holds an inherited history that I simultaneously wish was and wasn't mine. When I look back, across temporal distances that stretch beyond my existence, I become entangled with the seaweed of ancestry. These entanglements often leave me feeling ambivalent. Unmoored.

Whatever the seascape collects is, at least, honest. What enters and leaves, what lingers, what impacts its future – the sea has its own chemical and indisputable memory. A body of water does not lie. A body, my body, however, is its own discursive notebook. I seek that same kind of certainty and faithfulness in my own life, in the way I gather maybe-important things. Keepsakes from my own stratified depths. Photographs, voice notes, prayers, a screengrab of my father on a video call taken on a day when he is fine and smiling, a story about my grandmother, a square of patterned fabric owned by someone now gone, any digital heirloom with a timestamp. I convince myself I need these tethers to make sense of who I am.

In the stories that I craft for the onlooker, whether through poetry or prose, I often submerge into my memories and show kindness, even love, to every passed down narrative I encounter with my mind's tired eye. It sometimes feels like the movement toward self-love is the aim of all of this creative dredging – a marker of growth and recovery. But in the version of myself that is truer, though perhaps still not true, I admit my sadness and my anger. I don't allow myself to venture into the vastness fully. I avert my gaze from trauma, even if I avert my gaze in vain. I am hurting. This history is mine and I want it, *yes*, but is it also okay to say that I don't? It is love, *yes*, but it is also pain. Even after so much unlearning of what I have internalised, of seeking out radical joy and feeling out the meaning of reclamation, there are still all those moments where I want to shrink away from my very own body.

In my palms I can only hold so much water, and when held, this water can only reflect so much of my own face. An ocean of memory, then, can only ever engulf me.

*

I remember the hastily, sand-stricken, wiggling out of my fleece pullover. There are two other women on this stretch of beach. Their puffer jackets are sleek and black. Their two figures are far enough away that I can't tell anything specific about them, except that they are undressing too. We are discarding layers and layers while wrapped in towels, and finally emerge from our bundles in our swimsuits. When we enter the water, still however many metres apart, it is the ocean that connects us. This is the way I think about water: as an agent of separations and connections. Soon, we will be three bodies amongst the waves, held in the togetherness of sea swimming as passers-by look on. Water thrashes gently against all three of us, tangible and real.

In my notebook, I have written that this day is a Saturday and the tide is low at Portobello beach. Water drags along the coastline and there is a kind of morning sleepiness to the way it undulates. *Slippage.* The way the crests of waves, those small whirling peaks, come nearer and nearer until finally they break onto the shore.

In my diasporic imagination, the waves do not stop there. They keep moving, migrating into a new environment, one where they echo with their oceanic specificity in new ways. They are a little unfamiliar. Wet and silky across the sand, the waves move beyond the promenade, beyond the dogwalkers, and past Crumbs of Portobello. They cross the busy intersections, move up the stairs to the overpass bridge, and finally land next to the local pollinators in a field of wildflowers at Figgate Park. Waves and waves and waves and waves unfolding in places where another's imagination says they don't belong, moving in a way someone else might think is impossible.

In the water, the women appear closer than they did on the shore. They look over my way and I look back. I guess that we are smiling at each other. Just us linked together in the sea on a cool summer morning.

You walk into a warm café because you want to write this essay and your partner has an important meeting that morning. The space at home is too small for the both of you to work in privacy. At your table, you open one of your many notebooks and find fragments of your life written untidily on the pages. You read about your swim at Portobello Beach, trying to remember the calm you felt that cool summer morning. Memory ribbons over your eyes and your vision starts to blur until you can barely see your surroundings. The girl seated next to you is eating a full English breakfast and the scent of it makes you want to retch. You are suddenly too aware of the insides of your body. Your ears are too warm, they are ringing. It feels like hot air moves into them in a constant stream that travels straight to your heart. It is winter now, but somehow your insides are boiling. That day, you automatically assumed the two women smiled at you. Now, only four months later, as brown bodies are dehumanised relentlessly in mainstream media, you imagine every white stranger looks at you just a little differently than before. Slippage. The way the past slips into the bodily present and wrenches your day open like a loud December wound.

*

The sea is shaped by migration and migration is shaped by the sea.

Before my obsession with Lochend Park, there was my obsession with one of my ancestral homelands. There are over 14,000 kilometres between Edmonton and Dar es Salaam. This numerical displacement is deepened by imagination. I find a poem from six years ago where I envision the landscape of a place I had not ever visited. *I imagine my homeland when I am not there.* In it are descriptions of treelines and rose-ringed parakeets, of the Swahili Coast likened to a body on its side. This writing was informed by research. I remember looking up the chemical make-up of soils. The most common trees. Even the approximate cost of a ticket to the cinema in shillings, in the 1960s. This was the kind of searching that attempted to quilt together a story riddled with gaps and unknowns. But the place in that poem is not and can never be real. It will only ever exist in the imagination of a version of myself that could only find footing in a figurative landscape. A person I no longer am. And today, I cannot articulate how far from that self I have now drifted.

In 2019, I visited Tanzania with my father for the first time. And I unearthed information about my family and family history that sits in an uncomfortable and complicated place within me. Over those three weeks, I realised I needed to look further back, beyond the generations of my grandparents, to understand the ever present haunting of British colonialism, the migration of South Asians to East Africa, the familial disparity and loss, and all that, still, to this day, remains unspoken. The rose-ringed parakeet sounded so beautiful in the poem. Now I have to admit it feels wooden and unreal while I also acknowledge that, at one point in my life, the bird was symbolic of a genuine feeling. I remind myself that both are true.

At Coco Beach, I think of how a young girl met these waves and waves and waves and waves long before I did. I imagine she ran along the coastline in bare feet after a long day at school. Her favourite fruit was zambarau, black plum, jamun. I imagine her fingertips were always empurpled with it. I imagine pinkish, sweet, slightly astringent streaks of fruit juice ebbing from her skin into the sea. The water is collecting. It collects the aftertaste of a life lived in a first home. Both girl and fruit tree had an inherited history of migration. They found themselves at this shore, carrying in them a lineage that was rooted in an elsewhere place. Always another elsewhere place.

Fifty years after this imagined girl, who is a figuration of my mother, I don't run along the coastline, but I sit on a white plastic chair and watch the wild waves break onto rocks on the shore of Dar es Salaam. I am here at one of my ancestral homelands to engage with aspects of my heritage. This kind of travelling is a form of fulfilment, I think, for those of us with a history of migration. I am not sure if I feel fulfilled, exactly, but something draws me toward this coastal place that I have spent my whole life imagining. At the confluence of multiplicity, nothing is simple. But I feel peace at the cusp between land and water. I love where I am, next to family members I meet in person for the first time, in a country that had for so long tended to the childhoods of my parents. A place that knows them in a way I never will.

Looking out at the horizon, my memory decants into the water, and streaks of holographic, figurative, longing reach into its depths. Even those memories that double as imaginations filter through. Here are mirror worlds that host the inarticulable, innumerable losses tinged by forced departures. When I think of separations and connections, I am also thinking about crossings.

The sea is a poetics of movement and movement is political.

*

Yesterday at a book award ceremony, you smile and laugh and fall into step with applause. But you are lying when you agree the speeches feel powerful and political. Your life and body have always been politicised, so you are aware you have an unfair threshold when it comes to such things. But it is December 2023 and for the past two months, you have seen these words: none of us are free until Palestine is free. You wonder how it is possible to give acceptance speeches about the importance of the humanities in academia and say nothing about how all 11 universities in Gaza have been destroyed. You wonder how it is possible to talk about reproductive rights without once mentioning Palestine, when women in Gaza are having caesarean operations without anaesthetic. On the topic of marginalised languages, you wait, somewhat hopelessly, for anyone to speak of the gross mistranslations of Arabic in the media or the misrecognition of Islamic prayer as terrorist mantra. In this room, we celebrate the power of literature, the power of words, the importance of our craft and artistry – and yet there is a glaring, painful, gap in our own language when it comes to Palestine. The same day as the award ceremony, the poet Refaat Al-Areer is martyred. There is a line in your notes app from yesterday and it is about whiteness.

*

I have been spending my time reconstructing a girlhood from an assortment of memories. What emerges are broad brushstrokes and fleeting images – glistening ice on a quiet side street, the alpine green of mature spruce trees, the striated greys of a young tabby cat. Of course, ultimately, I fail at this task. When it comes to ephemerality, there is not any repeatable experimental design. There is no possible methodology for deciding which tendrils to keep and which to let fade away. But, still, the resulting assemblage is its own kind of truth.

A while ago in my reading, I came across a passage about truth and fact – or perhaps truth versus fact. Today, I cannot remember exactly where it was from or precisely what it said. I suspect it was informed by many other writings on the same concepts, and I wonder how much of it has also intermingled with my own positionality and my own thoughts. I think the knowledge of that passage must change with every iteration of myself too. It has become more of a feeling than a quotation from anything real. It is a remnant, a ghostliness, a dream of what might perhaps be hundreds of different interpretations.

Whether ghostly or not, these details are lodged everywhere in my body, and I attempt to loosen them. I swim in a river and emerge covered in its silt. I take up running. I go for long bike rides around Leith on old railway paths. But I discover that what works best is collaboration and finding in another artist, whether in their poetry or their sculptures or their choreography, the ink that fills in an unknown missing thing. But the beauty and the frustration comes from being unable to know what that missing thing is until I am deep within the process of creation. Through the mediums of other artists, I find memories of my own past and they burgeon in random and unexpected ways.

Sometimes even then, you purposefully look away. Perhaps it is an inherited shame, but you think that it is too easy to always blame the past for your feeling adrift. In piecing together your childhood, you skirt around your religious upbringing. The current onslaught of Islamophobia right now, a tactic used to justify war crimes in Gaza, sends you back in time. To the recollections of an old television set being rolled into your elementary school classroom. To the furious images of 9/11 on replay by every western media outlet. To the uncomfortable feeling of knowing your body came to (or always did) represent all the fears of your young classmates. There is so much in the white space between the lines of poetry that you cannot bring yourself to say. There is so much looking away even now, right here.

In early 2020, I wrote an ekphrastic poem titled after the short film *You Know it but it Don't Know You* by Welsh-Gambian artist Tako Taal. The poem was also informed by Taal's artistic processes – by notes and photographs dotted all over her studio space – and also by our conversations. In one of my notebooks, now tucked away in the drawers of a different home, I have written down all the things I thought were important at the time. But from my memory, I recall that we talked about fathers and saliva and the fractures that accompany growing up with a sense of cultural dissonance. Unsurprisingly, I remember coming away from her studio at the Edinburgh College of Art that day with the knowledge that this poem would incorporate water, specifically the waters between elsewhere places. The poem ends with the line *there is no irrigating a wound if that wound is the great sea.*

Perhaps in my work, displacement will always be linked to bodies of water in some way, just as migration seems intrinsically linked to the land.

However, what I did not expect were all the ruptures in poetic form. My response to Tako Taal's work pulled from me a different exploration, a structural one, where temporal and geographical distances – where memories, real and imagined – bled outside the imagery of water and more explicitly onto the physical contours of the page. The shape of a poem is itself an articulation, which I came to understand even more starkly through the confluence of text and visual art. All of this reminds me of an interview with poet Bhanu Kapil, where she asks the question: 'How can the poem's form – the shape that it takes, and the limits of that shape

– tell the truth (or one of the truths) about what it is like to be a human being in a given world?'

I still often think about the shape of one part of the sequence in particular. It materialised as a diptych where half the lines were in strikethrough text – still readable but crossed out. Before then, I had never formatted my own poems using this visual strategy in a sustained way, though I had seen it in other works. Even now, many questions linger in my mind about this piece and the *there-not-there* effect on those words. They all orbit this central inquiry: how does one voice silence? And what does it mean to use a visual cue that will deliberately draw attention to the text that I supposedly want to hide away.

*

I often use the words 'nature writer' in the context of my work. In fact, I throw it around with such frequency that it starts to feel meaningless, without any real definition. These words try to easily categorise a kind of work that is beyond easy categorisation. To understand my relationship to nature, I must delve into the past. I have to see through the lens of my relatives who lived in the forests of Mtwara long before I ever felt alienated in rural Alberta, a province in a country with its own violent colonial present. I must acknowledge the colonial history that placed human-made borders onto living landscapes.

Often, I get the sense that nature writing's popularity aligns with its palatable broadness – the way it can easily be framed as, to a degree, apolitical. After all, if it slips into the overtly political, it is easily categorised under the framework of *ecocritical writing*. This corralling of content into genre and subgenre allows audiences to find or avoid perceived neutrality in what they read.

~~Another arts institution says that it is apolitical, that it must remain neutral. It calls the devastation in Gaza and the murder of now over 17,000 Palestinians by the Israeli Military a complicated issue. We don't know enough about the conflict to comment, the director says in a private email. We have to let the board decide whether a statement is appropriate. You read excuse after excuse, and the underlying silence is loud in your heart. It tells you something you have always known about how bodies of colour~~

~~fit into the literary culture here in the West. On the other hand, through~~
~~the documentation and dialogue around Palestine, you become more~~
~~aware of ethnic cleansing throughout history and all over the world.~~
~~Genocides that you said and knew very little about. In this way, you~~
~~understand you, too, are the problem.~~

I think it is impossible to write responsibly about nature, about memory, without also considering the history of empire. The land and its natural water sources are being weaponised as part of environmental warfare or they are being exploited for capital. Often, these two things coalesce. Settler colonialism and the legacies of imperialism around the world have shaped and revised landscapes. And as a result, they have also played a key part in establishing the various relationships a person might have to the land.

*

The sea entangles with the roots of mangrove trees. These distinctive trees grow in brackish water, saltier than most tree species can stand. Their roots, thick and tough, anchor them in place along the coastlines of Zanzibar. Depending on the tides, a mangrove forest might look like its own, independent, floating island.

When I learned that I have family in Zanzibar, I added it to my travel itinerary in 2019. It was a bewildering revelation. I had what I thought was a fairly comprehensive knowledge of at least my aunts, uncles, and first cousins, even if my links beyond that were hazy and unclear. I had spent many years throughout my life imagining Dar es Salaam and Mtwara, places that I knew held my own familial roots. This recent information, however, was a newly uncovered strand of history attached to place, and I had to work its understanding into my admittedly already piecemeal sense of self. While I have no childhood memories of growing up in Tanzania, I have the stories my parents told me throughout my life. And I have the constructed imaginations, too — the remembrances that are not literal, but are real in that they are informed by the strong grip of desire to know one of the places I knew I was from. This appeal is itself perennial in nature, cropping up at intervals even when I think I have bested it, which is perhaps a condition of the second-generation immigrant.

When I visit Dar es Salaam, I find myself retrieving my first, and first lost, language after long decades of speaking only English. Kutchi is a language from the Kutch district in Gujarat. But growing up, I did not know this. It was the kind of information that I gleaned through pointed questions and archival research more recently. I still cannot trace my family's exact migration patterns on either side. A few years ago, my father told me the name of the village in India where his grandparents lived, but I was never able to find this place on a map.

You are reminded that you can still ask questions. You can still seek answers and find out this information. You can eventually know the paths your great-grandparents and grandparents took. However, the last time you asked your father about India, he always dovetailed the conversation back to Tanzania, his birthplace and the home he longs for still. It does not feel right to press for answers, especially to eventually relay them back here as content. You spent years interrogating whether you were writing for the white gaze, and what it means to pour out painful diasporic questions in your work. But now something in you is flourishing, some newly invigorated need to learn more and more and more in order to preserve your culture and your religion in your art, even if that means spilling out your trauma. You always say *sometimes you feel closer to your faith than others* and right now, as Islamophobic comments slither out in conversations with even your closest friends, you feel protective over your Muslim heritage. A poem by Palestinian-American poet Noor Hindi goes viral again in the wake of specifically anti-Palestinian racism, as again, in the repeated violence of settler-colonialism, Palestinians are murdered. *Fuck Your Lecture on Craft, My People Are Dying.*

I used to speak Kutchi fluently. Now, I can still understand it, keeping up with my father when we talk on the phone. But this language shrinks in my mouth and I answer him in English. I feel like my first language dissipates the longer I am in Scotland, the longer I am away from my family. But when I am in Dar es Salaam, Kutchi entwines around me like a scandent stem. After a few short days, I oscillate between two languages, and it is thrilling when, in my mind, I start translating Kutchi to English rather than the other way around. I think I even began to dream in it, this lost language of mine.

In Zanzibar, one of my cousins speaks only Swahili. My father is almost fluent and translates conversations between us. But when we are alone, we are unable to understand each other. She and I take many photos together because doing so is something palpable that makes us feel as close as possible despite the linguistic fault lines.

The mangrove forest is thick and alluring. When I'm on the island, after a long swim in the day, I find shelter in its shade. I learn that they are important for coastal ecosystems, reducing erosion where land and water meet. One day, I hear an unending creaking and I follow the sound. I am not sure what kind of omen this is, but eventually I see the tree snap and fall into the saltwater, clutching at mud all the while. Each stitch had been loosened for years as the mangrove was thrashed by the waves.

LUMPEN LIFE

James Brooks

No public figure in the UK can express old-school leftist politics without being labelled a 'firebrand' – a word implying an angry, rabble-rousing nature, which once invoked a person, damned to burn in hell. It is frequently appended to the name of veteran (perhaps retired, it's unclear) filmmaker Ken Loach, despite his softly spoken, avuncular demeanour, and it would be applied to Paul Laverty, too, if only more people knew who he was.

For Laverty, the scriptwriter for fourteen of Loach's fifteen last full-length features, its use would be just as inappropriate as for Loach; at least it seems that way from most of the interviews he's given. In the one tucked away under the 'extras' tab in the *My Name Is Joe* DVD, Laverty can be found sitting on a park bench next to a filming location (possibly near Drumchapel, one of the 'big four' post-war social housing schemes). He answers questions from his French interviewer in a quiet voice and with a friendly, if slightly guarded, manner. Laverty sounds almost apologetic as he stumbles his way to answering whether it's important to him that the film is set in Glasgow: 'It's not that Glasgow is any less or more complex or worthy than any other city [...] I'm from Glasgow so I can write Glasgow stories better than other stories, I suppose.'

But at the end of the clip, when he's asked if there's anything else he'd like to mention, Laverty becomes uncharacteristically emotive. 'Where we're filming this film just now there's forty percent unemployment,' Laverty says, before calling out the wider 'cosy consensus' in politics that if 'two thirds are doing OK, that's fine [even if] one third of the population are simply forgotten about'. He speaks of his anger at the inequality he observed out and about in Glasgow researching the film: 'one part is very, very successful and very rich and then there are other parts out of sight and out of mind, and there's people living there whose lives have simply been written off and seen as irrelevant'. All this, Laverty continues, despite the 'great talent and great energy' in such areas, along with the desire – people are 'desperate', he insists – to participate: 'I'm always amazed how much people want to contribute and how few people are given the chance, and I think that's probably true not only for the city of Glasgow, but many cities in Britain and Europe.'

Ken Loach is often described, indeed self-describes, as a chronicler of the working class. In fact, from his first films, *Poor Cow* (1967) and *Kes* (1969), through to *My Name Is Joe* (1998) and the similarly Clydeside-set and Laverty-scripted *Sweet Sixteen* (2002), his work has more often focused on the difficulties, passions, and, above all, cruel and restricted choices of the poor who are excluded from the traditional working class. All the descriptors for this group are pejorative, and that's without mentioning the vernacular ones. There's 'underclass', of course, but deploy Marxist terminology and we start talking of the 'surplus labour population' and its 'lumpenproletariat' (the 'ragged' proletariat). Marx gave this subclass of 'criminals, vagabonds, prostitutes', as he described them in *Capital*, short shrift, believing them bereft of revolutionary potential. (Other revolutionaries, from the anarchist Mikhail Bakunin to the Black Panthers, have disagreed.)

Over recent years there's been a resurgence of academic interest in the lumpenproletariat. The term is now frequently used to denote the entire unemployed or irregularly employed population which, in Marx's words, furnishes capital with 'an inexhaustible reservoir of disposable labour power [and where] conditions of life sink below the average normal level of the working class'. A handful of leftist writers and academics, for whom Clyde W Barrow's 2020 text *The Dangerous Class* is something of a touchstone, believe we are witnessing the dissolution of the traditional, salaried working class that, for all its hardships, had at least gained some contractual protections. They identify a tangled web of phenomena – diminishing profit margins in established industries, disintegrating welfare provision and labour protection, and the rise of platform capitalism (enabling the real-world 'gig economy' and its online companion 'microwork') – pushing populations toward economic disenfranchisement. In one word, 'lumpenisation'.

Loach's intertwined political commitments and his filmmaking career can be seen as a lifelong campaign against lumpenisation, well before that word enjoyed its resurgence. Two of Loach's most successful late-period films – *I, Daniel Blake* (2016) and *Sorry We Missed You* (2019) – tackle its corrosive effects on working-class lives directly. But it is his Clydeside pairing of *My Name is Joe* and *Sweet Sixteen* that, to my mind, remain his most powerful personal dramas, and his most politically damning depictions of lumpen life.

As Laverty would have known, Glasgow has been a place of wild contrasts of wealth and poverty for centuries. Even in the boomtimes, which often rapidly collapsed into busts, Glasgow held large surplus labour populations, first in tenements, which degraded into slums, and, in the second half of the twentieth century, in ill-conceived and poorly built brutalist tower-blocks, many of which were soon torn down. According to the Glasgow Care Foundation charity, Glasgow still has the highest concentration of people living in deprivation of any city in Scotland, with roughly a quarter of Glasgow's children below the poverty line. In what might be taken for a sign of creeping lumpenisation, in-work poverty in Glasgow is on the rise, the charity notes, and sixty-one per cent of poor working age adults now live in a household where at least one person works.

Shot entirely on location around Glasgow, *My Name is Joe* drops us quickly into the dilapidated milieu of its protagonists. After an opening scene in which lead character Joe Kavanagh (played by Peter Mullan, a Glaswegian socialist like Laverty) speaks at an Alcoholics Anonymous meeting, we rejoin Joe as he bangs on a dingy ground-floor council-flat door, pretending to be police, to flush out the lads in the amateur football team he coaches. He pops outside and lights a cigarette as they launch themselves out of windows to escape, his ruse having worked. Then we're in the back of the van with the squad, the soundtrack a chaos of sweary, testosterone-fuelled banter, as they unload the filthy contents of a kit-bag. The first shot through the windows to the outside world is of 'Zulu', the alleged ineffectual kit-washer, cycling down the street with an ironing board inexplicably under one arm, who is greeted with a barrage of abuse from his teammates. Zulu (an incidental character) is framed first against crumbling red walls painted with crudely written graffiti and then against grey low-rise housing blocks, which – this may only register subconsciously, so brief is the shot – appear to have most of their windows boarded up.

Use of long-focus lenses, as in the shots of Zulu, is a hallmark of Loach's style, and occurs frequently in *My Name is Joe*. It enables several effects both on the actors and on how the finished film is received by its audience. For the latter, as Charles Barr observes in a section on Loach in his primer on British cinema, the lenses 'flatten the characters against their unglamorous backgrounds [and work] to embed the characters in their environment, conveying their entrapment'. Such tableaux convey the message encoded in probably all Loach's films, and certainly in personal dramas like *Joe* – of the existential bondage enforced on the underclass by poverty and structural forces. 'Every fuckin' choice stinks doon here,' as Joe says in Laverty's original script (a line that did not make it into the final cut).

The long lenses, combined with his preference for dynamic (where the camera moves to track the action) over static shots, are also important in creating the strong sense of realism that vivifies his films. The camera – and viewer – remains at a distance, and the overall feel is one of observation of life going on, rather than an artificial recreation of it.

In addition, by keeping the camera out of the fray, and having it discreetly tracking its subjects' actions, Loach clears space for his actors to give unhampered, naturalistic performances. Discussing a scene filmed in this way on the *Sweet Sixteen* DVD commentary, Loach says he seeks to allow actors 'freedom to move as their instinct tells them without every move being preordained, and I think that can sometimes give you a fluidity and fluency and spontaneity that you lose if everything is nailed down exactly.'

This collection of characteristics – the on-location shoots, the responsive, distanced camerawork, the naturalistic performances – power the propagandistic effectiveness of Loach's films. They combine to induce obliviousness in the viewer that they are watching a scripted, directed, fiction film at all. Instead, the experience is more like watching a 'fly on the wall' documentary showing real people forced into lives of not-so-quiet desperation. Such verisimilitude heightens the emotional impact of Loach's films, and the viewer extrapolates unprompted to 'why isn't more being done to help these people?' at the very least – and possibly further to Loach's own socialist position. There's no need for him to resort to didacticism.

Most of Loach's films have done well at the box office, comfortably recouping their relatively modest budgets. Still, it's likely that the unjustified fear of attending a left-wing filmic lecture is precisely what prevents his oeuvre reaching an even greater audience. Loach's reputation for social realism may also led many cinemagoers to expect dour, 'kitchen sink' dramas, worthy in their ambitions, but about as appealing as cold porridge. Yet, largely thanks to the techniques noted above, Loach's best work is thoroughly engrossing. For me, frustratingly so. I saw both *My Name is Joe* and *Sweet Sixteen* when they were released in cinemas and both were personally formative films, living long in my memory. When I came to watch them again for this essay, in both cases it was only on the third viewing that I was able to extricate my brain from total absorption in the onscreen action and assess these technical elements. The characters are just too realistically drawn and acted, and filmed as if a camera crew had dropped into their neighbourhood unnoticed. We're eavesdropping on engaging, relatable people at critical junctures in their lives. Of course this is highly compelling cinema.

In *Joe*, the romance between the unemployed Joe and health visitor Sarah Downie is the strongly dominant theme of the film's first act, the main one for its second, and only recedes in the third, when an impossible situation in which Joe is embedded starts clattering down around him. Yet somehow, I remembered the romance as secondary. I think for two reasons. First, because of its profound naturalism; Joe and Sarah's relationship registered as completely true-to-life and was both engrossing and somehow unremarkable for that reason. Second, because of the extreme emotional impact of the final act, which culminates in what film scholar Jacob Leigh identifies as a recurrent trope in Loach's work – the death of an innocent. In his 2002 monograph on Loach's films, Leigh places Loach's films within a cross-genre categorisation named by the late film critic Michael Walker as the 'melodrama of protest'. Leigh draws upon Walker's description of these films, which include *Battleship Potemkin* (1925), Loach's 1966 TV film *Cathy Come Home*, and *One Flew Over the Cuckoo's Nest* (1975). In these films, Walker says:

> our sympathies are enlisted unequivocally with a group of people – defined by race, nationality, class or political creed – who are 'innocents', victims of persecution, exploitation or oppression [...] Like all melodramas of protest, these films are in effect propaganda. They all use the death of the 'innocent' or indeed, innocents [...] as an emotional device to rouse not just the people in the film, but those in the audience as well.

Regarding *Joe* and *Sweet Sixteen*, I would add some shading to the black and white picture painted by Walker. For one thing, while the petty criminals in both films are clearly products of their brutal environments, a couple of them are truly nasty pieces of work, and the audience is not 'enlisted unequivocally' on their side just because they too are of the underclass. For another, the main characters, those who we do empathise with, are not purely 'victims'. As we shall see, they do have choices, even if those are wretched ones. But Walker's overall schema remains valid. Both films rely heavily on the deaths of innocents for their ultimate emotional weight. In *Sweet Sixteen*, the death is metaphorical; in *Joe* it's real.

The train of events that leads Joe, and *Joe*, to calamity is grounded in a real-world one with which Glasgow has become synonymous – heroin addiction. (In his park bench interview, Paul Laverty speaks of Glasgow having the 'highest percentage of intravenous drug users in Europe', an unhappily credible statistic.) Liam and Sabine are a couple of heroin addicts supposedly in recovery or treatment. Liam, a former low-level dealer, is a player in Joe's hapless football squad. Immediately following the opening van scene, Joe stops off at the couple's flat to bring Liam to the match, just as Sarah is entering to check up on the couple and their one-year-old son. Joe and Sarah's romance starts there.

We come to learn that Sabine enjoys less success than her partner in staying off junk, and has returned to prostitution to pay for her habit. Not only that, she has racked up two thousand pounds of debt with local drug lord McGowan, by consuming the product she was entrusted to sell by Liam while her partner was in prison. After repeated warnings from McGowan's thugs and with the debt still unpaid, Liam is brought to McGowan's club and given an ultimatum: either pay the debt ('problem: he's nae money!' as Joe desperately tells Louise later), let McGowan pimp Sabine, or get both his legs broken. When Joe, who has known the manipulative McGowan since childhood, enters the scene, a fourth option is added: Joe can run two errands to the north coast to pick up a drug shipment, and the debt will be paid.

A critical juncture in Joe's downfall arrives when Sarah learns of Joe's deal with McGowan and confronts him over it. Joe's response is a blast of underclass self-disgust and victimisation, with sparks of anger shooting outwards at middle-class Sarah. He spits:

I'm really sorry, but I don't live in this nice, tidy wee world o' yours. Some of us cannae go to the polis. Some of us cannae go to the bank for a loan. Some of us cannot just move hoose and fuck off out of here. Some of us don't have a choice. I didnae have a fuckin' choice!

Judith Williamson's contemporaneous and mostly favourable review in *Sight and Sound* described Joe's outburst here as his 'keynote speech', noting disparagingly, 'in Loach films there is always a keynote speech'. True enough, moments where characters 'leak' didactic commentary to the audience do occur in Loach films, as Leigh notes in his monograph, but this did not strike me as a particularly egregious example. Partially that's thanks to Peter Mullan's compelling delivery, but partially it's due to Sarah's rejection of both the untrammelled victimhood that Joe describes for himself, and the naivety he ascribes to her:

Listen, I have seen babies rattlin', sent up to intensive care with expected brain damage... Have you ever seen a fourteen-year-old child choke on his own vomit crying for his mother who's out there screaming?

Joe and Sarah's exchanges in this scene, as much as their flirtatious and tender ones, belie not only their class difference but also the gender disparities in Laverty and Loach's version of mid-nineties underclass Glasgow. In short, and notwithstanding Sabine's destructive addiction-fuelled behaviour, the men mess up and threaten to boil over with rage, while the women cope and care. There's a keenly observed scene during the early days of the lead couple's romance where Joe pays a visit to the clinic where Sarah works. He pops his head round the door to hear Sarah deliver a talk on baby bathtimes for expectant mothers. An underclass male in a care setting, Joe's sense of unease is palpable. He looks far more at home in the grim, dangerous and ultramasculine setting of McGowan's club.

All this might make *Joe* sound like a tough watch, but it's not. Before its emotionally fraught final act, the film's mood is kept buoyant by humour. This comes in several forms – the football team's shenanigans, witticisms from the characters, absurd situations – some of which, like Joe's police-raid ruse in that early scene, may strain the genre confines of realism, but none break it. And one humorous scene is 'leaky' in the best possible way, offering oblique commentary on the disparity between the contrived version of 'God's country' promoted by the former Scottish Tourist Board, and that experienced by most Scots, certainly those surviving in Glasgow's toughest estates.

On his way back to Glasgow from his drugs run for McGowan, Joe stops to buy a cup of tea from a roadside kiosk. There's a brief but stunning shot of Joe from behind, with mountains rising up through the mist beyond, as he looks down on the path below. There, a grey-haired man in full highland dress is giving a shaky bagpipe rendition of Robert Wilson's unofficial national anthem, 'Scotland the Brave', to the obvious appreciation and ready cameras of the assembled tourists. As Joe takes his tea from the kiosk attendant, there's this exchange:

ATTENDANT: See that one? He only knows three songs – 'Scotland the Brave'...

JOE: 'Skyboat Song', I bet.

ATTENDANT: Right. And 'Flower of Scotland'.

[pause]

JOE: [sniffs] What are the odds he sells shortbread?

ATTENDANT: He does. He's selling it. [pause] Bonnie Scotland, eh?

JOE: Mmm, bonnie Scotland, yeah. Right enough.

The perfect rhythm of this dialogue, its laconic delivery, and our knowledge that Joe has an undisclosed weight of heroin in the boot of his car on its way to the sink estates of Glasgow, combine to make this vignette much sharper and neater than a similar scene in Danny Boyle's *Trainspotting* (1996). There, Renton (played by Ewan McGregor) and his band of Glaswegian junkies go for a walk in the Highlands and Renton rants that the Scottish 'can't even find a decent culture to be colonised by – we're ruled by effete assholes!' (He means the English, of course.) That line may have read well on the page, but sounds forced when shouted from McGregor's mouth.

If Laverty was right and *Joe* could have been shot in almost any similarly sized and poverty-stricken European location, the same cannot so easily be said of *Sweet Sixteen*, which is set 20 miles further up the River Clyde in Greenock. For starters, Greenock's smaller size, the greater prominence of the river there, and the sharp-angled hills behind combine to produce a stunning backdrop. As Loach says on the *Sweet Sixteen* DVD commentary track, the majestic scenery 'contrasts rather sadly with the quality of life' for much of its population. As a result, a particular atmosphere pervades the film, which would be difficult to replicate elsewhere. The characters in the film can seem haunted by the magnificent, distant landscape. It lurks as a constant reminder of the greatness that circumstance prevents them from attaining.

More prosaically, the barren scenery adds to the sense of Greenock as a post-industrial hinterland, which is again central to the feel of the film. Unlike Glasgow, which always had its dismal slums, Greenock's decline is within living memory. The town was bombed heavily in the second world war but recovered rapidly in the aftermath when its industrial capacity was rebuilt. Its heyday was short-lived, though, and its shipyards, the engine rooms of the local economy, were closed in the late seventies. (Greenock's fortunes have improved in recent years, thanks to the development and expansion of a container port and passenger terminal for cruise ships.) When Loach's camera crew showed up for *Sweet Sixteen*, according to the director, there was 'very little work [available] except in call centres and small electronic businesses'. The glimpses of the town centre we get in early scenes suggest it to be drab, damp, and uninviting.

But while the backdrop is altered, in many ways *Sweet Sixteen* is simply a harder, faster, more youthful rerun of Laverty and Loach's previous Clydeside venture, even down to some markedly similar plot points. In both films there's an act of vandalism which threatens to derail the main character's trajectory, but doesn't. There's a dicey entanglement with a local drug-lord. And there's the climactic sequence of an initial controlled explosion of male rage against a cherished female companion, followed by an unfettered and calamitous one against a more legitimate male target.

Thematically, *Sweet Sixteen* is a film focused even more tightly on male reaction to the cruelly restricted horizons of lumpen life than *Joe*. Indeed, while the earlier film just about passed the Bechtel test – which stipulates that two female characters in a movie should speak to each other about something other than a man – *Sweet Sixteen* does not. More favourably,

Loach's documentary-style techniques are used with greater daring and to greater effect in *Sweet Sixteen*. There are fewer pedestrian shot / reverse shots than in *Joe*, and our sense of eavesdropping on vital coming-of-age moments in the characters' lives is heightened.

Sweet Sixteen's protagonist is Liam (played by Martin Compston) a fifteen-year-old with a bright smile and cheeky disposition who we first meet tooling around Greenock. He slides into smoky pubs with his mate, the slim, red-haired 'Pinball', to hawk de-taxed cigarettes. Both Liam and Pinball — who is 'like a brother' to Liam, as he admits at one point — are from troubled homes. Liam's mother is in jail. He lives with his violent, drug-dealing stepfather Stan, and comically abusive — but still abusive — grandfather Rab. We know less about Pinball but come to understand that his father is a heroin addict.

So far, so Loachian lumpenproletariat. But this time around there is an added psychodynamic element to the drama — Liam's craving for love and approval from his errant mother Jean, and his desire to usurp the cruel Stan in her affections, with both motivations dictating his actions, and much of the plot. It's perhaps worth noting that had the film been transposed to a French bourgeois setting, and given production design to match, these powerful Oedipal undercurrents would likely have been foregrounded by critics in a way that they weren't at the time (American film critic Elvis Mitchell did pick up on them in an appreciative review in *The New York Times*, a year after the film's Cannes preview). There must be something about underclass lives, and social realist drama, that is just not worthy of such highbrow allusions.

Instead, much was made of Martin Compston's casting as Liam, and his undeniably brilliant performance. Loach, ever on the quest for authenticity, is known for picking non-professional players for his films, frequently preferring people whose experiences resonate with their characters' over trained actors. Michelle Coulter, for example, who gives a careful, controlled performance as Liam's mum, was a drug rehab counsellor, and went back to her job once the film had wrapped. Compston, meanwhile, was seventeen when he was selected from around five hundred local boys for his part, and he paused a nascent football career to shoot it, before subsequently pursuing acting professionally. He makes for an entirely convincing, energetic, and charismatic Liam, but the real wonder of his performance lies in its subtlety. In one emblematic scene, his older sister Chantelle tends to his wounds after a fight with three potential clients. (Liam has upgraded from selling contraband cigarettes to dealing heroin by this point, which Chantelle is unaware of.) 'How many times have I done this?' Chantelle asks, indignant, to no response from Liam. She talks of their time in a children's home:

> Remember you ran out and you fought three big boys. They all thought you were brave. But I didnae. I was screaming from the windae, and I heard your arm snap. They let you go and you still managed to laugh in their face. You didnae fight them because you were brave. You fought them 'cos ye jus' didnae care what happened to ye. That's what broke my heart. It's just another kicking for you. How can ye really care about us if ye don't care for yersel'?

This could so easily land as the kind of expository 'keynote speech' that Judith Williamson despaired of in Loach's work. What stops it doing so is Compston's subtle, muted reaction. He looks exactly like a boy who's heard this insight, if not the anecdote in which it is delivered, umpteen times before and for whom it holds no interest. With that, the whole scene rings true.

Chantelle is right, though. Self-disregard is a characteristic that Liam shares with his friend and drug-dealing partner Pinball. But whereas Pinball's indifference to his own wellbeing sucks him down a spiral of self-destruction, Liam's is converted into the resilience necessary to pursue his goals of wealth, and a better life for his sister and mother. As an underclass boy, out of school and stuck in the bleak hinterland of Greenock, he has no opportunity to achieve this legally. So, like many other young men in surplus labour pools around the world, he turns to the drugs game.

The film's oblique commentary on Scottish society is delivered not via comedy, as with the kiosk scene in *Joe*, but tragedy. As Loach says on the DVD commentary, picking up a theme tackled in a million rap lyrics, Liam 'knows how to run a business, he's full of ideas, he's an ideal entrepreneur really – it's just the wrong business'. In the drugs trade, Liam enjoys great success and seems to be on the cusp of realising his dream of a stable base for his sister and mother when his boss Tony gifts him a flat in a new development a few miles up the Clyde in Gaurock. 'Built-in oven, with microwave. Dishwasher. Very nice. Very classy,' Liam says as he shows his mum round the apartment, its echoey, hollow acoustics familiar to anyone who has visited a boxy, 'luxury' new-build in the last thirty years. But this scene plays out just a day before his eventual, tragic downfall. Liam's new prosperity was not built on firm foundations, but drug money. In that, it is just like the empty prosperity delivered by the financialised, neoliberal economy, Laverty and Loach seem to be saying; once modern, transnational capital has ripped apart the old ties of work, community and family, it cannot sustainably replace them.

On a more personal level, both as a member of the underclass and as an Oedipal character, Liam is unable to escape his fate. 'D'ye want to end up a waster like your old man?' he asks of Pinball, in an attempt to motivate his friend when the stakes of their drug-dealing escapades are upped. It is a question that Liam clearly cannot extirpate from his own mind, and we imagine he endlessly asks it of himself. Fittingly, when Liam unleashes the initial controlled explosion of rage that signals the beginning of his downfall, Chantelle, his female target, will answer it for him in the affirmative. Held to the floor by Liam, she yells:

> Just like Granddad, like our fathers, like Stan! Like all the other losers destroying everything they touch! Like a man! Join the club. Be one of them cos that's what ye are!

The metaphorical 'death of an innocent' at the end of *Sweet Sixteen* is Liam's – he finishes the film looking out over the Clyde and contemplating a likely jail term. 'Some people have said that the film strikes them as hopeless,' Loach says on the commentary track as the credits roll. But it's not, he says. There's hope 'in the resilience and character of people like Liam and Chantelle', he elaborates, and in the possibility that we could 'make that society happen where there is that security and a job to look forward to' for young people. He's talking about a reversal of lumpenisation, essentially, and the restoration of power and dignity to the working class – his lifelong animus.

Our society is speeding in the other direction. As long as that is so, Chantelle's words, spoken over the phone to Liam as he looks blankly over the Clyde, will be applicable not just to him but to the uncounted multitudes 'whose lives have simply been written off and seen as irrelevant', to reprise Laverty's commentary, in Greenock, Glasgow, and elsewhere in Scotland; in the UK, Europe, and places far, far beyond: 'What a waste. What a waste.'

ARTS AND LETTERS

FACES IN ROCKFACES

Muhammad Ameen

William, or Bill, Holmes – otherwise known as Muhammad Ameen – has been in love with rockscapes at least since the start of his eastern journeys in the very early nineteen sixties. He left school early, and therefore the London suburbs. The road provided his further education. He travelled through Kandahar and Sindh, Baluchistan, and the Hindu Kush. He started his career selling simple landscapes and lake scenes to the tourists in houseboats on Kashmir's Dal Lake.

Later, in a prison in Kuwait, he sold portraits in return for food and cigarettes. He said the *shahada* in Mauritania. Slipped into a trance at a Sufi *sama* in Urfa. His best-remembered journeys were with the Bedouin, mainly in Syria. Sometimes he crossed borders with them, not needing a checkpoint. He moved through a world which in many respects no longer exists.

For half a century since, he has settled in a part of Scotland whose bare brown hills and wildernesses remind him of the Syrian *badia*. He has painted in the Galloway uplands again and again, wrestling brevity as the light shifts and the colours change. He has painted faces in rock-faces – these have been his obsessive theme. He seeks to represent or at least to commemorate the art made by nature and time, by the wind and the wheeling sun.

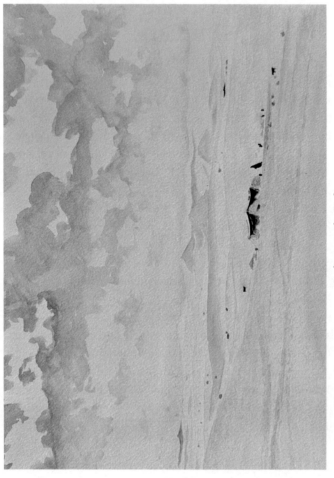

Bedouin in the Badia

Beehive Houses at Hakla, near Aleppo

The Old Grey Man of the Merrick

The Old Man at the Door, Cairnsmore of Fleet, Side Profile

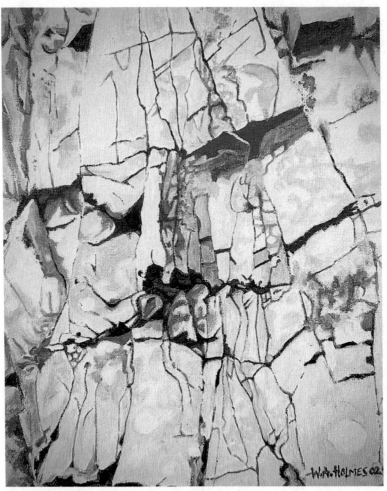

The Old Man at the Door, Cairnsmore of Fleet, Front Profile

Elephant Stone, above the Green Well of Scotland

Kiboko (Standing on a Rock Skull)

Craig of Knock Grey

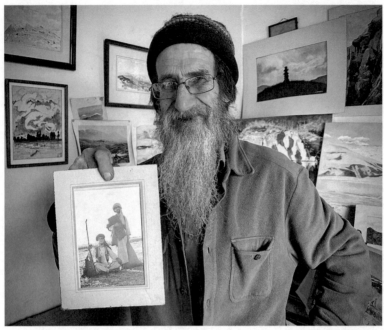

Bill holding a picture of himself and his brother outside Kandahar in 1968

THE DEVILS AROUND US

Shah Tazrian Ashrafi

Before, there were green hills. Now, narrow roads snake through layers of blackness and thick phantoms of smoke float up from the grounds as if the air is drawing out the past's vestiges. With tongues hanging out, dogs chase one another up and down those roads during territorial wars. The guttural whirring of trucks, excavators, generators, and engines is a stubborn presence like the sweat cruising down the workers' bodies. The nights ward away the day's heat, bringing with them an army of mosquitoes that feast on blood mixed with soot and hopelessness. In summer, when the sky bursts open and rain hammers down on the mutilated hills, the children stick their tongues out and let the drops wash the grime off their faces. They run up the slopes, climb up the amphitheatre-like hills, jump on black puddles. The adults bring out steel and plastic buckets, bottles, and bowls from their tin sheds to fetch the icy offerings. As the rain *taptaptaps* the inhabitants' skulls like inquisitive neighbours relentlessly knocking on doors, they are, briefly, swollen with a sense that this empire of smoke and soot will be rinsed clean and pepper vines and flowers will jut out from the black earth. But once the rain stops and the blackness still triumphantly stands before their eyes, their momentary optimism swims away. In the black rainwater zigzagging through the grounds, swishing into the drains.

Rajib emerges from the pit on a rickety ladder, his shoulders sagging under the weight of a jute sack loaded with coal. He unloads the sack on the wheelbarrow and exhales. He rubs his sweaty, dirt-stained forehead with his grimy hands. Rakib pushes the wheelbarrow away from the pit and towards the mound in the distance where the other kids have gathered, busy sorting impurities out from their shares of coal. Rajib trundles behind Rakib. They are fourteen, the youngest – and therefore the most disadvantaged – of the children working at the mine. The thought of encountering the older kids makes them both want to jump into the pit of darkness and heat and never emerge. After all, it is not unusual for the bigger children to tousle Rakib and Rajib's hair, land a punch or a slap, spit on their faces, thrash their backs with steel rods, and kick their abdomens and shins, among other things, in order to hijack their shares of coal. Rajib thanks God when he notices the other kids are done sorting their bits and are shrieking in excitement down the peak, brandishing threadbare sacks full of coal, chasing one another.

Rakib is almost done with his sorting. Rajib, being the naturally faster twin, has finished his three minutes ago and is now lying on the dirt, staring at the expanse of winding roads, black pools, yellow excavators, trucks, cranes, generators, and ant-like people armed with bags and trunks, going about their work. Amena, their mother, comes gasping, stones and gravel crunching under her boots.

'This merciless heat, o Allah!' she says, squinting at the sky. She opens the plastic water bottle and gulps down in quick successions. Her silver blouse sticks to her plump arms, revealing circles of sweat. 'Here, take it, kids,' she says. Rajib grabs the bottle first and drinks cautiously so that some water is left for Rakib.

At night, the white cigarette sticks out of their stepfather Majid's mouth like an abnormal tooth reluctant to stay in its position. He is lying on the cot in front of his shed. Kana, the one-eyed dog that has been a resident in the mining area for almost seven years now, is sleeping underneath in a sea of cigarette butts and maroon beer bottles, his plump body expanding and contracting as though he is a breathing heart out on display. He is Majid's only companion tonight. His friends – Akash, Jahid, and Sakib – have been thrown into the tyranny of prolonged extraction hours on account of skipping work last week (reason: second-hand Jack Daniels at the dank, urine-smelling, porn-broadcasting bar-cum-mini-movie-theatre, which is twenty minutes' walk from the area). It is their habit, trashing themselves with drinks and skipping work only to sentence themselves to extra hours. But this time Majid has been spared since he was able to pay off Khaled, the supervisor, from his six months' savings.

So, he lies there, eyes skyward, unbothered by droning mosquitoes bloating themselves with his blood, until he spots Amena, Rajib, and Rakib walk into their shed with steel bowls, plates, and mugs. Rajib turns the communal tap on while Rakib washes the utensils. Rajib feels Majid's eyes on the back of his neck. His stomach is twisting with hunger and he cannot deal with Majid's shenanigans now. He keeps praying to Allah, like he often does in sujood, to remove the Majid-shaped menace from his life. Majid groans, coughs, sits up, and straightens his white vest.

'Hey, boy. Come with me,' Majid says and goes behind the shed. Rajib gulps, convincing himself why he should go. The first time Majid took him there and did things to him – the same things the twins found him doing with Amena in the middle of the night – Majid said, 'If you speak a word of this to anyone, my friends and I will kill your mother and brother. Trust me, you cannot save them.'

Rajib follows him, bracing his core. After Majid is done, this time, a tower of pans and pots crumbles as Rajib's hands strike them down while vomiting.

'Who the hell dares to steal my things?' Amena comes with a red plastic broom. Seeing her son's pants lying in a corner over Majid's, her body softens.

The next morning, Amena packs the boys' bags and ships them off to Dhaka to work as garbage collectors. The job is arranged by her friend Shirin, a sweeper in the city.

'But Amma, why wouldn't you come with us?' Rakib says.

'I can't. Don't ask me these useless questions. Just go and call me when you reach.' She kisses their foreheads and hands bits of paper with Shirin's and her phone numbers. When the bus leaves the yard and slopes down the road sleek from rain in the morning – Rajib and Rakib's faces glued to the glass in her direction – her waving hands and smiling lips are seized by the agony of separation. She rests her head on a grey pole and curses herself for taking the loan – 30 lakhs – from Majid's sister, Ifa. As per the loan's condition, Amena had to marry Ifa's unmarriageable brother (unmarriageable on account of his rash drinking). Even though she had taken the loan to buy a new house for herself and the twins far away from the mining area, she lost it all when she deposited the money to her cousin who worked as a mason in Dubai (he said he knew the right people who could turn it into 60 lakhs in two months). When Majid's sister asked for her money back, Amena told her how she had been duped by her own blood.

'In that case, stay married to my brother for as long as you don't pay me back. I can't keep this drunken fool in my house,' the sister said.

The bus unloads the final passengers at the yard near the petrol station in the morning. Keeping Rajib in charge of their bags, Rakib goes to the kiosk at the farthest end of the yard selling biscuits and chips. Back home, Amena would prepare hot *rutis* and store them in a hotpot before they even woke up. He buys two packets of energy biscuits. Sitting on a stump behind a pharmacy's lorry with the bags at his feet, Rajib motions him to be fast. Rakib indicates with his small finger that he has to pee. He throws Rajib his share. He doesn't run fast enough to protect the biscuits from getting smashed. Rajib glares at him as Rakib limps his way to the bush.

Rajib hauls the bags when he goes to search for Rakib. When he goes behind the bush, a wall of urine smell smacks him. Torn slippers, chips' packets, condoms, banana skins, blades, and syrup bottles litter the grassy and slimy ground. He finds Rakib's biscuits, too. He oscillates between calling Shirin and Amena from one of the shops nearby. The vendor from the kiosk gently nudges Rajib's shoulder. 'What's wrong?'

At first, Rajib cannot say anything. His breath is stuck somewhere beneath his lungs. He breaks into tears and reveals he cannot find his twin. The man's face turns static. 'Son, you should complain to the police if you don't find him in forty-eight hours. It's very common here. Young folks like you get kidnapped all the time.'

A blaze of horror burns through Rajib. 'Who would kidnap my brother?'

The man grips his shoulders and rubs his sweaty hair to the right. 'They will kidnap anyone. They take out their eyes. Sometimes, legs or hands. And force them to beg on the streets.'

That night, Rajib stays with the man in his slum. He doesn't sleep at all partly because he fears the man might turn out like Majid and partly because he cannot stop weeping into his t-shirt thinking of Rakib being pinned down to the ground while someone takes out his eyes.

Two days pass without any hint of Rakib. The man finds Rajib work as a helper at his friend's mechanic shop farther into the city. Hasib, the shop's owner, regularly invites Rajib to his flat – above the mechanic shop – for dinner with his family (himself, a wife, and a fifteen-year-old daughter). Hasib has a dense grey beard that extends until his clavicles. He must have performed the Hajj, Rajib thinks. The green walls of the dining and living rooms are covered with photo frames of Masjid-al-haram, Medina, and the Shahadah in multiple calligraphies. Sharmin, his wife, wears a perpetual smile and an enthusiasm to serve Rajib. Farin, the daughter, is mostly silent and barely takes her eyes off her phone.

'Rajib, it's okay to fear for your brother. But remember, Allah is always with you,' Hasib says the first night after dinner, tapping his back.

'We will keep praying for him every day. You don't worry at all, Rajib, okay?' Sharmin adds, handing him a bowl of *firni*.

Before sleeping on the cot inside the shop, Rajib decides to call Amena with the blue Nokia feature phone Hasib has given him. He tells Amina that they didn't contact Shirin aunty because they hated the idea of working as garbage collectors in a landfill. When she scolds him for causing panic in her by not calling her all these days (*'If that merciless Khaled would let me take a leave, I would come there all by myself and give you two a loud whooping for acting so smart!'*), he says they were busy auditioning for better jobs. But everything is fine now because they've found employment at a mechanic shop.

Rajib fidgets on the cot thinking of Rakib. How everything would be so perfect if he were here. When he closes his eyes, memories of Rakib spill into the darkness. Here is Rakib, wielding a thick cable and stick, freeing Rajib from the clutch of the older kids back in the mining area who try to snatch Rajib's bucket of coals. Here is Rakib, saving a *shingara* and *samocha* for Rajib because he is down with a fever and unable to attend the *milad* at the masjid downhill. Here is Rakib, massaging Rajib's feet with a bottle of lotion he's stolen from the next shed because of Rajib's sprained ankle. Here is Rakib, fashioning a ludo board out of discarded TV cardboard because a rat has torn through their actual ludo board. Here is Rakib, fetching Rajib paracetamols by selling his watch because he thinks Rajib is quaking with high fever when in fact he's quaking because he's unable to forget the things Majid did to him just a few minutes ago.

The next few days pass by in a rush of activities. The other workers at the mechanic shop teach Rajib the basics of spray painting, attaching and pulling apart tires, tracing the engine coolant, and identifying the negative and positive terminals of a vehicle's battery. At the end of those days, he sleeps with the smell of diesel, grime, and chemicals burrowed deep inside his nose. The smell encloses him with long and thick fingers. The smell reminds him of life in the mine. Even though he wants to dislodge every painful memory from that gunmetal and smokey past, he cannot help longing for those days; at least, Amena and Rakib were there with him.

At first, Rajib thinks he's mistaken and perhaps seeing things due to the unforgiving sun and dehydration. He is buying lemons from the seller on the footpath for Hasib's household. Out of a sense of gratitude for giving him a place to stay without slashing from his salary, Rajib has happily taken to running their errands. He doesn't take the scrappy change from the seller, his neck straining towards the other side of the road. He squints through the haze of the heat bouncing off the sheds of cars and trucks. It is indeed Rakib on the other side. Legless. On a small wooden platform with wheels attached. A steel bowl on his lap. Raising his hands and pleading with words Rajib cannot make out when passersby cross Rakib. Rajib cannot decide whether it's a good thing that his legs have been taken out instead of his eyes, like the vendor prophesied.

'No, I can't just leave.' Rakib's smallness is staggering to Rajib's vision. Rakib used to be three inches taller than Rajib. And now Rajib has to bend or crouch to speak to him. He feels the universe has been realigned in all the wrong ways. Rakib is bald except for the uneven patches of hair growing from the sides. Red bumps fleck the skin. His elbows bear big and small bruises. Half-purple, half-brown. 'If I leave, they will hunt me down and abduct me again. I don't know what else they will take from my body this time.'

'But I've already filed a police complaint two days after you went missing. I am sure the police can do something.' Rajib pushes Rakib's platform farther away from the footpath and beneath a tree as passersby increase.

'Like what? Can they protect me if the men come hunting for me?'

'I am sure they can. I have to ask them first.'

'I can't even run. I shouldn't be expecting so much.'

'You just give me their address.'

'Why? What will you do?'

'Please, Rakib. Just do it.'

'I can't.'

'They won't even know you are behind the raid! Don't be such a fool now.'

'They will. You think they don't have cockroaches all over the areas where we beg? I bet they're monitoring that I am speaking to you and will question me about you.'

'Okay. I won't tell the police to raid. But still, mouth the bloody address to me, will you? In case I have an emergency or something.'

'And you think I will lead you to that place? So you could get kidnapped too?'

'No. I meant…what if Amma is terribly sick and I can't find you on the roads? How will I inform you then?'

'Don't utter such things! But okay here it is…'

Rajib can't sleep at night after the meeting. He ponders over how Rakib has changed so much because he is now pinned down by the incapability of doing something as simple as walking. If he had his legs, Rajib is sure Rakib could have freed himself someday, beating up one or two of the goons who run the racket of forced begging. He performs *wudu* in front of the water tap outside the garage. The combative howling of dogs outside and the wind of an incipient war among them remind him of Pinto, Rocky, and Silver, the dogs that pledged loyalty to Rakib and Rajib because they fed them biscuits after the night school. The trio ruled the mining hills, warding away outsider dogs with terrible howls that seemed to reach far out to the clouds. In his *sujood*, Rajib is seized by flashes of horrific things happening to Rakib. The warring dogs outside mix with the memory of the twins' feeding Pinto, Rocky, and Silver, and penetrate the flashes where Rakib is being beaten up by a rod, blood pouring out of his mouth. *'Who were you speaking to? Are you planning to bust us, huh?' the man says as he lands one strike after another.* In the morning, Rajib goes to the police station and gives the red-haired policeman Rakib's address.

After the raid, the city corporation provides the liberated beggars shelters in tents with communal washroom facilities behind the hospital. Hasib and Sharmin kiss Rajib when they hear the news. 'We are so proud of you! Such a young man and such a hero!' Hasib ruffles Rajib's hair. 'I am treating you both to *naan* and barbeque chicken tomorrow for this occasion.'

At the Kebab restaurant for Hasib's treat, Hasib licks his fingers clean, gets up from the table, and takes long steps towards the washroom. Rakib turns to Rajib, 'Who told you to act so smart? I trusted you. One of the idiots still hasn't been caught, by the way. What do you think will happen when he finds me?'

Rajib's happiness is deflated. He can feel it go phhhsssssssshhh around his lungs. He says, 'And what makes you sure he will suspect you in the first place?'

'Because, you fool,' Rakib hisses, 'he questioned me about you after I returned! I told him you were some guy who was new in the city and asking for directions.'

'You are overthinking,' Rajib retorts. 'That is not strong evidence to suspect you. Let's just enjoy na? Look, you have your own fan and a clean bathroom now! You get meals three times a day. Why are you still sulking?'

Rakib stares at him. 'That moron wasn't convinced of my answer. He said, "If I find something dirty, boy, see what I'll do...." '.

Rajib laughs and sprays a drizzle of Sprite on Rakib's face. 'Sorry, it reminded me of a Bollywood villain's dialogue. When did you turn out to be such a scaredy-cat?'

Hasib returns from the washroom and clumsily lands in his seat that makes a cringing noise against the mosaic. Guilt sloshes around Rajib's heart. He shouldn't have said that, he thinks. He didn't experience how it's like to live without legs. He wants to say sorry, but it seems like Rakib – now dipping his sheek kebab into a garlic-and-mayonnaise paste – didn't mind his words. Hasib takes a toothpick out of the transparent cup at the centre of the table and begins picking between two teeth in the corner.

'I was thinking...would you like to live with us, Rakib? You could assist Monju in book-keeping our shop's expenses. We could really use a hand!' Hasib says.

Rakib and Rajib stare at each other. 'Yes! Of course, I will!' Rakib says. He is consumed by the prospect of finally living with his brother. This is a prospect that seemed invisible during his days in the alleys where he and other children would be flogged with leather belts on certain nights for not earning enough on the streets.

It takes Hasib three days to sort things out with the Council. He fills up forms and convinces the Council – with bank statements and the transaction records of his mechanic shop – that yes, Hasib is indeed a legitimate employer and not another gang leader looking to exploit Rakib.

Rajib is off to fetch Rakib in the evening. Rakib wears the salmon shirt and the cargo pants – folding it up to the knees, where his legs end – the city corporation provided him. Rajib's Transformers t-shirt and discoloured jeans appear untidy beside Rakib's appearance. Rakib's luggage only includes a pink sack inside which all his clothes are entangled with one another. Hasib stretches his hands to hug Rakib as they step off the rickshaw in front of the mechanic shop. First, Rajib places the wheeled wooden platform on the ground, then positions Rakib on it. Rakib's face disappears in Hasib's beard. 'Come, come, you brave young men. May Allah shine His brilliant light upon you!'

The glass behind Hasib shatters when he opens the collapsible gate to the stairs. Rajib throws himself over Rakib. They slide under a car plastered with newspapers and smelling of new paint as a man from outside keeps firing. A commotion ensues. The gunfire has stopped. Local men have nabbed the shooter and are giving him a thrashing. Rajib slides out of the car first and sprints towards Hasib. Rakib shivers inside. Hasib's eyes are open and white tunic is gleaming red. Rajib jerks Hasib's unmoving arms. Hasib's head is heavy on Rajib's thighs. Everyone later learns that it is the same man who threatened Rakib on the day he reunited with Rajib on the road. "Missing fugitive attempts to murder former hostage," the newspaper headlines parrot.

'I will let you stay for another week. Find some other work. I can't risk my daughter's life because of your troubles,' Sharmin says to the twins the next day at the graveyard after Hasib's *Janazah* and burial have been completed. She faces his grave and mutters silent prayers as tears slip into her mouth, her hands firm on the just-built wooden fence. Rajib stops coming upstairs for dinner. Sharmin doesn't call him either. Relatives and friends bring fruits and boxes of food and console Sharmin, holding frequent congregational prayers in Hasib's remembrance. The scent of incense sticks descends from the flat on the garage and drives away the stench of petrol fumes and kerosene from Rajib's nose.

'He was a man of God. I am sure he's happy up there. He'd hate to see you cry, sister,' Rajib catches one woman saying near the garage and hugging Sharmin. Her words are true, Rajib thinks. He was such a kind man. No stranger has been this kind to him. With tears dangling from his eyes, Rajib runs to the masjid in the alley opposite the garage to make *wudu* and plead with Allah for Hasib's salvation in *sujood*.

'So, what are we going to do? Call Amma? Tell her the truth about everything?' Rakib spits out the seeds from his oranges.

'I don't know. I will have to do that. It seems like non-beggars like me aren't allowed to stay at the shelter with you.'

'I won't fill up the forms. I will go wherever you go. I am not staying at the shelter alone.'

'You are mad.'

'Maybe.'

'Sharmin Aunty isn't speaking to us. She won't even look at us. I wish we could ask her for jobs elsewhere once we are out of this garage.'

'Do you still have Shirin Aunty's number? Should we do the garbage collecting job?'

'I don't want to do that disgusting job. I want something like my previous job. I am great at being an assistant.'

'Well, we've got to do something! We can't call Amma. She will bring us back with her. And do you really want to face Majid again?'

'I guess no.' At the mention of Majid, Rajib's soul diminishes to the size of an ant, leaves his body, and scurries off somewhere he cannot picture.

The twins clear their belongings from their corner in the garage. Rajib touches the bullet holes on the wall behind the cot. The car under which he and Rakib sought cover was taken away yesterday by the client. He hands the keys to the garage and the collapsible gate to Farin, whose bitter eyes swallow him with spite as she yanks them from his hands, causing a scratch on his palm and thumb. He bites and sucks the scratched parts and imagines if he didn't facilitate the raid, Hasib would be alive and, perhaps, Rakib would not. He recalls what Hasib told him when he spotted him crying behind the wheel-less car that had come for repair in the morning. 'Whatever Allah plans is for the best. We can't change things no matter how hard we try.' Hasib's hands were welcoming. They didn't budge or shake in fear of turning black due to the grimy liquid smearing Rajib's t-shirt and neck. Amena had said the same thing when the twins asked her why they couldn't leave the hills. She'd added that besides Majid's sister, she owed Khaled (the manager) nine lakhs (with increasing interest) for their real father's cancer treatment (in vain). The twins scratched their heads as Amena told them about God's plans. That night, Rajib hovered above Rakib's face and asked him, 'So how exactly is Allah's plan of keeping us indebted going to help us?' Rakib replied, pulling up the tattered duvet over his face, 'I don't know. Go ask Him and let me sleep.'

The rickshaw takes them to the landfill site that Shirin told Rajib about on the phone last night. Men who have stayed at the masjids for an extended period of time after Fajr are coming out now. With their long beards and light tunics, they look like multiple Hasibs. Buses and trucks with musical horns and loaded with buffaloes, cows, and goats slowly increase on the main road. The shutters of eateries go up with clattering noises. Smells of dough and liver curries mingle with the lingering exhaust fumes. At the landfill, Rajib asks for a Sayeed bhai, like Shirin told him to.

'Over there. You will find a shed. Here are the keys. Leave your bags there and report back to me in an hour,' he says, squatting on the ground and dragging a cigarette.

The twins have to cross a big mound of garbage to reach their shed. Rajib carries Rakib on his back and holds the wooden platform in his right hand. Rakib's hands are wrapped over Rajib's shoulders. With his left hand, Rajib drags the surprisingly heavy sack containing all their belongings. Tires, bottles, artificial legs and hands, car doors, warped bicycles, and slabs of tin poke out here and there. Tufts of smoke appear on the horizon the same way they did back in the mining hills when the residents began preparing breakfasts. One red dog sniffs a small white one and rolls around its tail and ears. Behind them, a grey dog takes out the flesh of a dead rat. Watching them, Rajib is overwhelmed. He longs to leap from this moment to the one where Rakib still had his legs, and the twins fed biscuits to Pinto, Rocky and Silver. To see the good in God's plan, mapped out in high definition, against the smoky landscape in front of them.

BREAKING NEWS

Parand

The morning sun lights up Maryam's face through the gap in the curtains. She lies there with her eyes closed, enjoying the gentle heat. She knows she should get up, but her blanket hugs her whole body with kindness and forbids her from leaving the warm bed. It is a rare comfort: most days she has to wake before sunrise to get ready for work.

Work! The word gives her an electric shock. Suddenly she is sitting upright in bed, pulling her hair tightly back with one hand as she reaches to find an elastic band with the other. Oh, no, I'm late, she thinks. I've missed the office shuttle. Her husband turns to her and asks what's happened.

'I'm late. I won't make it to work on time.'

Mohammad chuckles and says 'Go back to sleep, it's Friday.' Maryam laughs. How could she forget it was the weekend?

Her husband tugs at her hand, asks to hold her, saying, come back and sleep. But she resists, she has a lot to do on Fridays – as she told him already a few days ago.

'At least try to sleep on Fridays,' Mohammad protests.

'I've many things to do and one day off in the whole week,' Maryam repeats, up and dressing now. 'I have to do the laundry, some shopping, and clean the house.' Mohammad is frustrated he can't go back to sleep with his arms around her. He pulls the blanket over his face and drifts off.

Maryam leaves the room. She takes the kettle from the heater, which it sits on all day to keep warm. She carries it to the stove and returns to the bedroom where Mohammad is now snoring. Without waking him, Maryam puts on her black hijab and headscarf, takes a few old banknotes from her handbag, and goes out.

The street is quiet. Apart from a man and woman going for a walk, water bottles in hand, there is no one. The couple's conversation drifts back to Maryam, walking slowly in their wake. The man worries about the Taliban's numerous daily announcements and how hard life has become for people in Afghanistan. The woman adds that life for women was already hard enough; the recent announcements of Sharia Law were needlessly cruel and could not possibly be justified. Maryam sharpens her ears, wondering if anything new has happened, but the couple move out of earshot until they disappear around a corner at the end of the street. Maryam forgets about them and goes over her list for the day. The rest of the way to the bakery, she counts her chores: she needs to prepare breakfast, then clean the rooms that have not been cleaned all week. Once this is finished, she can start a little sewing, and do some work for her artist's soul. Lost in thought, she reaches the nearest bakery. There are several on the street, as there are on every street. Bread is essential. Everyone eats it with every meal. She can buy it fresh-baked three times a day from the baker's assistant at a small, raised window. She goes up to the window but is distracted by the cry 'Bismallah'. A pedestrian has picked up a piece of bread from the street and is holding it up. Bread is holy and she sees he is treating it with respect. He places it carefully where the birds can eat it. She returns her attention to the baker's assistant.

'Aunty, how many breads do you want?' He rubs his eyes.

'Two loaves please.'

'With oil?'

'Just two normal loaves of bread.' The man skilfully wraps them in newspaper, and she returns home.

The tea water is boiling now, so she fills the thermos and adds some tea leaves from the glass jar in the kitchen cupboard. From a smaller jar, she takes a few cardamom pods. Biting them open with her teeth, she adds them to the tea. She smiles. When I die, there won't be tea at my grave for me. She wishes that after this complex life, she could have a thermos at her graveside every day. She laughs at the thought.

On the tray she places the glass cups her husband once bought her. She stops to admire the red flowers on the tray: she loves this tray because it ties her to childhood memories. It depicts a woman looking at the river from her balcony, and everywhere there are flowers. When Maryam was a child, she imagined herself as the woman on the tray. She felt the cool breeze from the river every time she looked at it. She had thought the picture was marvelously sophisticated and wondered how it had been composed so perfectly so as to give her this magical feeling. When she got married, she asked her mother for the tray to take to her new home, and it was included in the gifts from her parents to her new household. Now Maryam takes down the sugar and puts it on the tray with a bowl of walnuts and orange jam she made herself. She takes everything into the living room.

Mohammad is just waking. Maryam invites him to breakfast. He comes out of the bedroom rubbing his eyes. Then he returns to wash his face and freshen up. He emerges again and sits down, phone in hand. Maryam pours him a cup of tea and hands him the bowl of walnuts. She puts some homemade jam on a plate for him. While sipping his tea, Mohammad scrolls through social media on his phone.

'When we finish breakfast, I have to do the laundry and clean the house, after washing the breakfast dishes,' Maryam says. Mohammad looks up from his phone.

'Go slow.' He draws out the words.

Maryam laughs and shakes her head. She repeats herself again: 'You don't know! Today is Friday, my only opportunity. I'll be at work the rest of the week and the house won't be clean!'

A strange smile spreads across Mohammad's face. He gestures with his hand – seeming to suggest she has lots of time. This attempt to bring calm irritates Maryam further. She stares at Mohammad as if to ask him what he finds amusing. But he goes back to his phone, the smile still on his face. Maryam recognises the look – he doesn't want to say any more. But the smile remains.

She picks up her own phone, and, going to social media first, as usual, begins to scroll up and down for news. Once again, there are infuriating exchanges between men over a picture of a young woman. Then her eye is drawn to a post titled BREAKING NEWS. Underneath are many angry and sad emojis. It is a picture of a letter, but the print is too small to make out. She grabs her handbag, lying nearby, and fishes for her glasses. The picture is of an official document. It has the stamp of the Islamic Emirate of the Taliban and is signed by the finance minister. Maryam quickly scans the letter. It reads: 'Women are banned from working in any part of government or in non-governmental organisations until further notice'. It cites as a reason that women are not complying with official rules about wearing the hijab. International organisations are warned that if they do not comply, their license to work in Afghanistan will be rescinded.

Maryam slowly places her phone down, her hands shaking. She reaches for her glass of tea, but she can't drink it. She carefully puts it down. After a few moments in silence, her mind unfreezes. She realises what was in Mohammad's laugh, in the character of his smile: her husband wasn't happy that she worked out of the house and is pleased by the announcement.

Now Mohammad holds up his phone to Maryam. The same smile. 'Read what's written here.'

She takes the phone and pretends to read. Mohammad is waiting for her reaction. Her face flushes but she bites her lip to stop herself from crying in front of him. She tries to calm a volcano of anger rising within, and an equal despondency. She says, off-hand: 'Oh, I was waiting for this, I'm surprised they took so long to announce it. This is our situation: to be prisoners in our own homes and live purposeless lives.'

Mohammad tries to comfort her, but Maryam doesn't want his comfort. He tries again with that wry smile. 'Don't worry too much, this situation is only temporary, soon everything will change.'

Maryam does not reply. Her heart is on fire from two sides – from the loss of her agency and from her husband's horrible smile. She is more hurt by his smile than the news: the smile is the true sign of this oppressive code, passed from father to son without any official letter, book, or written law. Patriarchal thought sits deep in men's egos and is transferred from generation to generation in this land, she thinks. All this disgusting tradition in which men see their strength and survival in trampling on women – each day a new trick. They want us in their shadow. She jerks away from Mohammad. Even if it costs her life, she has to leave the room. Mohammad does not know how to give up and calls after her: 'Where are you going? Sit and drink your tea!'

'I am going to turn on the washing machine, but I have many other things to do after that,' Maryam says bravely. She opens the bathroom door. She walks mechanically towards the machine and puts the dirty laundry in.

If she could have done her chores as fervently as usual, that would have helped. But her hands are shaking, her body is lurching in pain. She fills a bucket with warm water and takes the washing powder down. She can't do the next step. She tosses the box aside and sits on the floor. She holds her knees and starts to weep. A strange conflict persists between her mind and her heart. Her heart wants to die from of all this injustice. But her mind will not. She retrieves the washing powder and resumes her work.

Translated from the Dari by Negeen Kargar

This story was developed through the Paranda Network, a global initiative from Untold Narratives and KFW Stiftung.

THE FATHERS OF GAZA

Zahra Wadia

Everything is gone so God sends him a memory.

Breaths shallow, eyes unfocused, he lets the ringing in his ears drown out the shouts and sirens, and grasps the gift like a lifeline. The memory plays in his mind: the first time his *akhee* taught him how to perform *wudu*.

Sleeves rolled up, he wrings his hands and tries not to wince as he runs them over his arms, making sure he reaches the hook of his elbow. He ignores the grime that coats the hair on his forearms, the black dirt under his fingernails, and the splatters of caked blood. He feels a desperate urge to feel clean, to feel pure, to feel steady. Clouds of dust occupy what was once vibrant and alive and the ground shakes every few moments; though an aftermath of the last or a warning of what is to come, he no longer keeps track.

He runs his hands over his mouth, his nose, his face, his ears. He doesn't know if his plea is enough to cleanse him of the words his lips have uttered, the screams his ears have heard, and the horrors he has seen.

His palms circle over his head, and he tries to imagine a cool stream of fresh water running across the back of his neck, instead of the suffocating fug that grips his throat and the stickiness that clings to his fingertips.

He looks at his blistered and raw feet. His right ankle has begun to swell and several toenails are gone though he does not remember how. It looks like it should hurt but his body feels too foreign to him. He runs his hands over them and focuses his gaze on the pile of rubble ahead of him instead.

His *akhee* had taught him that *wudu*, the act of washing his hands, face and feet, was to cleanse him of all he had witnessed and done, to purify himself before submission to the Creator.

And while he is no longer sure he believes it, he needs to hope that it is true.

Even if there is no water.

Because while water could wipe the blood, sweat, and dirt away, the ringing of screams of suffering, the smell of rotted flesh, the dust left from lives once lived: there isn't enough water in the world, a river pure enough, to cleanse him of that.

Allahu Akbar!

God is Great. He hears the chant and closes his eyes. It is a call to prayer, to action, to do the one thing that is possibly the only reason he is still alive. He clings to his faith, even if he had never done right by it before. Where there is no mercy, he needs His Mercy. Where there was no saving, he needs His Redemption. But where there is no hope, he is lost.

Allahu Akbar!

God is Great. His eyes catch a cherry red t-shirt caught between the rocks, a picture of your favourite superhero on the front. He stumbles and before he knows it, before he can stop it, he fights to not buckle to his knees and bile rises to his throat. Rooted in spot, his legs feel leaden as the images force themselves into his mind's eye. Your toothy grin, the curve of your cheek and the way your head would turn when he entered a room, repeatedly chanting, 'Baba, Baba, Baba!' until he picked you up and swung you around. The tight grip of your whole hand around his one finger. The exact way you would laugh, a mixture of giggles and snorts, is a sound he desperately tries to conjure but hangs on the periphery of his memory, just out of reach.

The memories appear in sharp flashes and they are not the act of a Merciful Lord, but rather the pleas of a broken and tired soul that taunts the abyss and begs for surrender. So desperately he wants to give in and remain in your remembrance.

Allahu Akbar!

The call jolts him. He cannot keep Him waiting.

He must adopt the character traits he named you after. He must rely on The Creation rather than a creation of his fantasy. He prays he can finally be the man that you, with your tight hugs and bright eyes, saw in him. Even if he's not pure and will never be clean again.

His steps gain purpose, every stride an act of worship, and he joins the others. Raising his hands, he makes a supplication.

God is Great.

He sinks to his knees and he clutches the rubble. With all the strength and hope that remains, he does the one thing, the only reason he remains in this moment.

He begins to dig.

GHAZALS

Deema K. Shehabi

Gaza

On his unearthed chest, she lays three thyme-braised ghazals.
History on repeat, she mourns like Al-Khansa', broken &
                                        splayed by ghazals.

Brown-eyed girl, wounded child with no surviving family, shakes
on camera, silencing her domestic rhythms & overplayed ghazals.

There's no room on the train for dark-skinned refugees;
pundits sing for a white Europe free of humane ghazals.

On the phone, Shadab says, *I believe*. Beneath the rubble, a child
sees an angel's oiled light opening a gateway for ghazals.

She retaliates for her neighbor's insult. Rudeness
can only be handled one way by practitioners of émigré ghazals.

'It's now or never,' he sings as the bombs fall on Gaza.
From a sunlit room, his deep-cigarette voice beats all plaintive ghazals.

Like this Far Mosque, you're always there for me. What name
do we give it, this rain light we bend for weighted ghazals?

November: Indian summer warmth lulls the poet to sleep,
but she wakes to a war-wind stir, parched leaves, crimson paper ghazals.

Home

On Highway 1, you belt me with: *there's no home outside home,*
but here's a sun hurtling on my chest & a Fairuz song rewriting home.

Thirty years since her death, I spread my body over her grave, two
sons watch, bleary-eyed. What's a mother but a magnified home?

O' love, I'm the only Umayyad left, the sole Abdel Rahman. On your
diaphanous collar bone, the New Damascus, our bona-fide home.

At dusk in a Fresno orchard, we identified Palestine's trees: Baloot,
Sidr, Qaiqab, Zeitoun, but we still couldn't override home.

Son, I lied when I said a sparrow saw you through the window;
there's no spoon full of sugar for my longing to keep you inside home.

Grenades erupt from your eyes when fatherhood chews you out.
Forget kisses behind the closet, secret darling, let's fly home.

I don't know how the human heart can recover from moral injury,
he said. How do I go on with none left beside me to define home?

Al-Ghazali: true friends are those who remind us of the One Friend;
What do you call these anemones leaning towards us on the ride home?

DO UNTO OTHERS

David Pollard

Among the ruins of conscience
the red crow blusters its battered wings
against the wind

hammers with its beak and claws
the rank air where it caws its prayers
to the same god grappling with itself

who left his cherubim archangels
thrones dominions seraphim
to fall under the blades of fire
and on beyond the gates of eden

to face the arms of amelek in the cities
of brickless doors and windows
horizons now as close as skin.

The thrum of blood in our ears
is the voice of god that reads our stars'
mythologies here in the rubble of life

and wields a sword so sharp that pock-marks
eyes to silence and the yad's failure
on the parchment of the world.

REVIEWS

OTHERING HEIGHTS

John O'Donoghue

At the start of 2017, Donald Trump enacted a series of Executive Orders and Presidential Proclamations prohibiting travel from a number of countries that eventually became known as 'the Muslim Travel Ban'. There were three Executive Orders and three Presidential Proclamations during his Presidency, the last Presidential Proclamation coming in January 2020, focused mainly on seven majority-Muslim countries – Iran, Iraq, Libya, Somalia, Sudan, Syria, and Yemen but also Venezuela, North Korea, and Chad. All travel restrictions enacted by President Trump were ended by President Biden on January 20, 2021.

In the middle of his legislative campaign on 11 January 2018 President Trump referred to Haiti, El Salvador, and African states – which ones is unclear – as 'shithole countries'. This choice epithet was reported by a Democratic aide who attended a meeting with a bipartisan group of senators at the White House in which President Trump was again engaged with the issue of immigration to the United States. It was later verified by two separate sources who had also been at the meeting. Trump later issued a denial on Twitter: 'The language used by me at the … meeting was tough, but this was not the language used'. For those who don't speak fluent 'tough' no translation of 'shithole' was provided.

My Life As An Alien, Seraj Assi, Tartarus Press, Coverdale, 2023

Palestinian author and scholar Seraj Assi's first person narrator never mentions President Trump, the United States, or the 'Muslim Travel Ban' once in the 214 pages of his debut novel. An academic who took his PhD at Georgetown University, Assi is an 'alien' who made it: he's now an Adjunct Professor of Arabic at George Mason University and also a Visiting

Researcher at the Center for Muslim-Christian Understanding (ACMCU) at Georgetown.

His novel is a kind of Othering Heights, set in a place of transition – it mostly takes place on board a United Airlines flight – where 'the alien' has an opportunity to reflect on Aliens and Humans, the Old Country, the New World, of flying to 'Humanland'. Here is the current bogey figure of political rhetoric, the migrant, the asylum seeker, the refugee, claiming their humanity in the only way they feel is left to them: by boarding some means of transport and leaving their 'shithole' country for another where humanity isn't so contingent, so provisional. As such this a timely and compelling novel, where those voices seldom heard by politicians and headline writers is finally given a chance to speak.

In choosing to describe himself as an 'alien' and in not giving himself a name or saying definitively where he's from, Assi's narrator gives voice to the kind of traveller the legend emblazoned on the Statue of Liberty was meant to welcome:

> Give me your tired, your poor,
> Your huddled masses yearning to breathe free,
> The wretched refuse of your teeming shore.
> Send these, the homeless, tempest-tost to me,
> I lift my lamp beside the golden door!

One gets the impression, however, that President Trump, with his stated preference for Norwegian immigrants to the United States, would not want the likes of Seraj Assi's narrator anywhere near 'the Land of the Free'. Of course, Humanland is viewed with a certain cynicism by Assi's alien:

> I see myself in a freer land, a dreamland, a Neverland, a promised land, a
> borderless land, a land where aliens roam free under the azure Western sky.

This riffing on 'land' – we get six variations on this evocative noun – is indicative of Assi's prose throughout the novel. For this is a *performed* text, for all of its nods here and there to canonical Western authors ('They say no man is an island; I say hell *is* other people' is perhaps the most representative of Assi's aphorisms). Assi's prose is closer to a monologue than a novel, a one-man show of a book that buttonholes the reader on a long flight and doesn't let up until 'the alien's' plane has landed and he is at the airport. Even then – a good 200 pages later – he is still nervously and excitedly gabbling away.

One of the most consistent riffs in the novel is on the word 'alien' itself. Take these passages for example:

> Nothing unites humans like the prospect of invading aliens. Nothing alienates the alien like finding himself adrift in a sea of mistrustful humans, for only when I gaze at them do I start to fathom the depth of my own loneliness.

> When good aliens die, we quip, they go to Humanland.

> There are two kinds of aliens; those who flee their homeland in horror and disgust with nowhere to go but Hell, and those who leave in pursuit of some paradisial fantasy. I'm huddled in the middle, in limbo, see-sawing, teeter-tottering, dangling midway between Earth and Heaven.

The dichotomy that pervades the novel – between humans and aliens, between those who are free and those who seek freedom, between the Masters of the Universe and the Wretched of the Earth – works also at a structural level, centred on the 'alien's' backstory and his nowstory. For 'the alien', stuck on his flight, not knowing if he'll be deported when he lands, has plenty of time to reflect on where he's come from, and fills in his backstory in a series of reveries:

> The shadow of gloom cast by my hasty departure refuses to leave me. My parents bid me goodbye. My father gave me his rather detached blessing: I could sense a mix of joy and sadness in his voice…'Write, son. Tell us about the Empire State, and the state of the empire.' To my father, the journey from wasteland to Westland is more than just a good pun. In a village where the mere mention of the West makes people shudder, his proclamation seemed rather biblical…

> My mother showered me with prayers, as if I were already dead.

Here is the 'quayside wake' re-enacted in the age of transatlantic flight, the final farewell given to a migrant son or daughter their parents knew they would never see again. These reveries punctuate the novel, and give an insight into the anonymous 'alien' en route to 'Westland'.

This switching between the 'alien's' backstory and their nowstory further emphasises the duality of his identity. At once they are an 'alien', but in leaving for Humanland with their sponsor's letter in their pocket they may just elevate themselves beyond the life, the identity, they've been ascribed. The 'alien' overnight – it may of course take a little longer than this – can finally become a 'human'.

And so we get very little of the traditional approaches to the novel in Assi's tale of the 'alien', none of the overstuffed parlours of Austen and Dickens, the pursuit of love, inheritances and 'great expectations', the virtuous rewarded, justice meted out to the venal, the palpable realist nineteenth century novel. Nor do we get more recent expansions of this formula, what James Wood called 'hysterical realism' in his essay 'Human, All Too Inhuman' back at the turn of this century. Wood accused novelists such as Salman Rushdie, Thomas Pynchon, Don De Lillo, David Foster Wallace, and Zadie Smith of writing novels that are 'excessively centripetal':

> ... different stories all intertwine, and double and triple on themselves. Characters are forever seeing connections and links and plots, and paranoid parallels...

> These novelists proceed like street-planners of old in South London: they can never name a street Ruskin Street without linking a whole block, and filling it with Carlyle Street, and Turner Street, and Morris Street, and so on.

Woods goes on to say: 'The conventions of realism are not being abolished but, on the contrary, exhausted, and overworked.' He blames a dizzying exponential proliferation of detail in these novelists' work on the obliteration of credible characters in their pages. Novelist and critic, Tom LeClair, has described the fiction of these writers as 'system novels', which deal with, as Christian Lorentzen in a recent essay on *Bookforum*:

> 1) too much information; (2) the inescapability of science; (3) the incomprehensible scale of things; (4) the limits of any man's perceptions; (5) the need to see things whole; (6) the impossibility of mastery even when it's the artist's duty.

Assi decides to abandon all of these approaches to writing a novel. Rather like a poet, he excludes most of the world to include only the lyric 'I', junking all the *stuff* we find in most novels – living rooms, houses, cars, cafés, pubs, plots, *systems* – to render not the human predicament, but the predicament of the *alien*, who must choose between the bombs and the bullets of the home they were brought up in, or trying to get away from this warzone to 'freedom' in a place where they may at least find safety. This simplification of the terms Assi decides to work within focus very clearly not on Le Clair's theses but on his own thesis, that anyone who is trying to escape from a 'shithole' will always be 'Other'. Aliens don't emigrate – they invade, and in seeking to humanise his alien, Assi forges a very different aesthetic from those Western novelists who have so dominated contemporary fiction.

If the mid-century American novel was the preserve of hyphenated Americans – Irish-Americans like John O'Hara, Italian-Americans like Mario Puzo, Jewish-Americans like Saul Bellow and Philip Roth, African-Americans like Ralph Ellison, Toni Morrison, and Alice Walker, Native-Americans like N. Scott Momaday, Asian-Americans like Maxine Hong Kingston – then here perhaps is the ultimate hyphenated American, the *Alien-American*, which is almost of course a contradiction in terms.

But perhaps my scrutiny of this novel by a Palestinian writer is distorted by Western goggles when I should be trying to look at his work through Eastern eyes. So here is Palestinian poet Mahmoud Darwish in an interview with Adam Shatz for *The New York Times* in 2001: 'Exile is more than a geographical concept... You can be an exile in your homeland, in your own house, in a room.' Substitute 'alien' for 'exile' and the very same sentiments can be found in *My Life As An Alien*.

Assi's novel is published by a small independent press based in Yorkshire, Tartarus Press, which was founded over thirty years ago. The press's USP up to Assi's novel has been the publication of 'the literary supernatural/ strange/horror fiction' by writers such as Arthur Machen, M. R. James, Robert Aickman. This is their first venture into the 'literary novel', and one can only wonder how a Palestinian scholar based in America found his way to Yorkshire. They are to be congratulated for taking a risk on Assi, for publishing his novel in such a handsome hardback edition, with cream jacket and embossed clouds on the boards, and a yellow ribbon to mark your place.

Assi's voyage from the Old World to the New – and the fictional representation of it in *My Life As An Alien* – is the dream of many a voyager in our contemporary world. It seems we live in times of great displacement. Here is a novel, an excellent comic, sardonic novel, in which the voices shouted down and shouted over, refused, excluded, abandoned, deported, finally get a chance to speak.

VOGUE AFRICA

Abdullah Geelah

Todd Webb, Untitled (44UN-7930-609), Trust Territory of Somaliland (Somalia), 1958 © 2021 Todd Webb Archive

In early 2021, a photograph in marvellous colour became viral on social media. Gen Z, mostly diasporic Africans, were hooked by its timeless appeal. It seemed to us a carefully choreographed Instagrammable shot taken during a throwback summer along the turquoise shores of the Côte d'Azur or the Cyclades. In fact, this was a picture-postcard of the Benadir littoral: two young women are walking on a pristine beach while a mutt, of probable terrier-collie pedigree, sits to their right. The young women, perhaps sisters of Hawiye or Darood lineage, are wearing matching yellow dresses in the popular fashion of mid-century urban Somalia: a style which gave way to the translucent and diaphanous voile of the *dirac* from risqué French Djibouti in the 1970s and thereafter the uniform of the Arabian-imported *jilbaab* in the 1990s and beyond. The dresses, with their embroidered patterns, are ostensibly handmade. Their white veils, loosely worn, waft in the midsummer wind of the Indian Ocean as they bask in effortless elegance on *il lido di Mogadisco*. This is Vogue Africa *ante literram*.

The photograph of the young women in the yellow dresses are one of several striking images in *Todd Webb in Africa: Outside The Frame*. Co-authored and curated by professors Aimée Bessire and Erin Hyde Nolan, the book features a collection of 200 hitherto unseen photographs from a UN assignment that took the American photographer Todd Webb (1905–2000) to eight African countries in 1958. The photographs are accompanied by essays from Western and African artists and scholars (some of whom from the countries Webb visited) which frame the images in a critical postcolonial context.

Aimée Bessire and Erin Hyde Nolan, *Todd Webb in Africa: Outside the Frame*, Thames & Hudson, London, 2021

Webb was no fashion photographer or photojournalist. The erstwhile stockbroker and Quaker-born Midwesterner only discovered photography during the Steinbeckian sojourns of his early 1930s. Neither are his photographs, beautiful and majestic, a mid-century *National Geographic* redux. As this book shows, Webb upends his UN-commissioned brief to 'document emerging industries and technologies'. This was too limiting for an artist who could not resist the power of his original oeuvre: to record everyday life and cityscape. And, in an African context gripped in the wind of change, he produced some remarkable results much to the chagrin of his UN patrons. Out of around 1,500 colour negatives which Webb diligently took on three cameras during his five-month assignment, the UN Department of Public Information published only 22 black-and-white images in a seven-page brochure. Those young women in the yellow dresses, and the images of many others, were lost for nearly six decades until their discovery by Betsy Evans Hunt, Webb's friend and manager of his estate, in a Californian basement in 2015.

The eight African countries were at varying stages of the colonial/postcolonial paradigm: two recently independent countries (Ghana and Sudan), a British Crown colony (Kenya), a British colonial federation (the Federation of Rhodesia and Nyasaland, now Zimbabwe, Zambia, and Malawi), a British protectorate (the Sultanate of Zanzibar) and three UN trust territories (Italian Somaliland, united with British Somaliland to form Somalia in 1960; French Togoland, now Togo; and British Tanganyika, now Tanzania following its merger with Zanzibar in 1964). Whilst most of these achieved their national liberation by the early 1960s, Zimbabwe only rid itself of its white settler government 22 years after Webb's visit. The UN trust territories, in particular, were a peculiar quasi-colonial set-up. These were either a hangover of the former League of Nations mandates or, in the case of Italian Somaliland, 'territories detached from "enemy States" as a result of the Second World War'. Trusteeship, with its seemingly benign connotation of fiduciary management, sought to prepare inhabitants for 'their progressive development towards self-government and independence'. Yet, it lightened the fetter of imperialist government only to fasten it firmly towards a form of endgame colonial administration, albeit with UN supervision. We are not sure why these African territories were picked. If economic potential were the likely factor in their selection, it would not adequately explain the omission of some politically comparable countries (say Nigeria). The inclusion of the trust territories, however, suggests expediency. The choice of first stop – Togoland – during its first elections following universal suffrage (stage-managed by the UN of course) was deliberate (consider Webb's studied appraisal in his journal entry dated 27 April 1958: 'the UN mission is vindicated and aside from the few here [i.e., the French] the country is in ecstasy'). As was Webb's photograph of the jubilant Togolese man waving a UN flag. And, offstage, the Somalis' choice of their independent flag two years later could not have been a bigger expression of approval in the UN's supposed good work.

Webb had a journal which recorded his views during his five-month assignment. These entries have been woven into the book to contextualise the photographs. The reader understands that, as a white American man in Africa,

Webb had preconceptions of the continent. These, on the whole, do not take shape in his photographs as something nefarious, even if the image of the bare-breasted Betammaribe women in rural Togo reinforces the primitive/modern dichotomy. On the face of it, Webb's preconceptions show the customary, almost boyish, excitement of visiting a new place. He interrogates his African romanticism, but without fully rejecting it. Socially conscious he may have been, he was still a creature of his time. While we neither infer in Webb a Marlow-like impetus to discover the 'wild Africa' nor observe some Damascene conversion in his later writing, his 'thrill in 'seeing Africa',' Bessaire points out in one of the essays, 'reads like a nineteenth-century adventure story'. It might be too convenient to dismiss Webb for his (tempered) romanticism. There is no ill-will. He shows a child-like innocence and an imagination informed by European culture and American exceptionalism — such as his displeasure when he realises that parts of Southern Rhodesia resemble the American Midwest. And, as he frequently displays in his journal, letters to his wife Lucille and photographs, he grapples with a set of conflicting emotions: the colonial horrors he witnessed, the humanity of the subjects he photographed and the biases he formed prior to his trip. We do indeed 'see Africa through his eyes', but we can also be sensitive to the complex perspectives he has provided, even if his understanding of 'Africanness' can be cringeworthy to contemporary readers.

Webb's wanton flouting of the UN brief yields some of his most interesting output. He breaks from such rigidity to explore what he viewed to be intellectually and creatively stimulating subjects and settings. Amidst the ubiquity of oil rigs and heavy industry, symbols not of the 'changing face of Africa' but of the ever-present colonial exploitation, his photographs of the quotidian are captivating because of their candidness and contrast: the Ghanaian Ewe chieftain in resplendent *kente* drinking Heineken; the uniformed Togolese attendant outside the Texaco petrol station; the Somali woman in her *guntiino* building a road outside the Italian Fascist-era parliament. He chronicles everyday episodes and elements that reflect reality: the cheek-by-jowl dynamic of the colonised and the colonial. And, accordingly, there is a sensitivity to the subject matter. Webb avoids essentialising Africans in his photographs, despite the commercial value and popular allure of doing so. The UN's defined brief to focus on industry and progress could have disrupted any wholesale attempt by Webb to engage in mythologised narratives of Africa, even if the UN mandate to document and aestheticise African progress was in itself reductive. The image of the Betammaribe women notwithstanding, Webb could have taken many primitivising visuals of Africa, brief or not brief, but he chose not to. Though the criticisms in the book of his being a white privileged man in Africa are compelling, we cannot ignore his subtlety of touch and quiet universalism. It is certainly easy to imagine that his upbringing amongst Friends in Detroit and Ontario might have influenced his views and work. His quest to record the everyday and his abhorrence by inequities and injustices in both segregated America and colonial Africa indicate that persistent Quaker principle to recognise the transcendent and precious in each person.

These photographs were taken by 'an outsider looking in' – a recurrent refrain throughout the book. The UN could have commissioned an African photographer or employed local ones in each of the aforementioned countries. In an interview which features in the book, the Ghanaian photographer, James Barnor, is dismissive: 'I could've taken the same type of pictures as Webb'. Recognition came much later in life for this nonagenarian, whose early shots of Ghanaian independence on a cheap camera and, subsequently, of 1960s Black Britain are mesmerising. Barnor was highly experienced, with local knowledge and credentials which superseded Webb's. He hailed from a family of Gold Coast photographers and had a vibrant studio in 1950s Accra. While Barnor acknowledges that 'perhaps [he] might have been able to go to places [Webb] couldn't', he confirms that 'we give home to foreigners too easily' and 'if anything, if you were a foreign photographer, you had all the equipment and the background'. It is simplistic to assume a racist underhand in Webb's selection. Webb was, after all, known to UN officialdom from previous commissions to photograph the General Assembly and Mexico. Besides, it seems that both he and his wife mingled in the same social set as them. But the criticisms still stand: the all-too-easy retreat to Black exoticism, the comfort of privilege and the continuing human-interest appeal of the white foreigner in the Global South. Barnor is correct that he, and other African photographers, could have had the access to local settings and subjects without the colonial or neo-colonial baggage. Some of the bemused and suspicious looks of Webb's subjects might have been replaced with more ordinary expressions, and most importantly, authenticity in the resulting photographs. Webb admits that while people in Italian Somaliland were hospitable and generous, 'as many were apparently resistant to his requests for posing'. Professor Ali Jimale Ahmed helpfully provides cultural background in the accompanying essay to the people's discomfort of the foreigner's lens, and indeed, the European gaze. The speed with which some of his shots are taken and the fleeting, almost blurred, results explain the subjects' reticence and raise questions of agency. It is difficult, however, to think Barnor and other Africans would have had the same access to the networks which Webb's privilege afforded, especially in places like Southern Rhodesia or at white-run, Black-manned plants where power dynamics were stratified. The best he managed to achieve, and the least damaging, was to capture what he found as he found them.

The sadness, and beauty, of the photographs are their anonymity. We are forced to give the subjects a backstory and speculate as to their futures. The historical trajectories of their countries are widely known; of their individual histories we know nothing. With the young women in the yellow dresses and the puppy, Ahmed deliberates – given Islamic ritual sensibilities around dog ownership – whether they are maidservants to an expatriate family. Or are they middle-class educated women who neatly fit into the UN's (and Webb's) aestheticised conception of African modernity? Our assessment of who they are, however informed, is pure guesswork. Yet the temptation to wonder what had happened to them is boundless and very human. What has become of the *jellabiya*-wearing members of the Cotton Growers' Council in Wadi Madani? Or of the young Togolese children on the cusp of a new horizon for their country? Where was the red-suited dandy off to in Mogadishu's medieval *Xamarweyne* quarter? Webb leaves us with little descriptions and no names. His life was indeed peripatetic but he was no photojournalist; he was just a man on a mission. And there is no immediate rush to identify or search for the subjects of his shots, despite my own fancy to think of one of the young women in the yellow dresses as my grandmother. The authors hope that the 'text and the photographs…make some noise'. Throughout the book, we hear the clatter of the copper mines in Zambia, the drone of the hydroelectric power stations in Tanzania, the 'cry of *ablode*! (freedom)' in Togo, the din of the Sinclair oil rigs in Somalia, the Last Post of European imperium. Webb's photographs are evocative and engaging, beyond the cacophony of a continent in transition.

FIVE MUSLIM MEMOIRS

Steve Noyes

Osman Yousefzada, *The Go-Between: A Portrait of Growing Up between Different Worlds.* Canongate, Edinburgh, 2022.

Mohsin Zaidi, *A Dutiful Boy*, Vintage, London, 2020.

Omar Saif Ghobash, *Letters to a Young Muslim.* Picador, London, 2017.

Mona Siddiqui, *My Way: A Muslim Woman's* Journey, I.B. Tauris & Co, Edinburgh, 2015.

Kamal Al-Solaylee, *Intolerable: A Memoir of Extremes.* Harper Perennial, Toronto, 2013.

The last decade or so has seen the publication of a number of interesting memoirs by Muslims. One expects to learn about the *ummah* and the individual soul in these memoirs. But one finds turbulence, displacement, and distance. Much has been written about the movement towards religious traditionalism as a response to modernity, and in these memoirs, there is certainly a tension between a more observant and less observant Islam. But that is not the only tension or division on display.

In the Western world, thanks to the post-structuralist thinkers, many have a more constructed view of the individual and the current fashion is to refuse 'the binary.' But the binary has a marked presence in these books, manifested by instances of *barzakh*, or barriers between modes of thought. There are divisions between inner lives and their surroundings; between more and less observant Islam; between the Western and Muslim countries; between women and men, straight and gay, between golden pasts and lapsarian realities—and plenty of false dichotomies.

Mohsin Zaidi's *A Dutiful Boy* begins with his father's *muharram* flagellation—fittingly, for over the course of the book, Zaidi's struggle to acknowledge and deal with his early-recognised homosexuality is often as wounding as any physical flail. From a few passages in the Qur'an (specifically 11:82) about the fate of Lot's people, and a singularly unhelpful book called *Morals for Young Shias,* Zaidi manages to construct a torture as wounding as any physical: he experiences the punishment visited on an entire population.

> I had told myself that my fantasies were a harmless indulgence that helped prevent me from going mad. But I had to stop these thoughts. It was unnatural. With the book clutched tightly to my chest, I imagined stones of baked clay crashing through my bedroom ceiling, solving all my problems.

How much different might have been his story had he turned at first to the ayah that says: 'Allah will not burden a soul beyond its ability to bear the burden' (2:289).

A central quandary is hereby set up: in order to realise his homosexual nature, he must embarrass his parents; in order to please his parents, he must deny his homosexual nature. His Oxbridge academic achievements make things worse. 'But I was building a prison out of my success. The more I achieved, the more my parents' eyes shone with pride for their boy – how could I tarnish this gleaming image?'

There are enough instances of Zaidi's family's good-heartedness and even their occasional tolerance of gayness sprinkled throughout—they find the gay American sitcom *Will & Grace* entertaining and funny; his brother, after learning that George Michael is gay, says 'I don't care. He's still my boy.' – that it is not surprising that his parents eventually come to accept his gay marriage:

> 'I...I'm thinking of marrying Matthew...but I don't want to do it without knowing you two are okay with it.' ....
>
> 'Okay with it?" My Mum leaned in towards me and grabbed my hand. "Mohsin, please hurry up before he dumps you!'
>
> 'And gets snapped up by someone else, my dad added.

Since Zaidi and Al-Solaylee both deal explicitly with men coming to terms with their homosexuality, their jihads or internal struggles, we can compare their respective techniques, the shapes of the narratives.

In Zaidi's book, the reader is dragged forward by a series of chapter-ending climaxes, much in the manner of a televised drama. Some of these effects are cheesy. The first chapter ends at the doorstep of the family home, where Zaidi has brought his male partner to meet his parents. The father answers the door, and Zaidi asks about his mother. There is a silence. What is the reader to think? That the mother won't see them? That she has died during the interregnum. Well, no, as we find out hundreds of pages later, she is there and reasonably happy at the reunion. Similar 'cliff-hangers' happen throughout. After his mother says, 'I can't help you if you don't tell me what's bothering you,' there is another silence, and she says,'You're not gay, are you?' and the chapter ends. Did anything interesting happen in the room then? We don't know: a flashy chapter ending has sufficed.

The huge upside of his technique is that Zaidi effectively evokes a whole range of emotional responses to his homosexual predicament at their highest pitch—self-castigation, horror, despair, hope, worry, shame, gratitude—and in doing so will probably tell other Muslim homosexuals who read *A Dutiful Boy*, that they are not the first to suffer in this way, and that they are not alone.

Whereas in Zaidi's narrative, the progression of his soul is forward and ascendant, towards a happy ending, by contrast, Al-Solaylee's predominant mode is lapsarian. His own escape from religious orthodoxy and gay-intolerant societies is not redolent of high drama; I found it rather frictionless. He gets a PhD in England; he emigrates to Canada; he succeeds as a journalist and academic. The more substantial aspect of his narrative is his distanced chronical about the fortunes of the family he left behind. Al-Solaylee is looking back at a privileged childhood and the cinematic glamour surrounding his father, a successful real estate developer in Aden.

> Mohamad escaping over rooftops and through back alleys to avoid getting caught in flagrante by a paramour's father, or, in some cases, husband. Or Father inviting unsuspecting females to his office to show off the plans for his next development. My favourite, because of its Mad Men sordidness (or is it

glamour?), my father flirting with flight attendants on the local airline. Aden was the Monte Carlo of the Arabian Sea, and Mohamed was its Cary Grant.

Great guy, eh? Just the sort that you would want in your community, a serial philanderer. At the risk of sounding prudish, I think he got it right with 'sordidness', not 'glamour': *Mad Men's* Don Draper is shallow from the get-go and gets shallower as the series goes on, to the point where he is copulating in alleyways with waitresses.

This glamour of a period of family vacations in a liberal upper-class Cairo, of meals in fine restaurants, of bespoke dresses, of a renaissance in the worlds of Arab music and film, a glamour that will, as the family is forced to move from Yemen to Cairo to Lebanon, back to Cairo again, and finally to a dangerous Yemen of civil war and reduced circumstances, will gleam all the more for its disappearance, and leave his family members shaken. For his sisters, it is a loss of privilege; for the mother, an alienating loss of community:

> They had every right to think of themselves as princesses. Didn't their father reign over Aden? They had their dresses made in Cairo and bought fine jewellery from the Indian and Jewish traders in Aden. Whether it was Arabic or Western music they listened to, they had the latest records on vinyl. Men competed for their affections, and they turned down many suitors.

And:

> (My mother) took part in the mythologising of Aden just like her husband and older children did, but her participation was often reluctant and punctuated with silences. When she was taken out of Aden, she lost her only safety net, her own three sisters and mother and a society that, despite its colonial moorings, was still tribal and village-like.

In both narratives these men drift away from Islam. They both forget how to pray. Al-Solaylee at a relative's grave in Yemen cannot even remember Al-Fatiha. Zaidi after many years finally prays for a much-loved uncle. Their own struggles have caused an estrangement from *diin*.

Al-Solaylee, having escaped from his family's straitened circumstances, feels this drift as a certain numbness, an anomie in the soul, perhaps a species of survivor's guilt. This passage is especially sad:

My path in life couldn't be just different from my own flesh and blood; I needed to be free of the legacy of guilt and abandonment I felt when visiting them. Their suffering forced me to examine a life that I didn't want for myself, and I could undo nothing to change it for them. I don't know when and how I became so heartless and selfish.... I saw no point in having this family as a compass for my life.

In a similar mood, once in Canada, Al-Solaylee does not dwell for long on the complexities of ending a long-term gay relationship, when a job opportunity separates them; he just slides away from it, in his typical transcendent fashion.

Al-Solaylee spares us no detail of how life constricts during times of increased piety and public morality, as his distant family suffer dislocations and then the privations of war. It is no fun at all. Perhaps it is fun if you're the one doing the policing of public morality. Restrictions affect his sisters: increasingly mandatory modest dress and narrowing life-possibilities. A brother becomes much more observant and berates the sisters about their morality. When the family finally returns to Yemen, they must deal with curfews, bombings and unpredictable power outages meaning they must cook at all hours of the night, when there is electricity. They turn to their religion to help them cope. Al-Solaylee responds with a sort of weary acceptance of their fate, without much curiosity about exactly how their faith is helping them survive, a potentially very interesting conversation.

I believe that my siblings have written off this life, hoping that they'll be rewarded in the afterlife, since they've been good and devout Muslims. Just a few years ago, I would have found that way of thinking not just defeatist but repellant. I can see it now as a natural conclusion of the intolerable journey they've been on.

In Zaidi, Al-Solaylee, and Yusufzaidi's stories, there is a theme of polarisation, of parts of the *ummah* separating and coming apart, like Pangaea, the formerly unified continent; coming apart, through immigration into discrete, somewhat insular communities bound by faith and honour. I liked this nice distinction that Zaidi makes about faith and honour: 'Faith and izzat are not the same thing, but, much like two languages with a shared history, they have a complex relationship with each other.' This insularity is very different from, say, Tariq Ramadan's vision of

Muslims playing a part in civic society. Within these 'island' communities, there is a religious mutual surveillance, one test of piety being comparative. Everyone watches everyone else for evidence of impiety.

Our writers deal with this theme differently. In Yusufzaidi's *The Go-Between*, this pious gossiping and shaming raise a relatively innocent schoolboy prank—he gets his pants pulled down at a sleepover—into a full-blown controversy and a meeting at the mosque. Al-Solaylee, visiting relatives in Birmingham is shocked and repelled by their Arabic milieu, because it 'represented a kind of immigrant experience that I'd spend the rest of my life avoiding: closed-off households that showed no interest in British culture or civic society'.

Al-Solaylee finds this stifling - it is what he has escaped from – whereas some might find this atmosphere interesting and comforting, especially when compared with the public drunkenness, smug racism and classism, near-nudity of hen parties, and ubiquity of betting-shops that comprise street-level British culture. But, as we learn in Yusufzaidi's telling, there are proximate causes to this closing-off: Margaret Thatcher's policies and resultant factory-closings that have deprived men of their purpose and identity and caused them to gravitate to the mosques. These are the Muslim equivalents of American coalminers, say, abandoned by the elites and emboldened by Trump.

"She is going to throw us out, send us packing, back to where we came from."

"We must continue to save and send money back home, buy land and build property, she won't let us build a home here, it will only be taken away."

We younger ones would listen, fearing the worst, or sometimes one of us would say, "she can't, we were born here, she can't just throw us out or send us back."

The Go-Between refers to the privilege Yusufzaidi was given as a child of going between the discrete masculine and feminine worlds of his Pashtun-speaking British community, and his gift for vivid imagery is well-suited to paint it for us.

Like storytellers, she and her friends would gather and listen to each other's heartbreak, even if they had heard it before. My closeness to this world of women was to come to an end as I grew older, but for now I stayed as close as I could. It was a full-blown epic, of tragedy, pathos, colour, jewellery and clothes, compared to the drab, smoky posturing of the men, who all seemed the same, who all dressed the same.

He can also with a few artful strokes draw the border between his family's world and the greater world as here where he describes the local prostitutes:

everything would play out like a slow-motion movie, the kerb-crawlers cautiously cruising up and down the streets, flashing their headlights, stopping under the bridge. I would watch, mesmerised, as the ladies glided by in satin negligees under their fur coats, and golden strappy sandals that dug into their pale skin on cold nights, the straps crisscrossing over their bright red-painted nails. Some of them wore long, thigh-high boots pulled over their knees. Car windows would scroll down, and these mermaids would bend forward to say a few words through the window.

The chapter titles give an indication of his method (Our Hood, Our House, and Mum's Sewing Salon; The Charpai, The Slipper, and the Jinn; God, Jelly and the Corner Shop), intending to bring these differing worlds into focus by a sort of layered triangulation. His ability to portray childhood with childish emotional responses is a remarkable literary achievement. He has a naïve but charming tone. He grievously laments the loss of his favourite sweets because of their haram ingredient of pork gelatine. On a visit to his ancestral Pakistani village, he narrowly escapes having to dive into a well to retrieve a polluting dead animal, but upon his return, writes a scary story of the adventure he didn't have, casting himself as a hero.

As he ages, his observations become more sophisticated and discerning, and many of these portraits and anecdotes are not flattering to these Muslims. We get an example of intended piety morphing into shocking dissociation when an acquaintance reasons that the Yorkshire ripper must have been a good Muslim because he killed prostitutes. We see his sisters entering purdah at the age of thirteen and getting taken illegally out of school; when the school investigates, the family smoothly lies about extended visits to Pakistan. We eavesdrop on his father's conversations with other men and learn that it is not only white people who are prejudiced, as they enjoy mocking Christians for their Christmas customs and beliefs.

And he vividly describes the change brought into the local mosque by stricter imams:

> Gone were the Sunday suits —worn with such pride in their new homeland — with which they had cut dashing figures in both the black-and-white and Kodachrome photos taken in their front rooms. Their dark, pomaded, old-Hollywood hair was now shorn and covered with handmade skullcaps. Those who had beards grew them longer so they were able to make a fist of them with their hands...

Mona Siddiqui's *My Way* also takes note of this move towards religious insularity, but she elevates the discussion somewhat, seeing the increased focus on conventional piety as a diminishment of *'ilm*, of knowledge, inimical to the 'bold and free inquiry' enjoined upon Muslims by the Qur'an. Siddiqui is an intellectual and she detects a strain of anti-intellectualism and *contemptus mundi* in the *ummah*. She suggests, as a Muslim scholar, that this sheltering from outward circumstances bears with it a cost: it has effectively dealt away some of the complexity and philosophical richness of Islam:

> I see a different kind of tension—the clash between religious knowledge and secular professions, the idea that spiritual growth comes from living apart from this world and that it is only religious knowledge which can strengthen our faith in God. I believe this has produced a cultural malaise in which basic books of theology suffice as learning and the dissemination of empirical and scientific knowledge, of literature, music and the arts, is seen by some as weakening the faith. I personally can't see this when I look at the rich history of Islamic civilisation or even the way the Qur'an commands us all to reflect upon the world, encouraging bold and free enquiry, not a closed and trapped piety.

Her own personal story is told within certain limits, a certain fastidiousness about how much she reveals of herself. Surely one can expect greater drama and personal information in a memoir? For instance, she alludes to disputes and disagreements within her own family but does not give any details; she comes to conclusions about the necessary ingredients of a successful marriage but reveals very little of her relationship with her husband. This is a quibble, not terribly important: it is likely that she is respecting her family members' privacy. One accepts the trade-off: less personal drama for more of her nourishing intellectual perspective.

When she does relate a personal anecdote, as here where internalised propriety encounters a breaching situation, the effect is even more startling.

> When I was leaving to return to the UK, he leant over to give me a hug. I remember recoiling, thoroughly embarrassed and ashamed of myself. How had I given such an impression, where a man felt he was at liberty to show me physical affection, even if it was just a friendly hug? It sounds so innocent, and looking back I sound so immature, but there are times when you know you have discovered something about yourself which can can't quite identify straightaway. On my return flight I kept thinking about why I had recoiled when I felt so comfortable with him. I realised I wanted all the experiences of life without feeling unsettled and that was impossible. I was a different person now.

We don't want to make too much of this anecdote—many other factors no doubt motivated Siddiqui to propel propelled herself beyond the overly parochial into her pursuit of inter-faith dialogue, for which she was awarded a CBE. There is a largeness and generosity of spirit that characterises her meditations on marriage, death, and the presence of Allah, and she brings in the Qur'an, Sufi thinkers, Christian thinkers, and secular philosophers.

She is not going to get sucked into the culture war, which she correctly identifies as a limiting series of skirmishes about politically loaded signs and symbols. The 'contemporary debate has limited the very concept of modesty to gender segregation alone, where women continue to be the primary repositories of sexual ethics and family values...unless Muslims are willing to actively engage with pluralism in all matters of life and religion, debates on Islam and the place of Islam as a public and private faith will continue to remain for the most part simplistic and uninspiring'.

Although she comments on the lack of lived experience in Islamic studies, and urges Muslims to engage, she doesn't have many concrete ideas about how to engage with those whose views are narrower or differently focussed than hers; engagement with British society *tout court* is the cure for narrowness, which begs the question. (So-called fundamentalists are also part of British society.) There is a consistent sense of being above the fray. A good example of this is her discussion with other Muslims women about modesty and dress; the women are looking for answers, and Siddiqui responds by saying that her job is to make them think, a sort of obstinate Oxbridge donnishness (or Socratic tactic, if you like) that doesn't address whatever tensions and disagreements there may be in such women's families about such matters.

Siddiqui alludes to and disapprove of a soft relativism (also noted by Tariq Ramadan), which would deny the essential truth of Islam, but does not entirely escape the soft-boiled language of 'relativism'. At one point she says she thinks of Allah as a permanent mental presence, but not in any ritual or performative way. It certainly must be at least tautological to call the *salah* performative, but leaving that aside, Siddiqui has put her finger on an important theme. A performance is done in public, and it is this being-in-public that constitutes Zaidi's struggle and A-Solaylee's urge to escape and causes both to fear punishment.

Siddiqui gently suggests that this concentration on punishment is a choice and that there are other perspectives available:

> We are turned off by the language of fire and brimstone; the vivid images of heaven and hell, although ingrained in our cultural consciousness, seem alien. But words which speak of grace and generosity, compassion and forgiveness draw us in and slowly we begin to imagine God in a different kind of language.

This is not a rejection of the Creator's message about the punishment and reward in the afterlife, and her clarifying comment is more subtle than it first appears: 'The relationship between this life and the afterworld lies in accepting that there is a place in time that has yet to occur ... this other world can be imagined but it is not imaginary.' *Jinnah* and *Jahannam* are real indeed, but portrayed in a way that we can visualise them.

If only Zaidi and Al-Solaylee had read Siddiqui; it would have saved them some grief. Or this quote that Siddiqui includes, by the Sufi theologian Ibn Qayyim al-Jawziyya: 'the Gnostic journeys towards on two wings, awareness of his own faults and recognition of his Lord's grace. He cannot journey without them, and if he be denied one, he would be like a bird that had lost a wing'.

The benefit of Siddiqui's deep Islamic knowledge is the precision with which she selects from other's thought to support her own. This is William Chittick quoting Ibn Arabi; the passage employs a brilliant metaphor that at once honours Islam as the final revelation, but acknowledges respectfully the contribution of other religions:

All the revealed religions are like lights. Among those religions, the revealed religion of Muhammad is like the light of the sun among the lights of the stars. When the sun appears, the lights of the stars are hidden, and their lights are included in the light of the sun. Their being hidden is like the abrogation of the other revealed religions that takes place through Muhammad's revealed religion. Nevertheless, they do in fact exist, just as the existence of the light of the stars is actualised.

Omar Ghobash's memoir/polemic, *Letters to a Young Muslim*, uses a literary conceit, a series of letters to his 'sons,' to deliver a progressive argument supporting a universalist and humanist Islam. A left-leaning, *Guardian*-reading person such as myself can find much to agree with: he wants his 'son' to think for himself, to resist calls to violence and a simplistic vision of a 'pure' or revanchist Islam. So far so good. My reservations have to do with how much Ghobash is willing to engage with countervailing arguments and with how little his polemic is grounded in the Qur'an and a more representative selection of modern Islamic thought: in other words, how much his screed leaves out.

It is entirely understandable that Ghobash is energetically opposed to violence, having lost his father at an early age to an assassination. His account of how he experienced this loss is unbearably poignant.

My siblings and I were told that there would be a three-day holiday and we celebrated. Back at the house, however, we returned to find my mother crying. Men stood in small circles outside in the garden. The women remained inside to watch a funeral broadcast on the family television … The house was crowded, hot, and I have a vague recollection of everything feeling saturated by tears. An Emirati flag covered the coffin. I asked whose funeral it was but received no answer.

Many years later I realised it was my father's funeral.

Early on there is interesting information about the sort of place that the United Arab Emirates were before the coming of oil wealth: hard-scrabble existence focussed on getting enough fish and rice. He portrays himself as a sincere yet skeptical participant in his own religion, telling us that he has felt religious fervour albeit while reciting the Qur'an badly in a singsong manner, but his self-portrait is tinged with a certain narcissism. Searching for role models as a young man, he looks around the mosques, and finds no one worthy or wise enough or with an adequate character. Really! In all the mosques?

It is not that he is incapable of giving good advice. I liked this exhortation to the 'son' to ground his faith in lived experience, for example:

> By purposeful experience I mean going out and placing yourself in positions where you are compelled by circumstances to take responsibility. Climb a mountain. Volunteer with children in a poverty-stricken country. Help a friend out of trouble. Defend someone less privileged than yourself. Teach someone to read and write. Speak in public and hear what people think of you. You will refine your understanding of yourself…

Now, I am not in any way agreeing with Muslims, or so-called Muslims, who attempt to solve political problems with violence (that often kills innocent civilians), but what I do object to in *Letters* is that it is extremely thin on Qur'an quotations and excessively thick on caricatures. He sets up the problem of violence by positing a certain type of ulema as a possible but easily knocked over solution to the problem:

> Could it be that the online ulema—or religious scholars of Islam—are correct`? Could it be that they are the living embodiment of what Islam can and should and will become? The path is clear, the language is straightforward and simple. When all the clutter of modern life is removed, the path opens up before you towards meaning and purpose.

There are indeed such clerics, devoted to a bellicose approach. (I thought of Yusuf Ali's comment in his 1907 *Life and Labours of the People of India*: 'Their dreams are centred in those nooks and crannies to which the light of modernity has never penetrated.') Hidebound, mumbling over their sacred texts. But there are others, who do indeed live in the modern world and use modern approaches. Could these online ulema be the same religious scholars, for instance, who wrote and published on the internet a point-by-point refutation of ISIS leader Al-Baghdadi's warlike theology?

Furthermore, Ghobash tells us that the battle between revelation and reason was lost over a thousand years ago. He is referring to skirmishes between the Mutazilites and orthodox Sunnism and to the ascendancy of *fiqh* over *falsifa*. The twin figures of Al-Ghazzali and Sayyid Qutb loom, the former approved of because of his turn to Sufism, and the latter despised

as a proponent of the nastiest type of jihad. This overlooks an entire
century of intellectual Muslim response to the West, such as one might
find in Albert Hourani's *Arabic Thought in the Liberal Age*.

One of Ghobash's stylistic tics is the posing of rhetorical questions.

> How can we stretch ancient concepts and attitudes without destroying our
> emotional and mental understanding? Should we turn back to our past, closing
> our eyes to what we can learn from others, insisting that we are special and
> different from all others?

And:

> What are we to do with the complex idea of being born with a predisposition
> to homosexuality? What are we to do with the idea of not having chosen one's
> sexuality? .... What if 'family values' hide tremendous injustice committed by
> patriarchal fathers against their wives and children, especially their daughters?

And:

> If we are Muslims and our religion is a one of peace, then why are there loud
> voices that have declared that we are at war? And that this war is one that has
> enemies everywhere and all the time?

But his pacific argument conveniently ignores that the Qur'an itself
defines necessary war (it is defensive, when you are persecuted and killed
for your religious beliefs) and lays down guidelines for its proper conduct,
including conditions for peace. A responsible discussion of the problem of
extremist violence must surely take account of that, and meet the
extremists' arguments on their own terms by referencing appropriate
Qur'anic verses. Consequently, his book has little of value to say to anyone
who perceives or believes they are at war.

As for the Qur'an, Ghobash rarely quotes from it. Instead, in a section
called "The Qur'an and Knowledge", he argues that the Qur'an is indeed
the word of Allah, but it needs other books to explain it and still others to
place it in a context. Then he skips to a relatively weak hadith (*Utlub bi-l-
'ilm wa law fii Siin*; Seek knowledge, even though it be in China) in order
to bolster the importance of knowledge.

Ghohash's often-deployed rhetorical method comes off as ill-suited to
his goal of encouraging his son to think for himself; too often, it sounds
more like he is telling his son what to think, because the answers are

contained within the questions; they are circular arguments that sometimes lead to dubious conclusions, such as here where, instead of referring to the Qur'an as *firqan*, a guide to right and wrong, he suggests that its guidance can ultimately be transcended:

> Points [for good and bad deeds] fit in well with the question-and-answer approach to moral conduct, which uses questions such as, Is this halal or haram? —allowed by Islam or not. *The balanced, principled person I want you to become no longer needs to ask these questions because he or she has absorbed the appropriate principles of behaviour.* (Emphasis mine.)

To be generous, this sounds a tad like Confucius's 'I could follow the dictates of my own heart; for what I desired no longer overstepped the boundaries of right.' To be less generous, it sounds like magical thinking: as Muslims, we will always need the Qur'an to guide us.

In this way, *Letters* reflects the preference or anti-religious bias of secular society (or the publishing industry), where religion is presented as a boiled-down set of moral concepts without connection to their sacred texts. *Letters* disappointed me because it seemed repetitive and smug, at times sounding like a training manual for the United Kingdom's Prevent programme, preaching to the converted, as unwilling to directly engage with opposing points of view as the Islamicists criticised by Abdou Filali-Ansari, quoted in Siddiqui's *My Way*.

> Today it is clear that fundamentalists and their supporters are completely closed off to even the most elaborate theological refutations of their views, even when produced by distinguished religious authorities. The first reflex of the fundamentalists is to withdraw from the mainstream, to build around themselves a shell that is impervious to any logic except their own.

After reading Siddiqui and Ghobash, it struck me that the polarisation I referred to earlier has made it difficult for more liberal Muslims to communicate with more traditionalist Muslims. That old *barzakh* again. Those on the left are also prone to only listening to those who agree with them. So: you out there, are you a Salafist, a Wahabbist, educated by the Jamat-i-Islami or the Muslim Brotherhood, with conservative views and interesting life experiences, but not a hater? We'd love to hear from you.

ET CETERA

ON INSULTING THE PROPHET

Mashal Saif

In December 2021, Priyantha Diyawadanage, a 48-year-old Sri Lankan employed as a factory manager in the Pakistani city of Sialkot allegedly tore down a poster from the factory wall. This seemingly innocuous act was reportedly spurred by the knowledge that the factory building was about to be cleaned. What ensued was the stuff of nightmares. Diyawadanage was beaten by a mob numbering around a hundred and then set ablaze. Videos of the incident, captured on multiple mobile phones, show some in the crowd celebrating and taking selfies with Diyawadanage's corpse.

What was Diyawadanage's crime? Allegedly removing a poster that bore Prophet Muhammad's name. For the mob that lynched him, Diyawadanage's act amounted to insulting the Prophet, a crime pithily described as *sabb al-rasul* in Arabic. The commonly used Urdu equivalent is *tawheen-e risalat*; English lacks this phrase and the act of insulting Muhammad is commonly expressed in English as blasphemy.

This gruesome incident is far from an exception. Extrajudicial killings for the alleged act of blasphemy have become increasingly common in Pakistan, as have officially registered cases of blasphemy under Pakistan's blasphemy laws. Between 1987 and 2020 at least 1,855 individuals have been accused of offences related to religion (including insulting Muhammad) under the country's blasphemy laws compared to just seven from 1927 to 1986. The past three decades have also witnessed an exponential rise in extrajudicial killings of alleged blasphemers, and particularly alleged Prophet-insulters. Only two alleged blasphemers were killed extrajudicially from 1946 to 1987. From 1987 to 2015, 57 alleged blasphemers were killed extrajudicially. Non-Muslim and Muslim minorities – Christians, Hindus and Ahmadis – are disproportionately targeted by these laws and gruesome extrajudicial acts. The laws are also used to settle religious and personal rivalries, at times by making false accusations.

In 2020, two hundred blasphemy cases were reported – the highest number in Pakistani history. The situation is currently so grim that it is not just the act of allegedly insulting Muhammad in this physical realm that merits punishment: in March 2022 three female teachers employed at a local religious seminary (*madrasa*) in Dera Ismail Khan in northwestern Pakistan murdered their colleague, Safoora Bibi. Their reason? One of the murderers' relatives, a 13-year-old girl, claimed that she had been informed in a dream that Safoora Bibi had insulted Muhammad.

These murders are not simply one-off killings of passion, or acts of mob violence, without any intellectual underpinnings to support the homicides. Many of Pakistan's most prominent traditional religious scholars (*ulama; singular, alim*) have publicly detailed the religious reasoning underpinning such acts and have vociferously declared that extrajudicially killing a Prophet-insulter is religiously acceptable.

The *ulama*'s consensus on this issue was most clearly apparent when Salman Taseer, the governor of Pakistan's largest province, Punjab, was accused of insulting the Prophet Muhammad in 2010. Taseer had critiqued Pakistan's blasphemy laws, amongst them Article 295-C that criminalises insulting Muhammad. Amongst the many *ulama* who termed him a Prophet-insulter was the scholar-activist, Mufti Muhammad Ashraf Asif Jalali of Jamia Jalaliyya in Lahore. Jalali is the founder of Tahrik Sirat-i Mustakim, a global movement for the propagation of Islam. He also heads the influential Tahrik Labbaik ya Rasul Allah, a movement for honouring the Prophet Muhammad and valorising those that protect his honour. Another illustrious scholar who shared Jalali's view was Zahid ur-Rashidi who is based in Gujranwala and belongs to the popular Deobandi school of thought (*maslak*). These prominent *ulama* declared that by insulting Muhammad, Taseer had removed himself from the fold of Islam and had become an apostate – a status meriting capital punishment. This view had also been publicly shared in a rousing sermon by the Rawalpindi-based scholar Mufti Hanif Qureshi, who teaches at Jamia Rizwiyya Zia al-Ulum and belongs to the Barelawi school of thought. Hanif Qureshi's sermon is said to have deeply inspired Mumtaz Qadri, Taseer's bodyguard.

On 4 January 2011, Mumtaz Qadri shot and killed Taseer in broad daylight, citing Taseer's crime of insulting Muhammad as rendering him deserving of this penalty. Even in death the *ulama* did not spare Taseer. No traditional scholar was willing to lead Taseer's funeral prayer. The *ulama* made their stance clear: as an apostate, Taseer could not be accorded the rites of an Islamic funeral. While condemning Taseer, in life and death, the *ulama* were largely united in their embrace of Mumtaz Qadri. They asserted that his actions were justified per Islam's ethico-legal code (*sharia*). When Mumtaz Qadri was arrested for Taseer's murder, many *ulama* spoke out in support of him. His legal team compiled a religious defence of his actions and when Mumtaz Qadri was eventually executed by the state in 2016, crowds thronged the streets with no end in sight. By some estimates, his funeral was attended by 100,000 people.

Many lay Muslims as well as most clerics in Pakistan embrace individuals who extrajudicially murder Prophet-insulters. But what are religious reasoning underpinning these gruesome acts and what, if any, alternative religious opinions are available to devout Muslims who wonder whether their religion really does require such violence?

A variety of terms are used in pre-modern Islamic legal texts to describe the crime of insulting Muhammad. These terms include: *shatam* (abuse), *sabb* (abuse, insult), *lan* (cursing) and *tan* (accusing, attacking). Even in Islam's early years, the act of insulting Muhammad was viewed by *many* scholars as meriting the death penalty as long as the insulter was a mentally competent adult who committed the act without duress. Many Islamic legal texts attest to this perspective. A case in point is the founder of the Maliki legal school, Malik ibn Anas (d. 795), who stated that anyone who insults the Prophet must be executed.

The earliest texts of legal schools did not equate *sabb al-rasul* with apostasy. This association began around the ninth century and has persisted. The thirteenth and fourteenth centuries were an especially important period for discussions of *sabb al-rasul*. The most prominent works of this era include those by the Shafii scholar Taqi al-Din al-Subki (d. 1355) and the Hanbali jurist and theologian Taqi al-Din ibn Taymiyya (d. 1328). Both al-Subki and ibn Taymiyya write in favour of the commonly accepted view of the time that *sabb al-rasul* by a Muslim renders the Muslim an apostate and the insulter must be killed. They draw on the Quran, *sunnah*, prior legal texts and events from Islamic history to formulate and defend their stance.

An event from early Islamic history that features prominently in ibn Taymiyya's arguments regarding blasphemy is an incident in which Umar, who would eventually be appointed as the second caliph, decapitated a Muslim who refused to accept the Prophet Muhammad's decision regarding a legal issue. The Muslim had first consulted Muhammad but was unhappy with his ruling. He (along with the Jewish person with whom he was disputing) came to Umar to discuss the same matter. The Muslim revealed that he was unhappy with Muhammad's judgment. Umar asked him to wait, then returned wielding a sword and decapitated him on the spot. The Muslim's crime: insulting Muhammad by refusing to accept his legal judgement. Ibn Taymiyya cites the above incident, amongst others, to conclude that it is a religious requirement to execute a Prophet-insulter. The above incident and ibn Taymiyya's writings in general are frequently cited by Pakistani *ulama* in asserting the religious validity of the extrajudicial killing of a Prophet-insulter in contemporary Pakistan.

Where do Pakistani *ulama* stand?

In his monograph, his speeches and sermons, Mufti Hanif Qureshi, who is often credited with spurring Mumtaz Qadri to murder Governor Salman Taseer, asserts a commonly held stance by Pakistani *ulama*: any Muslim who insults Muhammad is a Prophet-insulter deserving the death penalty. Moreover, for Hanif Qureshi and many other Pakistani *ulama*, any individual who kills a Prophet-insulter is to be lauded. Such an extrajudicial killing is a merit-worthy act, not a crime. In formulating his argument on this matter, Hanif Qureshi draws on the writings of the internationally renowned Pakistani scholar Tahir ul-Qadri who, like Hanif Qureshi, belongs to the popular Barelawi school. In his book *Tahaffuz-i Namus-i Risalat*, Tahir ul-Qadri also mentions the incident of Umar unceremoniously decapitating a Muslim who hesitated to abide by Muhammad's judgement. Qadri and Qureshi argue that this incident informs the revelation of Quranic verse 4:60, which states, 'Have you not seen those who claim to have believed in what was revealed to you, [O Muhammad], and what was revealed before you? They wish to refer legislation to *tagut* [unjust tyrants], while they were commanded to reject it; and Satan wishes to lead them far astray.'

Qadri and Qureshi turn to a variety of Quranic exegetical texts to substantiate their stance. These works include the multivolume compendium *al-Tafsir al-Mazhari* by the South Asian scholar Qazi Sanaullah Usmani Panipati (d. 1810) and the seminal Quranic commentary *al-Tafsir al-Kashshaf*, by the Central Asian scholar al-Zamakhshari (d. 1143/4). *Al-Tafsir al-Kashshaf* notes that Muhammad was incredulous when informed that Umar had decapitated a fellow Muslim. The *tafsir* explains that the Prophet's concerns were allayed when Quranic verse 4:65 was revealed. The verse states: 'But no, by your Lord, they will not [truly] believe until they make you, [O Muhammad], judge concerning that over which they dispute among themselves and then find within themselves no discomfort from what you have judged and submit in [full, willing] submission.' *Al-Tafsir al-Kashshaf* asserts that the verse was revealed in Umar's defence and absolved Umar of all blame by explaining that anyone who does not accept Muhammad's decisions is not a believer. *Al-Tafsir al-Mazhari* adds another layer of validity to Umar's act by stating that the angel Gabriel appeared to Muhammad to declare Umar's innocence by stating, 'Indeed, Umar has differentiated between truth and falsehood.'

This incident has become central to arguments by contemporary Pakistani *ulama* when they defend extrajudicial killings of alleged Prophet-insulters. For example, Mufti Muhammad Khan Qadri and Muhammad Khalil ur-Rahman Qadri – both affiliated with Jamia Islamiyya in Lahore – mention this incident in asserting the religious legitimacy of Mumtaz Qadri's killing of Salman Taseer. In fact, many *ulama* state that based on the above incident the killer of a Prophet-insulter should be commended, not reprimanded or imprisoned. Hanif Qureshi goes so far as to state that Islam encourages such killings.

There is a great deal of sensationalised coverage of this perspective – both in the international and local media. This discourse drowns out important dissenting voices and the diversity of Islamic perspectives on the act of insulting Muhammad.

A key figure who challenges the commonly accepted view is Ammar Khan Nasir, a Deobandi alim based in Gujranwala who is the grandson of the renowned Deobandi scholar Sarfaraz Khan Safdar and the son of the prominent Deobandi scholar Zahid ur-Rashidi . Nasir's academic credentials are impressive and lend his views a significance that cannot be easily dismissed. He undertook years of personalised religious education with his father and grandfather, and graduated in 1994 with his alimiyya degree from Madrasa Nusrat al-Ulum in Gujranwala. He currently edits the popular journal al-Shari'a.

In a treatise that spans over a hundred pages Nasir engages with the intricacies of Islamic legal literature on *sabb al-rasul* in formulating his arguments on the possible punishments for the act of insulting Muhammad. He constructs his argument along a variety of key register and challenges the commonly held position as well as questions the validity of the Umar incident.

In addressing the question of what punishment should be meted out to a Prophet-insulter, Nasir explains that Muslim and non-Muslim Prophet-insulters were classified differently in early Islamic legal texts. Non-Muslims living in Muslim lands entered into contracts whereby they paid taxes in exchange for protection. Nasir acknowledges that for the majority of legal schools insulting Muhammad terminates the contract of protection and renders a non-Muslim *mubah ad-dam*, that is, a person who can be killed extrajudicially without the killing being considered a crime.

Importantly, Nasir explains that the Hanafi legal school – the legal school to which the majority of Pakistanis belong – held a different opinion. Early Hanafis viewed insulting the Prophet as an expression of unbelief. A non-Muslim Prophet-insulter was already a disbeliever. Hence in the eyes of the early Hanafis, a non-Muslim's act of insulting Muhammad did not change the insulter's status or terminate their contract of protection.

Nasir provides copious references from established sources to convince his readers. One amongst the many quotations supporting Nasir's perspective is that of the North African Hanafi scholar Abu Jafar Ahmad ibn Muhammad al-Tahawi. Al-Tahawi states: 'If a non-Muslim, who has entered into a contract [of protection with the Muslim ruler], insults Muhammad, his contract is not broken. He will be told not to repeat the act. If he persists, he will be punished, but he will not be killed.' Nasir also rightly notes that Ibn Taymiyya, in his work The Unsheathed Sword Against Whoever Insults the Messenger (al-Sarim al-Maslul ala Shatim al-Rasul), acknowledges that in Hanafi law, a non-Muslim Prophet-insulter is still due protection and should not be harmed.

The importance of Nasir's arguments and interventions cannot be overstated. Recall the case of Priyantha Diyawadanage, the Sri Lankan who was beaten to death by a mob in December 2021. If Nasir's arguments and findings are amplified in the contemporary Pakistani context and begin to be accepted as an established Hanafi position, it would mean that the killing of non-Muslims such as Priyantha Diyawadanage would be understood as religiously impermissible.

Nasir's writings also feature detailed discussions regarding the Muslim Prophet-insulter. He explains that classical Hanafi scholars viewed a Muslim who insults the Prophet as having become an apostate. The rules that apply to all apostates then apply to the Muslim Prophet-insulter. Amongst these rules is forgiveness for apostasy if the criminal repents. As with his discussion of the non-Muslim Prophet-insulter, Nasir provides references from highly regarded Sunni scholars to bolster his argument. Amongst the scholars he mentions is Ibn Taymiyya, who writes that a Muslim Prophet-insulter is allowed to repent. Similarly, Abd Allah ibn Abbas, an important scholar of the Qur'an and *sunnah* features in Nasir's work. Ibn Abbas states explicitly: 'Any Muslim who insults God, Muhammad or any other prophet has committed an act equivalent to apostasy [i.e. an act of apostasy]. He will be asked to repent. If he does so, then all is well, otherwise he will be killed.'

In sum, Nasir's detailed evidence-laden treatise effectively argues that the extrajudicial killings of Prophet-insulters and the carefully crafted arguments of many contemporary Pakistani Sunni *ulama* are a deviation from early Hanafi teachings on *sabb al-rasul*. Moreover, Nasir details that a shift occurred in Hanafi opinions on *sabb al-rasul* in the fourteenth century whereby the possibility of repentance for the Muslim Prophet-insulter came to be replaced by a mandatory death penalty for the crime. Nasir's characterisation of this shift is supported by secondary scholarship. Ibn al-Bazzaz, a Crimean scholar, is often cited as helping to establish the now-common view that a Prophet-insulter should be executed without recourse to repentance. Ibn al-Bazzaz's stance was adopted by Ottoman jurists, amongst them the chief *muftis* of the empire (*shuyukh al-Islam*). Around the fifteenth century, the view that the Prophet-insulter ought to be executed without recourse to repentance had become the dominant position of the Hanafi school.

Several key Hanafis in later centuries worked tirelessly to discredit this innovation. Amongst them were Husam Chelebi and Ibn Abidin. However, their efforts largely came to naught and, amongst most later Hanafis, insulting Muhammad became a crime for which there was no possibility for repentance.

Nasir's factually correct position on the early Hanafi view and the possibility of repentance for the Muslim Prophet-insulter is supported in contemporary Pakistan by Nasir's own father Zahid ur-Rashidi, who has marshalled evidence in defence of his son's perspective. This evidence includes statements from one of the most well-regarded Hanafi scholars of South Asia, Ibn Abidin, as well as from a key early Hanafi, Imam Abu Yusuf. Abu Yusuf was one of the two most famous students of Abu Hanifa, the founder of the Hanafi legal school. Both Ibn Abidin and Imam Abu Yusuf clearly state that a Muslim Prophet-insulter who repents is spared the death penalty.

In addition to the above-mentioned trove of evidence refuting the view that it is always religiously necessary to execute a Prophet-insulter, Nasir also mounts an additional attack. He challenges the veracity of the oft-mentioned incident of Umar decapitating a Muslim who insulted Muhammad.

Breaking from conventional appraisals of this incident, Nasir asserts that the authenticity of the Umar event is dubious. He undertakes a rigorous analysis of the *isnad*, the chain of transmission used to determine the veracity of a report about the Prophet's words and actions. Nasir powerfully and dexterously marshals the methodology of *hadith* verification to challenge the Umar incident. He shows that both of the chains of transmission by which this incident is passed down are broken. In other words, the incident's historical veracity cannot be conclusively determined and the unverifiable incident cannot be used to definitively conclude that all Prophet-insulters should be killed. Moreover, Nasir asserts, that logical thinking leads to the conclusion that the incident is baseless and fabricated. In particular, Nasir argues that Umar was not a rash person; and the alleged decapitation of a Muslim would have resulted in mass unrest. Nasir details that there is no record of this unrest in historical or exegetical works of the time. Thus, Nasir concludes that the Umar incident is fabricated. In sum, Nasir's extensive treatise on *sabb al-rasul* convincingly posits that a prominent, established perspective within Hanafi law does not allow extrajudicial killings of Prophet-insulters.

A different strand of argumentation that also arrives at the conclusion that extrajudicial killings of Prophet-insulters are un-Islamic is articulated by some contemporary Pakistani *ulama* who formulate their arguments around the issues of anarchy and lawlessness. This strand of argumentation is concerned solely with extrajudicial killings, unlike Nasir's detailed critique.

The general maxim of recognising state authority and according it due respect is popular amongst Pakistani ulama. The journal al-Shari'a's March 2012 special issue discusses this topic in detail. The views of several dozen contemporary Pakistani ulama feature in the special issue – these ulama draw on Islamic legal sources to condemn anarchy and argue against vigilante justice.

Several renowned *ulama* who view Islamic law as condemning lawlessness also explicitly apply this prohibition against lawlessness to extrajudicial killings of Prophet insulters. Amongst these *ulama* are the Barelawi *alim* Irfan Mashadi, the Deobandi *alim* Mawlana Tahir Ashrafi who chairs the Pakistan Ulema Council, and the Deobandi *alim* Mufti Muhammad Naim, who teaches at the renowned seminary Jamia Binnoriyya in Karachi. Commenting on the issue of extrajudicially killing a Prophet-insulter, Mufti Muhammad Naim stated that, 'from an Islamic ethico-legal (*shari*) perspective, no individual person has the right to take the law into his own hands. If men start killing each other, there will be lawlessness and anarchy in the country … So it was not right for Mumtaz Qadri to commit this act.'

Nasir's meticulously researched and reasoned critique of the commonly accepted position amongst contemporary Pakistani Sunni *ulama* appears to have had little impact beyond igniting debate in scholarly circles. Even in scholarly circles, Nasir's views have frequently faced resistance. For example, Nasir's father Zahir ur-Rashidi – while defending the veracity of his son's facts and the intellectual merit of Nasir's arguments – states that he himself believes that the most stringent of punishments, the death penalty, ought to be meted out to Prophet-insulters.

Importantly, there is a key grass-roots initiative in Pakistan promoting the same general perspective as that of Nasir. Leading the helm of this initiative is Arafat Mazhar, who founded the organisation Engage, which aims to study and reform religious laws in Pakistan. Mazhar has written several detailed public scholarship pieces on blasphemy in *Dawn*, one of the leading English-language daily newspapers in Pakistan. One of his articles aims to highlight the permissibility of repentance for the Prophet-insulter as – in his words – the authentic Hanafi position. In another of his articles, Mazhar notes that Ahmed Raza Khan Barelawi (the founder of the Barelawi movement), Mahmud Hasan Deobandi (a key early figure of the Deoband movement), and about 450 other *ulama* from around the world signed a juridical opinion (*fatwa*) on blasphemy. A copy of the *fatwa* can be accessed in the book *An Explicit Victory and a Warning Against the Wahabis (Fath al-Mubeen Tanbeeh al-Wahabin)*. The *fatwa* details that a non-Muslim Prophet-insulter is not deserving of death unless they insult habitually and frequently. In other words, according to the key figures of the Barelawi and Deobandi movements, the hundreds of non-Muslims who have recently been killed in Pakistan for allegedly committing one act of insult did not deserve to die since their insults were not habitual and frequent.

Arafat Mazhar also describes the uphill battle he faces in convincing *ulama* and religious leaders of other backgrounds to come out in support of the position that blasphemy is a pardonable offence. In one of his articles, he details how the scholars he met agreed with his stance and the research on which the stance is founded. However, they refused to sign, stamp, or endorse this position since they did not think that it would serve the public good (*maslihat*). Their reasoning was that publicising the possibility of pardon for blasphemy would promote the agenda of 'secular' forces.

While Mazhar and Nasir face an uphill battle against many religious leaders set in their views that blasphemy must be punished by death, it is not clear to what extent the Pakistani public is open to accepting the early Hanafi path of repentance and non-violence. As more public scholarship is published and additional outreach campaigns directly targeting the public are initiated it is possible that extrajudicial killings, such as those of Safoora Bibi and Salman Taseer, might decline. I therefore end by reiterating Nasir's important voice and those of likeminded Muslims, who highlight the diversity of Islamic legal opinions on the issue of *sabb al-rasul*. Crucially, they bring to public notice that some long-held and firmly established opinions within the Islamic legal canon actually condemn the killings of Prophet-insulters.

DANGEROUS LIAISONS

Amandla Thomas-Johnson

How did it come to pass that twenty years after neoconservatives launched their 'war on terror', self-proclaimed Muslim leaders were queuing up to ingratiate themselves to a mainstreamed far-right headed by Donald Trump? Forget those four to five million people who were killed as a result of the 9/11 wars, better we embark on a 'war on woke'. To be sure, the 'war on terror' had cast Muslims as both external and internal enemies, severely curtailing their political possibilities. As imams self-censored, politics disappeared from the Friday pulpit. A supposed war against Islamism made every Muslim a potential target. Meanwhile, under the guise of 'counterterrorism', a new generation of Muslims, born after 9/11, was integrated into the American nation-state – domesticated. Muslim politics turned inwards to the private realm.

Yet the intellectual Guantanamo in which Western Muslims found themselves confined after 9/11 was but one reason for the pivot to the hard right. According to the recent book by the Islamic studies scholar, Walaa Quisay, *Neo-Traditionalism in Islam in the West*, Muslim leaders such as the American traditionalist Hamza Yusuf felt Muslim-Left-wing alliances forged in the early days of the war on terror had skewed the 'metaphysical lens' of Muslims. 'Our discourse is troubling,' Yusuf cautioned young Muslim students in 2017, 'they seem to derive from dark luminaries as Derrida, Foucault, and their influence from Karl Marx.' Instead, Yusuf sought an 'alliance of virtue' with willing evangelical Christians and Jews. He even took up a seat on a human rights panel set up by Donald Trump, a man he described as 'God's servant'.

Hamza Yusuf is just a symptom of a rising tendency among Muslims on both sides of the Atlantic to find allies on the hard and far right. This includes the Canadian psychologist Jordan Peterson and the English Conservative Philosopher Roger Scruton who were both courted by Yusuf. Andrew Tate, the self-proclaimed 'misogynist' influencer has found an audience with younger Muslim males. But as Yahya Birt, the eagle-eyed British historian writes, this snuggling up to brazen reactionaries comes while Euro-America is going 'through a wave of populism that is pandering to ideas around Western superiority and white ethno-nationalism.'

Like many in the West, Muslims fear that the pace of social change has become overwhelming. Certainties are being challenged and traditional norms – about family, gender, and identity – upended. Space for religious expression has evaporated in the face of a marauding, triumphant liberal secularism. I doubt that these are necessarily recent phenomena, but they are being felt (or made to feel) as such. With this in mind, some feel the need to take sides. Even though the Western order has its shortcomings, best not to abandon to the barbarians at the gates. We are in spiritual decline. The end days are at hand.

Since Ancient Greece, just who the barbarians are remains unclear. Republicans baying to dismantle environmental protections in the world's largest polluter? Or those Muslims, natives of so-called 'shithole countries' and victims of Trump's 'Muslim ban'?

The Islamophobic pronouncements of some of his hard-right interlocutors have failed to deter Yusuf. Instead, his sights have been firmly set on 'victimhood culture', of which anti-racism is a supreme avatar. For Yusuf, injustice and inequality is a metaphysical fact we should learn to accept and live with, a test from God. Black Lives Matter protesters should just suck it up. Other neo-traditionalists, such as Abdul Hakeem Murad of Cambridge Muslim college, have turned to Italian far-right philosopher and fascist metaphysician, Julius Evola for guidance. Evola thought Mussolini rather too mild. For Murad, Evola's thought helps to explain our current age of moral decline, far away from the halcyon days when God was in charge and Gregorian chant rang through gothic abbeys. According to Murad, Evola presages the 'last of days' where 'the current breakdown of tradition, monarchy, order, natural hierarchy, and a sense of the sacred' are upended. The post-Christian angst, shared with Evola and other

Conservative forces, means that this alliance goes beyond the politics of the here and now and appears more as an alliance of worldviews. A problem with this take on Western spiritual decadence is that the highpoint of old Christendom coincides with the old anti-Jewish pogroms, the Crusades, and the Spanish Inquisition, before African enslavement and indigenous genocide in the Americas. What Yusuf and Murad and their allies view as a harmonious past is one replete with historical crime. Little wonder efforts to address the legacies of those crimes – such as the Black Lives Matter movement – generate an almost apocalyptic foreboding.

None of this, of course, means that the current state of the world is above reproach. But retreating to an ostensible metaphysical realm to describe it is fanciful at best and dangerous at worst. It gives their opinions on everything from history, to politics, social justice, race, and gender – their entire description of the world as it is – a Godly sanction, even when they rely more on fascist thought than holy writ or social analysis. It betrays an embarrassing anti-intellectualism, at odds with traditions of Muslim thought.

Their decline and fall of Western civilisation thesis or Muslim millenarianism does not account for how our current economic order has served to alter identities and culture, as for example, has been argued by Fredric Jameson in *Postmodernism, The Cultural Logic of Late Capitalism*. Ziauddin Sardar has critiqued the cultural imperative and imperialistic tendencies of postmodernism, as well as its 'mission to destroy, absorb and relativise all claims to reality and truth.' However, it would be hard to make such powerful arguments without invoking Marx – and the neo-traditionalist have either no awareness of these arguments or chose to ignore them because of their dislike of left leaning scholars. Rather, some twenty years after the war on terror appeared to bring into view what some navel-gazing Western strategists imagined was a clash of civilisations, Anglo-American neo-traditionalist chose to forge alliances with the far right and unsavoury American conservatives.

On 7th October 2023, as they roused for morning prayers, they found knives in their beds.

As news of a Palestinian attack on military positions and settlements in Southern Israel began to emerge, I was on my way to Communist Cuba, to speak at a conference at the University of Havana. While the US's full-blooded support for Israel's blitzkrieg butchery had yet to fully dawn, its commitment to the slow death of Cuba was all too evident. Food shortages, power cuts, and a lack of medical supplies, resulting from the longest blockade in US history. Backed into a corner, the Communist Party are making capitalist market reforms which could soon mean 'the game is up', the British journalist Ed Augustin told me. Inequality has grown amid claims of governmental corruption. Since 2021, half a million people – or 5 per cent of the population – have left.

Knowing that left has become a filthy word in the popular Muslim discourse, here was my chance to see what a leftist state was actually like. Anti-communist propaganda would have us believe that Cuba would be full of human automatons, phalanxes of armed police patrolling the streets, and portraits of Fidel Castro swinging from old crucifixes outside shuttered churches. But here I was in a communist state that has been the most enduring symbol of resistance to the wiles of US imperialism; one that has been a consistent ally to the Palestinians in their struggle for decades. Still, I wanted to take up Yusuf and Murad's vantage point and ask what came to view through Cuba's metaphysical lens.

Santería, salsa, and cigar smoke aside, It was hard to see much in the space of a week. But it was telling how little Cubans, as hard-up as they were, begged or bothered us for anything. I felt almost unwelcome in a street market when the sellers showed little appetite to hawk me their cigars and trinkets. Taxi drivers didn't take up the opportunity to rip us off. Our Cuban friends were shy to ask and shy to receive. The dignity and integrity I saw in Cubans was best summed up by an Algerian Muslim cashier I spoke to on the night I arrived back home to Ithaca, the Upstate New York town in which I live. 'Those Cubans, ah, they have great *akhlaq!*', an Arabic word that in Islamic terminology means etiquette.

While Muslim leaders had above all else drawn attention to the secular elements of some leftist discourse, they have ignored the basic material wellbeing has on the spiritual. Not that the Cubans, queuing for bread beneath crumbling porticos, had much to show off about. But it is possible that by meeting their basic needs in the form of free healthcare, free education, and affordable housing, the Communist Party may have prevented their people from falling into an overwhelming spiritual despair. Structural inequalities and dispossession in the United States, most terrifyingly manifested in soaring rates of black men swept from their families into prisons or native American reservations beset by alcoholism, not to mention babies separated from their mothers at the border with Mexico, can only be the source of acute spiritual malaise. Yet the 'woke' activists have been made into the problem.

It was also clear that Cuba's metaphysical lens had been scrubbed somewhat clean of capitalist excess and its attendant spiritual afflictions in stark contrast to the US. To be sure, no place, Cuba including, is perfect, and free of the cardinal social sins. Violent *machismo* was wickedly displayed one night in Havana's old town with a loud slap across a woman's face. Anti-black racism is still deeply embedded within the society, a Caribbean ambassador informed me over lunch.

Yet, it seemed ironic that the atheist communists may have understood the link between the material and spiritual well-being of a people more than today's self-proclaimed 'Sheiks' and Muslim leaders. Such a tradition stretches back to the early days of Islam with Umar Ibn Al-Khattab's attempt at redistributive justice and the creation of a welfare state.

This is so easy for Yusuf and Murad to miss because these two middle-class highly-educated white male converts to Islam take for granted who they are and where they are speaking from. It is one thing to think about the future of the Muslim world from the comforts of the United States, whose shaky moral foundations, of enslavement and indigenous genocide, cause constant shivers of existential dread even when – as we are now seeing in Gaza and Yemen – it can, at the flip of a dime, wipe the poor, the damned, the other, from the face of the earth. The United States is a place that prods its citizens to assimilate and dislocate from the rest of the world.

To view the Muslim world from Cuba reveals solidarities and longings suppressed by an unholy obsession to anathematise anything remotely 'left'. Cuba, unjustly designated a 'state sponsor of terror' by the US; the site of the Guantanamo Bay detention facility; and as the only country in the Western Hemisphere to not recognise Israeli sovereignty over Palestine. Cuba, whether we like it or not, as a primordial guerrilla to US hegemony, is a beacon for a different kind of world.

From Cuba, 'left' looks very different – more like us.

I arrived back in the US from Cuba in mid-October, to sensations and scenes reminiscent of those I had felt in the months and years after 9/11;

ones I experienced as a Muslim teenager, a student, then as a reporter. Calls for unbridled vengeance; the likening of human populations to animals; the exclusive demand for Muslims to condemn; and unbridled Western support for yet another war in the Middle East, passionately supported by a spineless media. The war on terror has returned.

Back at Cornell, an Ivy league university in Upstate New York, where I study and teach, students had begun to organise in response to Israel's 'complete siege' of Gaza city, where there would be, in the words of the far-right Defence Minister, Yoav Gallant, 'no electricity, no food, no fuel' and everything would be 'closed'. They were further riled by a number of impulsive statements released in the wake of 7 October by university president, Martha Pollack, which had run into difficulties mentioning the word 'Palestinian'. Meanwhile, Zionist students rallied, holding vigils and hanging posters for the Israeli hostages in campus corridors.

The situation quickly escalated after Russell Rickford, a brilliant and conscientious Black historian and perhaps the most vociferous supporter of the Palestinians of any faculty, came under fire for comments made at a pro-Palestine rally. A video of his speech where he had said that Palestinians had 'challenged the monopoly of violence' had circulated on social media, but with the parts that provided the vital context to his words strategically muted, the captioning paused. A campaign for his dismissal – egged on by the *Daily Mail* and the Murdoch-owned *New York Post* – intensified with multiple petitions, protests, and high-level meetings of university officials, while a billboard truck with his likeness next to the words 'antisemite' drove around the campus. It seemed that many ordinary people and political elites in the US were implacably pro-Israeli, unrepentantly Zionist.

Two events convinced me otherwise.

One was the march on Washington, the largest pro-Palestinian march in history, where I saw indigenous people, Black people, Euro-Americans, Latinx communities hold placards and chant freedom 'from the river to the sea'.

The other were the students at Cornell. They followed the tactical masterstroke of cutting off the billboard bus and bringing it to a halt at road junction using hire bikes with the strategic one of forging the Coalition for Mutual Liberation, an alliance of students– including Jews, Latinx, Euro-American, Black, and Asian students – committed to eradicating oppression across the board. The Muslim student body which had limited their activity to social events and religious observance, thankfully, also joined the coalition. After a three-day campus occupation that made national headlines (including again in the *Daily Mail*) the Coalition won concessions from the university which vowed to crack down on doxing, the odious slandering of pro-Palestinian activists online by Zionist students and organisations like Canary Mission. (Cornell students were so afraid of doxing that they wore covid masks and hoodies to hide their identities during television interviews.) The university has also agreed to meet with students about divestment from companies supporting the Israeli war and occupation.

Things were different at other top-tier universities. After testifying at a congressional hearing on pro-Palestine activism and alleged antisemitism on their campuses, then coming under pressure from wealthy Conservative pro-Israel donors, the presidents of the University of Pennsylvania and of Harvard, resigned.

These aggressive campaigns to stifle activism and debate on campuses show that American elites have lost ground at the very institutions that are supposed to replenish their number, ensuring their dominance. Universities like Cornell and Harvard, Jamaican critic Sylvia Wynter argues, help to cultivate, the 'inner eye' with which future leaders will view and in effect, decide the fates of vast human populations – as much the Palestinians as the Israelis as their own elite segment. Their fears are borne out by seismic demographic shifts in attitudes toward Israel and the Palestinians, with recent polling showing the majority of young Americans backing the Palestinians, with those over 30 supporting Israel.

Cornell's student coalition is a reminder that there is a global majority in support of the Palestinians. The apocalyptic anxieties of US conservatives, which neo-traditionalist 'Sheikhs' have adopted as their own, are as much to do with a shift to a multipolar world – where China, Russia, and India, as well as South Africa, Turkey, Pakistan, and various developing nations need no longer adhere to US foreign policy directives – as it is about a perceived unravelling domestic situation.

Should we turn to these rising giants for succour in these awful times? As multipolarity opens doors it closes some: ask the Uyghurs about the Chinese, Muslims and scheduled castes in India, or victims of Russian massacres, be they in Ukraine, Syria, or Mali. By flouting its own rules and norms, the West may have enabled the BRICS. But by what rules do the newcomers play?

There are few viable political options within Western countries where multiparty parliaments have fused into one-party cartels backing Israeli no matter what it does, how it violates human rights and norms of human decency - from Berlin to Canberra to London to DC. That we can witness a genocide streamed live over Aljazeera and on X – not to mention others in Congo and Sudan and Ethiopia that are taking place in total silence – is a damning indictment of Western culture and civilisation. Sylvia Wynter, argues we need to create a new kind of human, beyond the Euro-American model of 'man' who has been so violently imposed on the world: a 'man' who is chiefly motivated by economic self-interest. Muslims pinning their hopes on an unravelling Western project betray a worrying lack of self-confidence and perception. I am not the first to say that Muslims need to draw on their tradition while remaining open to the world as it is, to stimulate fresh thinking, ideas, and knowledge, not just for themselves but humanity at large. It may be a thankless and perhaps unpopular task, but a necessary one.

In his recent book, *Islam and Anarchism*, Mohamed Abdou, North African-Egyptian interdisciplinary activist-scholar, attempts to do just this, drawing on the spirit of the Prophet Muhammad's Medina charter to think about what he calls 'affinity-based' solidarities, enduring alliances between communities and cultures that are based on shared decolonial and ethical commitments rather than ones reactively cobbled together whenever the need arises. Instead of rushing to integrate into an American Dream in a country that then uses their tax dollars to strafe the very countries they fled from, Abdou calls on Muslim migrants in the US and Canada to understand their complicity in settler-colonialism and predatory capitalism, and identify with indigenous and Black movements who are seeking land back and reparations respectively. Abdou's book, which has gained traction since it was published in 2022, will force us to think beyond the frames we take for granted, of nation-states, political parties, and governments, of left and right, and far beyond the options recent history has presented to Muslims: an inevitable clash of civilisations or a convenient alliance with far-right and ultra conservatives.

TEN SCOTTISH THINGS

What distinguishes Scotland from the rest of the world? If you were to ask people at random, a flurry of responses are likely to emerge. The Scottish folks themselves would try to differentiate themselves from their neighbours in England – who they often outshine. Here is our list of ten things which while not uniquely Scottish are nevertheless Scotland writ large.

1. Midges

The midge is Scotland's equivalent to the mosquito. It may be even worse than the mosquito, and is worst of all in the west of Scotland, especially over peaty soil (the east, on the other hand, excels in tics). The midge is never found in the singular, but in the mass – it's not the midge, but midges, clouds and plagues of them. They crawl over faces until minds are lost. They are capable of penetrating clothes, and aim unerringly for the warmest, most sensitive spots, for groins and armpits and the like. Tourists are hereby warned not to visit the Highlands in the summer months when the midges are out in strength. Spring and autumn are safer. But if you are foolish enough to experience the Scottish summer, be sure to be inside at dusk, which is the midging hour – or failing that to stand above a very big bonfire. You might choke on the smoke, but that will seem to be the better option.

2. Novelists

For such a small country, Scotland has produced a very large number of successful novelists. They include classical figures like Tobias Smollett and Walter Scott, and writers whose creations are known globally – such as Robert Louis Stevenson, who invented Dr Jekyll and Mr Hyde, and Arthur Conan Doyle, who invented Sherlock Holmes. There's also the crime writer Ian Rankin, and the chronicler of the ugly underbelly, Irvine Welsh. And the literary-fiction blockbusters AL Kennedy and Ali Smith. And many more. *CM* recommends in particular James Kelman, and his prizewinning novel *How Late it Was, How Late* – tragic-comic, brutal, and entirely written in Glasgow dialect – which does take some getting used to.

3. Scientists

As with the arts, so with the sciences – Scotland has often punched above its weight. James Watt (steam engine), Alexander Fleming (penicillin), John Logie Baird (television), Alexander Graham Bell (telephone), and James Clarke Maxwell (electromagnetics) are some of the world-changing inventors and thinkers to originate here. And why is tarmac called tarmac? Because it's a kind of tar invented by John McAdam. The world's first stretch of surfaced road is near McAdam's old house at Carsphairn, in south west Scotland.

4. Haggis

A haggis is a mix of oats, spices, and chopped-up offal stuffed into a sheep's stomach. It should be cooked, and served with tatties and neeps, that is potatoes and turnip – or what the English call suede. Like many 'national' dishes, haggis was once a meal of the poor. Today it's a delicacy, as well as a chip shop favourite. To try the authentic version, buy it from a recommended Scottish butcher, not from the supermarket. These days there's no excuse to shirk the adventure. Not only are there vegetarian and vegan versions of haggis, there's a halal haggis too!

5. Whisky

As far as we're aware, there's not yet such a thing as halal whisky – but this hasn't dented its popularity in Muslim countries any more than anywhere else. There's long been a whisky black market in Saudi Arabia, for instance. Like cocaine, the reach of this substance is global. Bottles of Scotch turn up in Southeast Asian village shops as surely as they do in European airport outlets. Once, every other Highland home housed its own still. Today –

after centuries of state regulation closing out the little man, whisky is an industry worth six billion pounds a year.

6. Fish

Not much of Scotland is arable land. It's too rain-sodden or peaty or windswept or bare. Only rugged breeds of sheep and cattle do well in its fields. But there is a compensation: its rivers contain perch and pike and salmon and trout. The latter two fish in particular are rich enough in oily nutrients to make up for any deficiencies implied by geography and climate.

7. Water

It's no surprise that Scotland is abundant in fish when it's so abundant in water. It has rivers, lochs (lakes) and sea lochs, as well as lochans (small lochs), and ubiquitous burns (streams). Look on the map and you'll see that the northern third of Scotland is almost separated from the rest by a continuous line of lochs. The North Sea and the Irish Sea, meanwhile, pound against its cliffs. Western Scotland is one of the rainiest places on earth. In the winter it can rain for days without a break. In the summer, the dripping humidity and the abundant greenery gives corners of the country a tropical feel. Scots make good use of their watery resource, and not just for drinking, fishing, and swimming. Grand hydro-electric schemes cover the country, as do wind turbines. In 2022, over ninety percent of Scotland's energy was generated from renewable sources. As for the non-human inhabitants of the country, sea and river birds, and seals, dolphins, and whales, all benefit from our still reasonably clean water.

8. Oil

Oil is yet another of Scotland's valuable liquids – though this one these days is more controversial than whisky. From the 1960s to 2014, an estimated 42 billion barrels of oil were extracted from the North Sea. The profits flooded British state coffers in the 1980s, helping to fund Mrs Thatcher's privatisations and tax cuts. If only – nationalists mutter – an independent Scotland had invested then in its own national oil fund, as Norway did, then Scotland today would be as comfortable as Scandinavia. Somewhere between 12 and 24 billion barrels of oil are estimated to remain under the sea. They could potentially enrich an independent Scotland in the future, but nobody really wants to say so. Unlike Rishi Sunak's Westminster government, Scotland's local rulers understand the dangers of fossil fuels. The Green Party is part of Scotland's coalition government, after all.

9. Schemes

Scotland certainly needs enriching. Despite the profits from oil and whisky, and from natural power and tourism, poverty and social deprivation persist. They are most apparent in the schemes – or what in England are called housing estates. Most were built between the 1950s and 1970s, and were supposedly intended to improve the lives of working class people previously crammed into inner-city tenements. The old tenements were demolished, which left space for redesigning the inner cities. But the residents were generally moved out of the cities to more isolated locations – like the notorious Easterhouse scheme. The new residential blocks were poorly designed and constructed, and usually had no shops or recreational facilities in the vicinity. Unsurprisingly, the inhabitants suffered disproportionately from health and social problems. In the 1980s, for instance, Scotland had both the highest murder rate and the highest AIDS rate in Europe. The AIDS infections were in turn a symptom of terribly high levels of heroin addiction. Addicts shared needles – and disease – in the 'shooting galleries' in the basements of tower blocks.

10. Festivals

In the last three weeks of August each year, the Edinburgh International Festival showcases music, dance, and drama from everywhere. When the Fringe Festival – at which anybody can perform, not just recognised artists – is added to the International Festival, Edinburgh's is the largest performing arts event in the world. In 2022, for instance, over 3,300 shows were performed by artists and companies from 63 countries. It isn't easy to find a place to sleep in Edinburgh in August, but if you do find accommodation, you don't need a lot of money to enjoy the acts. Alongside the expensive formal events, there are free street performances, and thousands of very cheap plays, concerts, and comedy shows. Scotland also offers the Wigtown Book Festival in October, and a range of small-scale music festivals. Of these, CM recommends the Knockengorroch Festival (at the end of May), for its friendliness, non-commercial atmosphere, and location in the Galloway uplands.

CITATIONS

Introduction: Highlands and Lowlands
by Robin Yassin-Kassab

Scotland's involvement with slavery is considered in Stephen Mullen's *It Wisnae Us: the Truth about Glasgow and Slavery*. The Royal Incorporation of Architects in Scotland, 2009. There is also a website based on the book: https://it.wisnae.us/

The *Trainspotting* Highlands scene can be watched at https://www.youtube.com/watch?v=29-LRuuqFT0

I recommend the following books on Scottish nationalism: T. M. Devine. *Independence or Union: Scotland's Past and Scotland's Present*. Penguin. 2016; Gerry Hassan. *Scotland Rising: The Case for Independence*, Pluto Press. 2022; and Michael Kenny. *Fractured Union: Politics, Sovereignty and the Fight to Save the UK*, C. Hurst and Co. 2024.

For a comprehensive treatment of land ownership issues, read Andy Wightman. *The Poor Had No Lawyers: Who Owns Scotland (And How They Got It)*. Birlinn Limited. 2015.

Scotland's brief attempt at independent imperialism is covered in John Prebble's *The Darien Disaster*, Pimlico, 2002.

You don't need to be a whisky drinker to profit from Neill M. Gunn. *Whisky and Scotland*. Souvenir Press. George Routledge and Sons. 1935. Gunn's modernist novels are also recommended.

My awareness of Hebridean history, religious disputes and faeries was greatly expanded by reading Alastair McIntosh's *Poacher's Pilgrimage: A Journey into Land and Soul*. Birlinn Limited, 2016. McIntosh has written several books on community stewardship of land, the environment, and spirituality – all are worth perusing.

While walking in Glen Affric I met volunteers planting trees. If you wish to spend a holiday rewilding the Scottish Highlands (and if you're ready for midges, tics, and lots of rain), contact them at www.treesforlife.org.uk

My Love for Scotland by Jeremy Henzell-Thomas

I have referred to the following sources:

HRH Prince Alwaleed Bin Talal Centre for the Study of Islam in the Contemporary World, University of Edinburgh, at https://www.ed. ac.uk/literatures-languages-cultures/alwaleed;

'Scottish Inventions.' *Scotland* at https://www.scotland.org/about-scotland/culture/scottish-inventions; Olivia Sterns, 'Muslim inventions that shaped the modern world', *CNN, Inside the Middle East*, 29/1/2010 at https://edition.cnn.com/2010/WORLD/meast/01/29/muslim. inventions/index.html; National Geographic, '1001 Inventions: The Enduring Legacy of Muslim Civilisation', 2012; Bashir Mann, 'Islam and Scotland', *Islamic Tartan*. https://www.islamictartan.com/islam-scotland. php; Donald MacLeod, 'Calvinism in Scotland', *The Aquila Report*, 10/2/2014 at https://theaquilareport.com/calvinism-in-scotland/; Khadijah Elshayyal, 'Scottish Muslims in Numbers: Understanding Scotland's Muslim population through the 2011 Census', Alwaleed Centre for the Study of Islam in the Contemporary World, University of Edinburgh, 2016, at https://www.ed.ac.uk/files/atoms/files/scottish_ muslims_in_numbers_web.pdf; Nafeez Ahmed, 'David Cameron's illiterate proposal to counter radicalisation by targeting Muslim women', 18/1/2016, at https://medium.com/insurge-intelligence/david-cameron-s-illiterate-proposal-to-counter-radicalisation-by-targeting-muslim-womenf6069bfee942#.xxsxte2lw'n; Aysu Bicer and Muhammed Enes Calli, 'Scotland's new first minister inspires young Muslims, but challenges lie ahead'. *AA (Anadolu Ajansi): Politics,World, Europe*, 31/3/2023, at https://www.aa.com.tr/en/europe/scotlands-new-first-minister-inspires-young-muslims-but-challenges-lie-ahead/2860110; Chris Rojek, *Brit-Myth:Who Do the British Think They Are?* (Reaktion Books, London, 2007), 10; 'Scotland is more open to Muslims, claims senior police officer', *The Scotsman*, 13/8/2018; 'Just how welcome are Muslims in Scotland?' *The Herald*, 26/8/2018, at https://www.heraldscotland.com/news/16599716.just-welcome-muslims-scotland/; Stefano Bonino, *Muslims in Scotland: The Making of Community in a Post-9/11World* (Edinburgh University Press, 2016); 'Agenda: Stefano Bonino on the huge changes sweeping through Islam in Scotland', *The Herald* 2/5/2016; Severin Carrell, 'Edinburgh teen admits racially aggravated stabbing of Syrian', *The Guardian*, 19/7/2018; Bashir Maan, 'Islam and Scotland', *Islamic Tartan,* at https://www.islamictartan.com/islam-scotland.php; 'Bashir Maan – Times Past', *Glasgowlife* 30/3/2022 at https://www.glasgowlife.org.uk/libraries/family-history/stories-and-blogs-from-the-mitchell/times-past-blogs/bashir-maan-times-past; 'Obituary: Bashir Maan, CBE, politician and Scots-Asian community leader', *The Scotsman,* 14/5/2020; 'Five Scottish philosophers who helped shape the world', *The Scotsman*, 11/4/2016, at https://www.scotsman.com/whats-on/arts-and-entertainment/five-scottish-philosophers-who-helped-shape-the-world-1478966; *Stephen Lyons*, 'Birth of a Legend', NOVA, November 2000, at https://www.pbs.org/wgbh/nova/lochness/legend.html; Nicholas Witchell, *The Loch Ness Story,* (Penguin, 1975); Kevin Quinn, 'Rosslyn Chapel visitor numbers rise to near record level', (*Edinburgh Evening News*, 10/1/2020); Alistair MacDonald, 'Scottish enlightenment', *British Council*, July 2016 at https://www.britishcouncil.org/research-insight/scottish-enlightenment; R.A. Houston, *Scottish Literacy and the Scottish Identity: Illiteracy and Society in Scotland and Northern England 1600–1800* ((*Cambridge Studies in Population, Economy and Society in Past Time* 4 (New York, Cambridge University Press. 1985); Dennis Rasmussen, 'He died as he lived: David Hume, philosopher and infidel', *Aeon*, in association with Princeton University Press, 23/10/2017, at https://aeon.co/ideas/he-died-as-he-lived-david-hume-philosopher-and-infidel

Saving the Environment by Nayab Khalid

Works cited include, Zoe Todd, 'Indigenizing the anthropocene', in Davis, H. and Turpin, E. (Eds), *Art in the Anthropocene: Encounters Among Aesthetics, Politics, Environments and Epistemologies*, Open Humanities Press, London, 2015; and Alastair Mcintosh, *Riders on the Storm: the Climate Crisis and the Survival of Being*, Birlinn Books, Edinburgh, 2020. On the confession of RDLS founders, see Persephone Pearl, Rachel Porter and Emily Laurens 'On Racism and Environmental Practice – Reflections on a Journey', at https://www.lostspeciesday.org/?p=1458

Zarina Ahmad's co-authored academic paper is worth a mention here. It analyses the role of Muslim intermediaries in environmental policy: Zarina Ahmad et al, . (2023) 'The religions are engaging: tick, well done' in *The invisibilization and instrumentalization of Muslim climate intermediaries*, Policy Studies, 44:5 (2023)

The Muslim Connection by Saqib Razzaq

Interviews and life stories of pioneers mentioned can be viewed at the Colourful Heritage website: www.colourfulheritage.com.

For background history, see Bashir Maan, *Muslims in Scotland,* Argyll Publishing, 2014; Peter Hopkins, *Scotland's Muslims: Society, Politics and Identity*, Edinburgh University Press, 2017; and *Scotland's Lascar Heritage,* Glasgow Museums Publication, 2023

For Islamic tartan and to obtain your halal kilt, see https://www.islamictartan.com/

Gaelic by Kirsty MacDougall

Charles Withers's *Gaelic Scotland: The Transformation of a Culture Region* is published by Routledge, London. (1984). For further detail, see: William Gillies, *Gaelic and Scotland = Alba agus a' Ghàidhlig.* Edinburgh University Press (1989), Kenneth MacKinnon, *Gaelic: A past and future* prospect,

Saltire Society, Edinburgh, (1991); and Wilson McLeod, *Gaelic in Scotland: Policies, Movements, Ideologies*, Edinburgh University Press (2020). See also: Fiona O'Hanlon, et al. 'Gaelic-medium education in Scotland: choice and attainment at the primary and early secondary school stages'. Celtic and Scottish Studies, September 2010, University of Edinburgh, which can be accessed at: https://www.gaidhlig.scot/wp-content/uploads/2018/06/OHanlon-2010-Taghadh-coileanadh-FtG-CR09-05-GME-choice-attainment.pdf

Lumpen Life by James Brooks

Commentary quotes and film dialogue from *My Name is Joe* (FilmFour Video, 2002) and *Sweet Sixteen* (Icon Film Distribution, 2007) DVDs. Lumpenproletariat quotes from *Capital Volume 1*, Karl Marx (Penguin Classics, 1990). Statistics from 'The Current State of Poverty in Glasgow', Glasgow Care Foundation website, 14 March 2023, http://tinyurl.com/478ywr8b. Long-focus lens quote from *British Cinema: A Very Short Introduction*, Charles Barr (Oxford University Press, 2022). Script quote from *My Name is Joe*, Paul Laverty (ScreenPress Books, 1998).

Melodrama of protest quote from 'Melodrama and the American Cinema', Michael Walker, *Movie* (Summer 1982), cited in *The Cinema of Ken Loach: Art in the Service of the People*, Jacob Leigh (Wallflower, 2002). 'Keynote speech' quote from 'My Name is Joe', Judith Williamson, *Sight and Sound* (November 1998). Renton's rant in Trainspotting can be viewed on YouTube at http://tinyurl.com/yc7wnh99. 'Streetwise Son with Heart, Played by a Young Natural', Elvis Mitchell, *The New York Times* (16 May 2003), is available at http://tinyurl.com/2c3c6j68.

Othering Heights by John O'Donoghue

James Wood's essay 'Human, All Too Inhuman' was published in *The New Republic* 24 July 2000. On Tom LeClair notion of 'systems novel', see his 1987 study *In the Loop: Don DeLillo and the Systems Novel* and *The Art of Excess: Mastery in Contemporary American Fiction* (1989). See also: Christian Lorentzen, 'Shocks to the System', *Bookforum* Summer 2023.

Last Word: On Insulting the Prophet by Mashal Saif

Works referenced and cited in this essay include (in order of appearance):
'Pakistan: Killing of Sri Lankan accused of blasphemy sparks protests,' *BBC News*, December 6, 2021, accessed July 20, 2022, https://www.bbc.com/news/59501368.

Kalbe Ali, '89 citizens killed over blasphemy allegations since 1947: report,' *Dawn*, January 26, 2022, accessed July 20, 2022, https://www.dawn.com/news/1671491.

Arafat Mazhar, 'Why blasphemy remains unpardonable in Pakistan,' *Dawn*, February 19, 2015, accessed July 20, 2022, https://www.dawn.com/news/1163596/why-blasphemy-remains-unpardonable-in-pakistan.

Sana Ashraf, *Finding the Enemy Within: Blasphemy Accusations and Subsequent Violence in Pakistan* (Australia: Australian National University, 2021).

'Blasphemy Cases Have Inflated in 2020, says CSJ,' *Dawn*, February 5, 2021, accessed July 20, 2022, https://www.dawn.com/news/1605527.

'Women madrassa teachers slit colleague's throat,' *The Express Tribune*, March 29, 2022, accessed July 20, 2022, https://tribune.com.pk/story/2349940/women-madrassa-teachers-slit-colleagues-throat.

'Punjab Governor Salman Taseer assassinated in Islamabad,' *BBC News*, January 4, 2011, accessed July 15, 2022, http://www.bbc.com/news/world-south-asia-12111831.

Salman Siddiqui, 'Hardline Stance: Religious bloc condones murder,' *The Express Tribune*, January 5, 2011, accessed July 15, 2022, http://tribune.com.pk/story/99313/hardline-stance-religious-bloc-condones -murder/.

Ashraf Aṣif Jalali, *Ghazi Muhammad Mumtaz Ḥusayn Qadri ke Rihai ke Baray Mein Shari Fatwa* (Lahore: Dar al-Ifta Jamia Jalaliyya, October 20, 2011).

'Qanoon Namoos e Risalat SAWW, An Exclusive interview with Maulana Zahid ur Rashidi,' YouTube, video uploaded by adeel arif, August 17, 2011, accessed July 15, 2022, http://www.youtube.com/watch?v=xs2zAUmrx30.

Ismail Khan, 'The Assertion of Barelawi Extremism,' *Current Trends in Islamist Ideology* 12 (Oct. 2011): 51-72.

'Hanif Qureshi's sermon which made Mumtaz Qadri to Kill Salman Taseer Gustakh e Rasool khanqah dogran,' *Youtube*, video uploaded by

almujtaba100, August 27, 2011, accessed July 15, 2022, http://www.
youtube.com/watch?v=8QEtLWYY6Tk.

'Top prayer leaders deny Taseer his rites,' *Pakistan Today,* January 6, 2011,
accessed July 15, 2022, http://www.pakistantoday.com.pk/2011/01/
top-prayer-leaders-deny-taseer-his-rites/.

Asad Hashim, 'In Pakistan, a shrine to murder for "blasphemy,"' *Al Jazeera*,
February 10, 2017, accessed July 25, 2022, https://www.aljazeera.com/
indepth/features/2017/02/pakistan-shrine-murder-
blasphemy-170206103344830.html

Madeeha Anwar, 'Convicted Murderer's Grave in Pakistan Becomes Shrine
for Some,' *Voice of America*, March 25, 2017, accessed July 25, 2022,
https://www.voanews.com/a/convisted-murders-grave-becomes-
pakistan-shrine/3781717.html.

Lutz Wiederhold, 'Blasphemy Against the Prophet Muhammad and his
Companions (Sabb al- Rasul, Sabb al-Sahabah): The Introduction of the
Topic into Shāfi'ī Legal Literature and its Relevance for Legal Practice
under Mamluk Rule,' *Journal of Semitic Studies* 42, no. 1 (1997): 39-70.

Taqi al-Din al-Subki, *al-Subki fi Furu al-Fiqh al-Shafii* (Lebanon: Dar
al-Kutub al-Ilmiyya, 2004).

Taqi al-Din ibn Taymiyya, *Kitab al-Sarim al-Maslul ala Shatim al-Rasul*, trans.
Muhammad Ijaz Janjua (Lahore: Nuriyya Rizviyya Publications, 2010).

Mufti Muhammad Hanif Qureshi Qadri, *Qalm Kuch aur Likhta hai, Zaban
Kuch aur Kahti hai* 2nd edition (Rawalpindi: Shabab-i Islami Pakistan, 2012).

Tahir ul-Qadri, *Tahaffuz-i Namus-i Risalat* (Lahore: Minhaj al-Quran
Publications, 2002).

Malik Muhammad al-Rasul Qadri and Mufti Muhammad Khan Qadri,
'Muhaqiq Al-Asr Mufti Muhammad Khan Qadri se ek Interview,' *Sue Hijaz*,
Lahore 17, no. 10 (Oct. 2011): 52-53.

Muhammad Khalil ur-Rahman Qadri, *Ghazi Muhammad Mumtaz Husayn
Qadri ka Iqdam: Islam, Iman aur Qanun ke Rushni mein*, 34-36.

Muhammad Ammar Khan Nasir, *Barahin: Muasir-i Mazhabi Nuqtah ha-yi
Nazr par Naqd va Tabsirah* (Lahore: Dar ul-Kitab, 2011), 443-604.

M.S. Wagner, 'The problem of non-Muslims who insult the prophet
Muhammad,' *Journal of the American Oriental Society* 135 no. 3 (2015):
529-540.

Zahid ur-Rashidi, 'Tauhin-i Risalat ki Saza ke Hawalay se Jari Mubahisa,' *Roznama Pakistan*, October 2, 2011.

'Salman Taseer Gustakh nahi or Mumtaz Qadri Qatil hai by Irfan Mashadi,' *Youtube*, video uploaded by HaqiqatKyaHai, April 28, 2012, accessed July 24, 2022, http://www.youtube.com/watch?v=8wp6S_AFvx0.

'Salman Taseer ku Mumtaz Qadri nay najaiz Qatal kia by Allama Tahir Mahmood Ashrafi,' *Youtube*, video uploaded by Blasphemy Law, October 17, 2011, accessed July 24, 2022, http://www.youtube.com/watch?v=RExcm8l_8RE.

"'Mumtaz Qadri did not right, it was his individual act" by Mufti Naeem,' *Youtube*, video uploaded by Blasphemy Law on October 17, 2011, accessed July 24, 2022, http://www.youtube.com/watch?v=XbJ0v5V2vzw.

Arafat Mazhar, 'The untold story of Pakistan's blasphemy law,' *Dawn*, December 9, 2104, accessed July 20, 2022, https://www.dawn.com/news/1149558/the-untold-story-of-pakistans-blasphemy-law.

Arafat Mazhar, 'The fatwas that can change Pakistan's blasphemy narrative,' *Dawn*, January 4, 2015, accessed July 20, 2022, https://www.dawn.com/news/1154856/the-fatwas-that-can-change-pakistans-blasphemy -narrative

Arafat Mazhar, 'Blasphemy and the Death Penalty: Misconceptions Explained,' *Dawn*, November 2, 2015, accessed July 20, 2022, https://www.dawn.com/news/1215304/blasphemy-and-the-death -penalty-misconceptions-explained

See also: Mishal Saif, *The 'Ulama in Contemporary Pakistan: Contesting and Cultivating an Islamic Republic*, Cambridge University Press, 2020

American Diary: Dangerous Liaisons
by Amandla Thomas-Johnson

The quotes from Walaa Quisay's *Neo-Traditionalism in Islam in the West: Orthodoxy, Spirituality and Politics* (Edinburgh University Press, 2023) are from p17 and p34, respectively. Hamza Yusuf quotes can be found at: https://parliamentofreligions.org/blog/the-alliance-of-virtues-for-the-common-good/; https://www.middleeasteye.net/big-story/hamza-yusuf-and-struggle-soul-western-islam; and https://www.bbc.com/news/uk-64125045

Yahya Birt's citation is from his article 'The Unbearable Whiteness of Being' on the Islamic Human Rights Commission website: https://www.ihrc.org.uk/the-unbearable-whiteness-of-being-convert-leaders-in-the-west-and-the-new-ethno-nationalism/

On Hamza Yusuf and victimhood culture, see https://renovatio.zaytuna.edu/article/cultural-devolution; and the Abdul Hakim Murad quote is from Quisay, p160.

Fredric Jameson's *Postmodernism, The Cultural Logic of Late Capitalism* is published by Duke University Press (1992); Ziauddin Sardar's *Postmodernism and the Other: The New Imperialism of Western Culture* is published by Pluto Press, London (1997). The quote is from 'Modernity, Postmodernity and Judgement Day'. *Futures* 25 (5) 493-506 (June), which can be accessed at: https://ziauddinsardar.com/articles/terminator-2-modernity-postmodernism-and-other

Mohamed Abdou's *Islam and Anarchism: Relationships and Resonances* is published by Pluto Press (London 2022). See also: Sylvia Wynter, 'No Humans Involved: An Open Letter to My Colleagues,' *Forum N.H.I.: Knowledge for the 21st Century* 1, no. 1 (1994): 42–73; and for the American support for Palestine poll, see: https://www.washingtonpost.com/world/2023/12/21/us-support-israel-palestine-poll/

CONTRIBUTORS

• **Leila Aboulela** is the author of six novels, of which the most recent, *River Spirit*, is a *New York Times* Editors' Choice and Best Historical Fiction Book of the Year • **Robin Ade**, artist, writer and fisherman, is the author of *Fisher in the Hills: A Season in Galloway* • **Muhammad Ameen/Bill Holmes** is an artist and firewood forager living in Scotland • **Shah Tazrian Ashrafi** is a writer based in Dhaka, Bangladesh, his first collection of short stories, *The Hippo Girl and Other Stories* was recently published by Hachette India • **James Brooks** is a science journalist • **Abdullah Geelah** works in a large City firm • **Jeremy Henzell-Thomas** is a regular contributor to *Critical Muslim* • **Nayab Khalid** is adrift in the real world, having recently completed a PhD in pure mathematics from the University of St Andrews • **Kirsty MacDougall** is a native Gaelic speaker from the Isle of Skye and lecturer in Gaelic language at Sabhal Mòr Ostaig, the National Centre for Gaelic Language and Culture in Scotland • **Steve Noyes** is a Muslim novelist and poet • **John O'Donoghue**, poet and writer, is author of the memoir *Sectioned: A Life Interrupted*, which was awarded Mind Book of the Year 2010 • **Parand** is a screenwriter, essayist and novelist living in Afghanistan • **Alycia Pirmohamed** is a Canadian-born poet based in Scotland • **David Pollard** has published eight volumes of poetry and a novel, *Nietzsche's Footfalls* • **Arusa Qureshi** is a writer and editor based in Edinburgh, and the Music Programme Manager at Summerhall • **Saqib Razzaq** is Project Manager and Head of Research at 'Colourful Heritage' – the largest organisation preserving South Asian & Muslim heritage in Scotland • **Mashal Saif** is Associate Professor in the Department of Philosophy and Religion, Clemson University, South Carolina • **Deema K. Shehabi** is a widely published Palestinian poet, writer and editor • **Amandla Thomas-Johnson**, a journalist working for Aljazeera and *Middle East Eye*, is travelling the Americas • **Zahra Wadia** is a British Pakistani writer living in Ontario, Canada • **Robin Yassin-Kassab** would happily spend the rest of his life exploring the wild corners of Scotland.